GENERATION X

GOES
TO
COLLEGE

Gordon D. Venturella

GENERATION X

GOES
TO
COLLEGE

An Eye-Opening Account of Teaching
in Postmodern America

Peter Sacks

OPEN COURT
Chicago and LaSalle, Illinois

Open Court Publishing Company is a division of Carus Publishing Company

Copyright © 1996 by Carus Publishing Company

First printing 1996
Second printing 1996
Third printing 1997
Fourth printing 1997

Printed and bound in the United States of America.

Library of Congress Cataloging-in-Publication Data

Sacks, Peter.
    Generation X goes to college: a journey into teaching in
  postmoden America / Peter Sacks.
       p.   cm.
    Includes bibliographical references (p.   ) and index.
    ISBN 0-8126-9314-0 (pbk : alk. paper)
    1. College teaching—United States. 2. College Students—United
  States—Attitudes.   3. Generation X—United States—Attitudes.
  4. Postmodernism and education—United States. 5. Education,
  Higher—United States—Aims and objectives. I. Title.
  LB2331.S17 1996
  378.1'25—dc20   96-10985
                                                CIP

Contents

Gratis

Author's Note   vii

Introduction   ix

Part One: The Sandbox Experiment   1

Chapter 1: Coming into Teaching   3

Chapter 2: Culture Shock   8

Chapter 3: The Castle, with Apologies to Franz Kafka   31

Chapter 4: Reflections on the Worth of Teachers   39

Chapter 5: "We Are Grownups Now"   44

Chapter 6: Where All the Kids Are (Way) Above Average   54

Chapter 7: Hooked on Hand-holding   60

Chapter 8: "Hey, Dad, Put It on Pause!"   66

Chapter 9: The Sandbox Experiment   81

Part Two: Education in Postmodern America   105

Chapter 10: The Postmodern Revolt   107

Chapter 11: The Balkanization of Knowledge and Power   122

Chapter 12: The Postmodern Spectacle and Generation X 142

Chapter 13: Postmodernity and the Entitlement Society 154

Chapter 14: Adapting to a Postmodern World   171

Epilogue   188

Notes   191

Index   203

Author's Note

I have changed all names and many incidental details in part one of the book. This story is simply a true portrayal of my experience as a teacher. However, the book is not meant to focus criticism on any specific individual, group, or institution.

This book has endnotes for those readers who wish to consult them. I did not want to clutter up the text with numbers or asterisks, but for those who want to check on sources, please refer to the notes section beginning on p. 191.

Introduction

It's coming up on the end of summer, and I'm at a campsite in the Rockies, reflecting on the past few years since I quit my job as a newspaper reporter to become a college teacher. At this moment, I can say that I'm satisfied, for I've discovered some important insights and lessons about succeeding as a teacher in the age of Generation X. But, in the story that follows, you may judge me harshly for the Machiavellian tactics I employed to arrive at this position of knowledge. In my defense, let me say that becoming a teacher was like falling off a cliff as I struggled to re-orient myself to the strange and sometimes grim realities of teaching in the 1990s.

In taking leave from the world of daily journalism, I didn't have a clue about what I would be getting myself into as a college teacher. But at a large suburban community college in the West, I learned how Generation X goes to college. And I discovered how an effectively corrupt educational system, also struggling to come to terms with profound cultural changes in students, often rewarded and encouraged laxity and mediocrity. I entered the classroom knowing about the cancer of mediocrity afflicting America's public schools. The stories of such appeared frequently in the press. And I'd always heard that community colleges were not bastions of intellectual rigor, to say the least. To be sure, I anticipated that. But I would see far worse conditions than I would ever have expected, and I would conclude that this wasn't simply a problem with my community college or community colleges in general. It was a problem with our society and its relationship to its young people.

As I look back, the results of this misunderstood problem were perhaps predictable. The cancer in our public schools we've all read about had crept into the realm of the collegiate enterprise. As an outsider looking in, I discovered that nobody in the system had much of a stake in shoring up educational standards. Indeed, I would find that just the opposite was the case, and my experience is testimony to this unfortunate fact.

Of course, I hear what you're saying: "What do you expect? You're not talking about Harvard or Yale. This is "A-Mart" College, higher education for the masses, where A's and B's are easy and standards are low."

To this, I say, you're right. And that's exactly what's so scary. The Harvards and Yales have always been outstanding schools for the elites, and they will always remain so. The elites will have access to the best in education and everything else. But we should be as worried about mediocrity at the colleges for the masses as we are satisfied with the excellence routinely obtained at elite universities. "A-Mart" College, as the college of the masses, can be considered a barometer for the nation on a multitude of fronts—politically, culturally, and economically. If the elites aren't taught how to think and how to distinguish truth from lies, then the result is somewhat less effective government bureaucracies and Fortune 500 corporations. The inability of ordinary people to think for themselves is far more profound in its implications for the health of the republic. If ordinary people at ordinary colleges aren't encouraged to think critically and to take responsibility for themselves, then they will become dupes of the likes of Rush Limbaugh, Louis Farrakhan, and other popular demagogues who prosper from widespread ignorance and their ability to manipulate public opinion. I'm afraid that the state of higher education for the working classes is a much better indicator of where the country is headed than George Bush's alma mater.

To be sure, "A-Mart" College has never been held in very high regard among educational institutions, and therefore one would certainly expect mediocrity. But in talking to other instructors at my college and even at more prestigious institutions, I discovered that the situation was getting worse, to the point that many teachers believed the system had reached a crisis point. The college and university teachers I talked to had seen student culture change in profound ways in recent years, to the point that many teachers saw an increasing number of students as practically unteachable, raising fundamental questions whether the existing model of higher education even applies any longer to teaching this generation.

The story that follows is about my journey to become a teacher. It's a story of my confusion and bewilderment trying to teach Generation X and how I ultimately came to understand the true source of my confusion and frustration. It's also the story of how I ended up using the cover of my position as a teacher in order to gather, and report to the outside world, information about academic life that normally would be inaccessible to most reporters and members of the public. I didn't make this decision lightly, being well aware of the ethical dilemmas that I faced acting as both reporter and teacher at the same time. I left daily journalism with the intention of trying something different, looking for a new challenge. As I went deeper into the world of Generation X, I decided that this was a story I had to tell. I decided that my story was compelling, and that members of the public, who have certain assumptions and expectations regarding public higher education, had a right to know what was really going on inside such institutions.

And so I played the role of the college instructor, and I tried to be the best teacher that I could. Confronted with my own questions, I went about investigating what it would take to succeed as a college teacher in the 1990s. I went through what all new instructors went through, and I became a candidate for tenure. Thus, an important part of this story is how college teachers are evaluated for tenure, which at the college at which I taught, like scores of other small teaching-oriented colleges around the country, meant being evaluated by the very students who might have a hard time getting out of bed to get to class, or trouble distinguishing a comma from a semicolon in written English. So I hope readers will bear with me as I tell what it was like to be evaluated for tenure, as well as what it was like teaching Generation X, for the two subjects are really opposite sides of the same coin. On one side were the very unusual (to my manner of thinking) ways that many students approached college. And on the other side was the tenure process, and that included the power the institution had given students in the process. As I went undercover, being granted tenure became sort of a game for me. I ended up manipulating the system in order to see if I could win the game. Getting tenure, really, wasn't that important to me; I was more than willing to get back into the newspaper business. But I found myself in a very interesting position as an investigative reporter. I wanted to understand just what it meant to be considered a "good" teacher. The answer I discovered might not conform to what most people would wish to believe. And the answer isn't encouraging for the state of higher education.

Indeed, I would discover that my own manipulations were not unusual, that teachers were manipulating students, and students were manipulating teachers, and all this symbiotic game-playing was really about one thing: grades. You've heard about grade inflation, I'm sure, and all the hand-wringing that goes on inside and outside academia about the seemingly inexorable rise in grades, rendering them as a practically meaningless indicator of performance. Doonesbury has ridiculed it; newspaper pundits and politicians talk about it as if it were a force of nature beyond anyone's control. Now I know, having been on the inside of higher education, exactly why grade inflation occurs and why it's not some mysterious process that nobody can do anything about.

I discovered that the college where I taught was a battle ground of a culture war, and I'm not referring to clashes between races, sexes, or people of different religious beliefs. I'm talking about something perhaps more fundamental than these often-discussed conflicts of multiculturalism; I'm talking about a culture war between generations, and race and gender don't matter in this war. The culture war I discovered was between college teachers, typically Baby Boomers like me or older, and members of Generation X.

But this was no ordinary "generation gap." I witnessed a cultural divide, which I now believe to be the result of a quantum break between past and future—in essence, a break between the modern and postmodern worlds. The problems I saw stemmed from educators, reared under the tenets of the modern age, confronted and bewildered by a new reality: a generation of young people who had emerged from a radically changed, postmodern society. But arriving at this conclusion was no simple matter for me. It was only after some three years of searching, trying to make sense of my experience and the experience of other teachers, that I came to this understanding. Part one of this book recounts the experiences I went through that helped me reach this conclusion.

For their part, students were by no means oblivious to this culture war. But they were a generation that appeared to be sharply divided. On one hand, some students accepted the traditional roles, expectations, and responsibilities of themselves as college students; sometimes they were as angry and frustrated as their teachers that many students weren't living up to their end of the bargain. It seemed that the student body at my college was typified by what I would eventually call the "postmodern student." Like McDonald's customers expecting neatly packaged $1.99 Big Macs, these postmodernists harbored a strong sense of being entitled to easy success and good grades, even though they were often unwilling to work to achieve them. And, these postmodern individuals were quick to put the entire blame for failure on the shoulders of their teachers.

The system, for its part, erred on the side of mediocrity. My college, without seriously considering the implications or the reasons behind its policies, made huge allowances for this postmodern mentality of consumerism, while largely ignoring the needs of more serious and motivated students, which would have been unheard of in decades past. And the system was somehow locked into this position, incapable of changing, because the cultural forces preventing change were far too powerful.

In part two of the book, I explore postmodernism and education in America, trying to place my story into its broadest possible context, and analyzing the cultural and economic forces that have shaped the postmodern generation. A member of this generation is a conundrum of contradictions. He or she wants desperately to trust, but refuses to trust authority, institutions, knowledge, facts—all the traditional sources of legitimacy and value in higher education. The postmodern student knows the value of learning but expects to be entertained. He has a keen sense of entitlement but little motivation to succeed. That is the essence of Generation X, the first true generation of the postmodern epoch. She is being torn apart between the traditions and expectations of the past and the profound uncertainty of the future.

Much is being written and said nowadays about Generation X, including the latest attempts of some to counter the supposedly false stereotype that this is a generation of slackers. But having been on the front lines of a clash of cultures as a college teacher, and having investigated the Generation X phenomenon as a reporter, I've concluded that this could be a generation in trouble, foreboding possibly scary times for our country, unless the educational establishment clearly understands that a new reality has arrived on the cultural landscape. Thus, in the final chapter, I discuss what it means for educational policy and reform once educators understand and confront the conflict between the postmodern generation and an educational establishment often entrenched in the ways of modernism.

In the following chapter, I recount my decision to quit the newspaper business and begin my journey into teaching. Then I go on to explain the contrast between the professional world I left and the brave new world I found as a college teacher, and how I struggled to understand and conform to this world. As my journey into teaching reached a climax, I discovered what worked and what failed as a teacher in postmodern America.

Thus, if you want a peek at the future, take a look at the place I call The College, where I became a teacher. It could be your college in your neighborhood, town, or city.

PART I

The Sandbox Experiment

CHAPTER 1

Coming into Teaching

Before I got the job at The College, I had been living in California, working for a large daily newspaper, generally enjoying my job and the perfect seaside weather. The job was one of several I had held in the newspaper business, in a career that had taken me all over the country. I was fairly typical of young, ambitious journalists, moving to increasingly bigger papers, covering bigger stories, earning more money and a bit more prestige. In California, I was doing what I loved, or at least what I was good at.

I'm telling you all this because I think you need to understand where I was coming from when I became a teacher. I was coming from a completely different world, the professional one, going into a shockingly different subculture of America, it seemed. Deep down, I think I will always be a reporter, looking for the compelling story. Though I took the job at The College with the best intentions, I would eventually end up more or less posing as a teacher, becoming the proverbial fly on the wall, in order to report back to the outside world what I saw and experienced in my journey into teaching. I was able to become a part of the subculture and yet to view it from the perspective of an outsider, an opportunity few people had, and I decided to take advantage of it. But I'm jumping ahead in my story.

Though I loved working for newspapers, the business of newspapers had been troubled during the late 1980s and early 1990s. I left the East Coast for California just as the northeastern economy was collapsing. Then the same recession finally clobbered California. Plus, I was getting burned out in the newspaper business. Colleagues complained that their jobs weren't as satisfying as they used to be since cost-conscious executives started meddling in the nation's news rooms. Newspapers were trying almost anything to stem the loss of readership and advertising dollars. Good journalists who got into the business because they loved to chase big, important stories found themselves continuously dissatisfied with the ho-hum, pre-packaged stories editors were dumping on them. Dan, a reporter at my paper, once told me, "I'm just not having any fun anymore." People were getting out of the business, taking buy-outs, going into public relations, or teaching, or whatever. Indeed, after I announced my resignation from the paper, another colleague, John, collared me and picked my brain about how he might also find a teaching job.

About that time, my partner, Sandy, then in her last year of medical school, got word on where she'd been matched for her three-year residency program, and it became clear that she would have to move to a new city in another part of the country. I was faced with a decision: try to stay at a newspaper in an industry some believed was a dinosaur or follow Sandy and try to find a new job. We decided that I would try to join her, but we weren't sanguine about my prospects. When she left me in June, we'd already bought four round-trip tickets so I would visit her on long weekends and scope out jobs in the new place. When I began my job hunt, I soon discovered that I was far from alone. Scores of Californians were trying to cash in their holdings in the Golden State and find a simpler, saner way of life in states like Oregon, Washington, Idaho, Utah, Nevada, and Colorado. I visited one medium-sized daily in the area and talked to an editor who used to work at the *Orange County Register,* and he too had followed his wife and her career. I was beginning to feel like just one of the crowd of former big-city journalists trying to get a job in a smaller town or city. I couldn't get a foot in the door at one major newspaper in the area, which seemed to have its pick of journalists who wanted to leave bigger cities.

One day I got a telephone call from a contact who knew well the politics and ways of The College, and he told me about a teaching job that had opened up there. He read me the job announcement over the phone. The College was looking for someone to teach both writing and journalism. "Sounds interesting," I said. "But I haven't got any teaching experience. I haven't taught since graduate school, and even then, it was hardly what you'd call being a real teacher."

But given my poor luck until then at finding a job in the area, I decided to apply—I and some 150 others, I would later find out. Amazingly to me, about a month later I was invited for an interview, and I was to fly up a week later. At that stage, I was dealing only with the personnel office, which told me I was to prepare a brief lecture "appropriate to a beginning journalism class." I didn't have a clue what to do. I called a former colleague who had taken a teaching job. Since he taught beginners, I figured he might be able to help me. He was full of ideas, but they didn't seem quite right for the occasion.

I finally hacked out a lecture on how reporters use public documents to gather information for stories. I remember being sort of proud of the lecture. I was able to tell the fictitious class—who turned out to be some eight faculty members on a hiring committee—how as a reporter I would gather information from public documents. Ross Perot was in the news a lot then because he was running for president, and I spiced up the lecture with some examples from his background that became public because of court papers. As I prepared my little lecture, I found myself really wanting the job. The weekend before the interview, I practiced my lecture in the park with Sandy as my audience.

Even now, I don't really understand why I was hired at The College. I have trouble comprehending why the hiring committee would have picked somebody with so little teaching experience, especially since they had their pick of experienced people to chose from. True, I had an extensive background as a journalist. I had the kind of real world experience too few teachers probably have. My little lecture to the hiring committee seemed a perfect example of this. I could see the looks of pleasure on the faces of the members of the committee, as if to say, "This guy knows what he's talking about." But, I would discover once I got into the real classroom what a hiring committee of faculty members considered interesting was a far cry from what would hold the attention of the X Generation.

Other than my little lecture, the interview consisted of the members of the committee asking me questions. Anita was the acting chair of the journalism and writing department, a tall woman in her fifties who'd been teaching at The College for many years and had accumulated as much influence as any member of the faculty. And she asked me the most interesting question. "What are the books which have played the most important role in shaping who you are as a writer?" she wondered. I remember babbling something incoherent about Walt Whitman and also a book called *The Word,* written by a former Associated Press staffer about journalistic writing. In fact, I could hardly say that latter book shaped me in the slightest, because I'd never read it, but it was one a former editor of mine suggested I use in my lecture. An honest answer to Anita's question would have been to talk about Kafka or Camus, but I thought better than to bring up existential angst during a job interview. So I coughed up the baloney about *The Word,* and I watched one of the committee members, Beth, nod appreciatively.

Beth, a stout woman who looked younger than her fiftysomething years, had once worked as a reporter on a small daily. I would later come to see Beth as a leaf blowing in the wind, reluctant to take firm positions on anything. She preferred to just nod, it seemed, like she did in my interview, trying to make you or students—but especially students—feel comfortable, even when she's driving you crazy wondering what she is really thinking. I would later discover that her nurturing approach was her key to success as a teacher.

But if there had been anybody in a position to inform me then about the culture shock I would be in for by leaving newspaper work behind for the world of teaching eighteen-, nineteen-, and twenty-year-olds, Beth, herself a former reporter, would have been the one. But she didn't. Nor did Anita or anybody else on the hiring committee. And I admittedly was clueless. To ask questions about students at The College and how college students in general had changed since I was in school never crossed my mind. After all, this was college, wasn't it? And college was, well, college. You had certain expectations.

After the interview, things happened fast, too fast. I got the job offer at a substantial cut in pay. But I decided to take the job anyway. I think I had already made my decision to accept any reasonable offer when I applied for the job. I wanted to give teaching a try. I saw it as a good opportunity to try something different. After all, journalism, though it turned out to be my calling, was actually my second career. Before that I'd worked as a research consultant. I was still looking for the perfect job. There was something about college teaching I'd always admired and had seen myself one day doing. I had looked up to my college teachers. They were smart and usually at ease with themselves. They seemed to like their jobs; and they didn't have to wear a tie. People who knew me as a journalist from time to time would tell me things like, "You'd make a great teacher." Shellie, a former colleague of mine, used to say that when I'd help her on stories she was working on. Yeah, I knew I could be a good teacher. I imagined young, bright, ambitious students who hung on my every word about being a good reporter and writing compelling stuff. Perhaps it was my fatherly instinct revealing itself when I imagined students in my own image, wanting to be like me, respecting me for my knowledge, experience, and talents. You know the drill: I could "give something back" to the system that had given me so much. In such a world, I knew I would be a great teacher.

There wasn't much time for thinking. The first day of classes was less than a month away, and Anita called me to give me my teaching assignments for the coming term. So I had to select my textbooks and plan two courses in a matter of just a few weeks, which turned out to be nearly impossible for an inexperienced teacher.

I remember the day I went public at the paper with my intention to leave and take a teaching job. As I said, some people in the news room wondered how I went about getting the job, thinking they too might like to give teaching a try. Others simply congratulated me for being able to get out of the newspaper business. But I remember one comment most vividly. It came from James, another reporter on the staff. He was a few years older than I, and had been in the newspaper business about twenty years. At about five feet six inches tall, with bright red hair and a short-cropped beard to match, he was a sharp, blunt reporter. On an unsaid but deep level he seemed to understand how I operated and where I was coming from as a reporter. The day I announced my resignation, people were sitting around desks in the news room talking about my career move, and the words that came out of James's mouth hit the proverbial nail on the head. "But you don't even *like* eighteen-year-olds, do you?" he asked. That was a good question. I wasn't sure if I liked eighteen-year-olds. I hadn't spent any time around them since I was eighteen myself.

CHAPTER 2

Culture Shock

The first day of classes arrived, and I went through what every other new teacher goes through on The First Day. Even Anita, as smooth an operator as there ever was, who'd been teaching for some three decades, told me a couple of days before school began that she got a bit jittery on the first day. But I should tell you that the first day for me was probably more painful than for most people. I know I'm a quiet, introspective person. Some people might say I'm slightly introverted. And the last thing a shy guy like me wants is to stand before a group of thirty or forty highly critical people and expose himself to their scrutiny. That's probably why I was so comfortable as a reporter. I could go into my cave, as it were, talk to sources on the phone, read whatever interesting documents were relevant to my story, talk briefly and tersely with other reporters or editors, and essentially just be left alone to write my stories.

One of the most striking things I discovered during those first few months as a teacher was that there was no place to hide up there in front of a classroom full of people staring at you. You were out there, and if you flubbed up or weren't entertaining enough or otherwise crossed students' sensibilities, or if you showed any weakness, students would smell blood and like sharks would devour you. I know that sounds like a horrible attitude. I didn't go into the job thinking that way, though. But after my trial by fire, I changed, and that very cynical attitude was the unfortunate result.

On that first day, I met with my beginning writing classes and my introductory journalism class to introduce myself, pass out the "syllabus," or course outline, and generally tell the students what to expect. I had heard that the journalism class had been considered a joke in the past because it was so easy. I figured a good start would be to tell students a bit about my background as a journalist, and then to start right away suggesting that people who didn't want to work hard find another class. I was determined that my class wasn't going to be considered a joke.

I scanned the classroom and the unaccustomed sights before me. My first impression was that most of the students seemed quite young, with a good 80 percent between eighteen and twenty years old. I continued to look around the room. I saw young women trying very hard to look like models in fashion magazines, with their big hair and big lips. (This should be interesting when we start discussing magazines and their influence on popular culture, I said to myself.) Then I saw something I hadn't seen before, at least in the context of an intellectual endeavor. Scattered mostly in the back and far side rows were young males with professional sports baseball caps, often worn backwards. Completing the uniform of these guys was usually a pair of baggy shorts, a team T-shirt, and an ample attitude. Slumped in their chairs, they stared at me with looks of disdain and boredom, as if to say, "Who in the hell cares where you worked, or what your experience is, or what you know? Say something to amuse me."

I would encounter this look and The Attitude often. It was a look of utter disengagement. At first, I was confused and bewildered by it and thought there must be something terribly wrong with me and the way I taught. But even after I began to strategically adapt to my situation, I would continue to get Those Looks accompanied by The Attitude. And I eventually would conclude that I was a good teacher, that it wasn't me who was the problem but a culture of young people who were born and bred to sit back and enjoy the spectacle that engulfed them. They seemed to resent that I obviously couldn't measure up to standards for amusement that they learned on *Sesame Street* in their formative years, standards later reinforced by *Beverly Hills 90210*,

Cosmopolitan, Nirvana, and Pearl Jam. What's more, they were conditioned by an overly nurturing, hand-holding educational system not to take responsibility for their own actions. But until I began to accurately assess my new environment, I often reacted with a visible irritation to such scenes as bored guys with backwards baseball caps. I would learn that this was a classic case of people who could dish it out, but who couldn't take it; and the trouble for me was that these young people collectively held a great deal of power in this place, a rather key point that I didn't fully comprehend at first. Until I understood this, my relationship with some of my classes developed at times into all out war.

By now, you're probably wondering why I refer to my college as simply, "The College." I've chosen not to pinpoint the place because I don't want you, the reader, to be distracted from the larger issues I believe my experience reflected. The College looked and acted like any number of smaller public colleges whose mission was devoted to teaching undergraduates. The College had several thousand students and was located in a middle-class to lower middle-class suburb. Students were mostly white, but that was changing rapidly, and most were straight out of high school. Although enrollment was open, allowing academically poor students in high school a second chance at college, many others were capable of going straight to a four-year school. Indeed, some students could have done well anywhere; their biggest reason for going to The College was clearly that they weren't as wealthy as their peers who went to more prestigious colleges and universities.

Meanwhile, as a new teacher I had high hopes and aspirations, for my students and for myself. I had some ideas about education that I was excited to put into action. For example, I had always despised traditional college textbooks because I thought they were dumb-downed versions of original works and interesting ideas, and besides that they were often just plain boring. And in journalism I found no shortage of such textbooks, particularly for introductory courses in the mass media. There was a blizzard of them.

But I was wary of trying anything too different in the beginning. Not knowing what to expect at The College, I took the easy way and did what countless college instructors do: I found a mediocre textbook to foist upon students. (But later, I would find that students had come to expect such textbooks, in order to regurgitate its contents on tests, and often didn't know how to react to a real book.)

I'd had about a month to move a few thousand miles and then figure out what in the world to do to keep three classes moving forward, five days a week, fifty minutes per session. In any sane system, a professor would meet with students no more than three times a week. But state law demanded that professors maintain a certain number of so-called "contact hours" with students, and so those five days a week were carved in stone. I found this requirement daunting. How, in just a few weeks before classes were to start, would I fill up that much time?

Gearing up for my first journalism class was especially problematic. I figured that I needed to teach the students about the mass media—the conventional history of newspapers, magazines, cable TV, broadcasting, advertising, ethics, and so on. And to be sure, that's what students had come to expect of such survey courses: to be spoon-fed facts so that they could regurgitate them on multiple choice tests. So I lectured. The problem was coming up with—in just a few weeks—lectures for a course I'd never taught before. I'll admit it—and this is another of the teaching profession's little secrets—I borrowed material heavily from a textbook, which covered essentially what the students' assigned text covered. I augmented those canned lectures with some of my own creation on subjects I was interested in. But even with the help of a textbook, it was impossible to come up with five lectures a week, for some eleven weeks. So, to complement my lectures, I decided the students would do most of the work. In fact, out of my own sense of survival, I had unwittingly found myself doing what was increasingly becoming the fashion in some higher education circles, eschewing lectures in order to make students take greater responsibility for their learning. I had the students analyze and critique different types of media, including magazines, newspapers, and television shows, then to do oral presentations on their critiques. Miraculously, it all came together pretty well. I knew I wasn't a gifted lecturer, but I was providing them solid material, backed up with examples from my own experience. I'd improve my lecturing skills with time.

The problem of preparing for my first classes was more easily solved in the writing course: I'd have the students do a lot of writing and working with each other in groups. I'd been a professional writer, but I had never taught people *how* to write. Frankly, I didn't have a clue how to teach people how to write, and I'm not sure I do even now. I'm not convinced many other writing teachers do either. I would never admit this to my students, but I'd never even taken a bonehead English composition course in college. (Though I do wear this fact as sort of a badge of honor.) Maybe that was during the free-flowing 1970s when such regimentation was frowned on. In my undergraduate days at a large university, I took what was called expository writing, and we just wrote stuff. I say "stuff" because that's how formless it seemed to me. I got away with writing page-long sentences for assignments in a class I took from a poet. He would write "bravo" when I did that. After toying with a lot of English classes, I went to graduate school, worked as a researcher and consultant for several years on the East and West coasts, then went on to write news and feature stories at newspapers for several more years.

My point is that I didn't have the slightest idea what traditional English teachers meant by "rhetorical modes," "expanded definition" papers, "diagnostic essays," or "cause and effect" essays. Such terms were of little use to me in the newspaper business. Okay, I'd make the students do some writing, but what would they write? Fortunately, I stumbled onto an excellent textbook for my writing classes, that I found at the bookstore. (I'll admit that there are a few worthy textbooks out there.)

Essentially, I followed the author's methods and his assignments almost exactly. He taught me a trick that I found useful for using up the requisite amount of class time while keeping students busy and amused: having students work in groups to critique each other's work. It turned out that students liked talking to each other more than they liked listening to teachers. Group work used up time and kept students busily entertained. Of course, neither the textbook's author nor other writing instructors would ever admit to using group work so cynically. But when I got to The College, I found that the group feedback method was widely used in our department. Though I would come to seriously doubt that students who couldn't compose a complete sentence could give useful feedback about writing to other students (who also couldn't write a complete sentence), that insight seemed lost on most of my students; and whether other teachers in my department believed as I did was beside the point; students working in groups was useful, because it used up time, and kept them busy. Indeed, as I dove deeper into the ways of The College, I would conclude that excellent classroom teaching was measured almost exclusively in terms of what "worked" to keep students' attention, rather than the actual content of the learning. Nearly everything we did and talked about as college instructors seemed to revolve around what "worked" on such terms.

I entered the classroom having made certain assumptions about college and college students. I figured they would read the assigned books, take notes when I lectured, and show up for class. I expected students to be adults and that I could therefore treat them as adults. I now realize just how naive I was. I had given no thought to the possibility that these assumptions might be way off base.

At first, I took the idealistic position that attendance policies were puerile, certainly not how one should treat adults. But there were times in my writing classes, which had enrollments of about twenty-five people each, when half the class would be absent. This wouldn't have mattered much to me except that such absences were embarrassing when other faculty and administrators would come to watch me teach.

What's more, my writing students simply refused to read. Reading the essays in the book was an important part of my approach to trying to teach people how to write. But I wasn't in favor of coercing people to read by concocting phony, make-work quizzes testing them on the readings. I shared an office with a woman who taught writing and literature, and I used to overhear her conversations in which she'd mention quizzes on the books in her creative writing class. I was flabbergasted that she had to resort to quizzes in a creative writing class; it was so far removed from my expectation that college students should not have to be hit over the head to do what's in their best interest. I learned that such trivial quizzing was common at The College. And that's exactly what the students expected; otherwise they figured reading the books wasn't worth their time.

So on days that we'd break into small groups to discuss the readings in the book, silence would reign. Why? Because my students would be busy reading the homework assignment during class time. I once asked a student as informally and non-threateningly as I could, "Why don't people read the assignments?" He said, "If you gave us something to *do* with them we would. Give us some questions on the readings and make it count on the grade." Perhaps I was too headstrong, but I didn't heed his advice. I recalled my own writing and literature classes in the 1970s; we were never quizzed in such a petty fashion. And I wasn't going to start down that slippery slope.

But my first-quarter culture shock was fueled as much by small things as by the big stuff. A lot of students had the habit of always asking the same questions on what I considered trivial matters that should have been resolved with a single question or by students just *reading* the course syllabus.

For instance, on days my writing classes turned in their essays, two or three students, apparently in the habit of high school, would invariably ask me, "Do you have a stapler?" And I would always say, "No, I don't carry a stapler with me." Sometimes I would give variations of the same answer, trying to indicate my annoyance that they hadn't gotten the message. "No, I'm not a walking office" or I'd say, "No, that's your job. I teach writing. I don't provide staplers." But perhaps I should feel lucky. I told a colleague about my stapler problem, and he said, "I had a student come up to me once and ask me for a Kleenex."

Then there was simply plain rudeness. That first quarter I noticed that some students would read newspapers—the baseball hat guys immersed in the *USA Today* sports page or textbooks from other classes—while I was talking. Often, some students would pair up as if they were back in high school, and maintain their own little chatty powwows while I was trying to teach the class. I had a pair of nineteen-year-old women in my writing class that first quarter who introduced me to this trait. When I would interrupt them and ask them to pay attention, they'd give me these looks like *I* was the rude one for interrupting them. But I don't mean to single out the women; just as often two guys would pair up and chat away, not really trying to lower their voices, as if their conversation was the main act and the class and I were mere sideshows. Quite often, I would see a student who decided he or she had better things to do and would simply get up and leave in the middle of class, without regard to whether I was talking. The clever ones would leave when my back was turned.

I began to wonder, just how much detail did one have to cover in the syllabus regarding expectations that would normally be assumed of thinking, responsible, considerate adults? Expecting a world of higher education in which students pursued ideas and knowledge because they wanted to improve and enrich their lives, I instead found what I regarded as a very mean and nasty Skinnerian world in which students wouldn't do anything unless it specifically and directly affected their grade. Thus, while students' reading the books for a class would affect their grade indirectly, they wouldn't read the books unless you quizzed them on the material, and then only if the quizzes counted as a significant percent of the grade. Students wouldn't attend your class unless you deducted points for absences. I wondered what else needed to be linked to the grade. Did the course syllabus need to spell out that for each instance of rude behavior a student's grade would be docked so many points? I began to regard the syllabus less as an outline of the course content than as a legal contract. Besides content, you had to specify appropriate behavior in a college classroom, and then create an elaborate system of penalties and bonuses in order to elicit appropriate behavior from students.

But chances were, my students wouldn't read the syllabus anyway. On the syllabus for my writing course, for instance, I spelled out that each essay was to be three to five pages, typed, and double-spaced. Yet each time I made a new essay assignment, somebody would blurt out, "How long should it be?" That first year, having answered the same question over and over, I would answer tersely, trying without success to keep my irritation in check, "It's in the syllabus."

While many students refused to read, they weren't shy about bringing new consumer technology to class, and I'm not talking about calculators, PCs, and Macs. Technological gadgets had increasingly become part of students' classroom experience since I had been in college during those now-ancient days when slide rules were the gadgets of choice.

From time to time, phone pagers would scream out during class. The implicit message that emanated from The College was that such technological interruptions were okay, simply because technology was good. For example, one day on our bulletin board in the department office, I saw a memo tacked up from a dean's office, informing instructors of the phone number for students to fax in their homework. "If they can't attend class and turn it into me personally, they can't turn it in," I remarked to whoever was standing there as I read the memo on the wall.

But that was minor stuff compared to what happened in my writing class. One morning, we had just broken up into groups to go over the students' drafts. They had finally settled down to work and things were humming along when the electronic pulse of a modern phone pierced the air. A student named Jeff pulled out his cellular phone—one of those very small, very cool folding types, and he answered it, and the entire class stopped dead in its tracks to watch him do his thing on the phone. "I can't believe this," I said. "Okay, folks, you all have seen a phone before. Please get back to work." Then I walked up to Jeff and said very quietly and very forcefully. "Put that damned phone away. I never want to see that in this class again." He said lamely, "I forgot to turn it off."

My tales of consumer technology invading the classroom paled in comparison to a story one of my colleagues told me. Jill, the instructor, told me about a student of hers who had come to class one day, not to listen to the lecture or to participate in class activities, but . . . to watch TV. He set up one of those tiny portable TV sets on his desk and started watching it during class, as if this were his morning ritual. "I told him to shut it off and put it away," Jill said. "So he says to me, 'I've seen this show anyway.'"

If a college student watching TV during class is beyond comprehension, consider Caitlin, a student in my journalism class one quarter. Caitlin, struck me as earnest but her thinking skills were poorly developed, at least judging by her muddled writing. She struggled to understand simple concepts of journalistic writing, but she would often leave me with the impression that any weakness she had in this regard was simply my not liking her "style." She wasn't alone in this rather relativistic sort of thinking. I had many students who believed there really weren't legitimate standards of excellence in writing but that it was always a matter of opinion. If you figured out what "style" the teacher wanted, then you'd do okay.

Caitlin's strange notions (to my way of thinking) didn't stop with the subject of writing. One Monday, class members were scheduled to turn in the drafts of their restaurant reviews. Caitlin came up to me as the students were passing me their papers and said, "I've had a cold all week, and so I don't have any tastebuds. I can't taste the food. Do I still have to do the assignment?"

I was awestruck. I almost broke down laughing, or crying, I'm not sure which. I looked at Caitlin for a moment with a bemused smile, thinking I've now heard it all, wondering what in the hell I was going to say to her. All I could muster for a response was: "I'm sorry, Caitlin; I can help you with a lot of things, but I really can't help you with your tastebuds. And yes, you still have to do the assignment."

To be sure, dealing with the students' rudeness, narrowmindedness and lame excuses was inconsistent with my idea of teaching college-aged adults, and I often reacted to what I considered juvenile behavior with visible irritation. I didn't learn—until it was almost too late—that my negative reactions and resistance to bending had broken an unwritten rule: A faculty member at The College must exert near Herculean effort to make the necessary accommodations to ensure that students are happy.

By now, you probably think I was some kind of old fashioned, highly conservative fuddy-duddy. That certainly wasn't how I saw myself. First, I wasn't old. In my late thirties, I was actually quite young compared to most of the teachers at my college. I had a lifestyle closer to that of many of my students than most teachers and other professionals who had children and mortgages to worry about. While my peers were having children and taking out home loans and buying new cars, I was driving an old Volkswagen mini-bus and spent my extra money on bicycles and skis. And I spent my spare time using both. My politics? I'm a liberal, a "progressive" as we liberals like to call ourselves. I voted for Carter, Mondale, and Jesse. As a reporter, I was always plugging for the underdog whenever I could. I had always distrusted authority and hated the abuse of power, U.S. government power and corporate power especially.

And so, I was truly taken by surprise when I told one professional acquaintance about some of my more interesting encounters with students and she more or less called me an old prude. "That's how kids are," she said. But she had given herself away. "Kids?" I said. "These aren't kids I'm talking about. They're not six-year-olds. Last time I checked, twenty-year-olds were grownups just like me." I later realized that this acquaintance had adopted the same attitude toward students as had many teachers and administrators. To the extent that many twenty-year-olds were behaving like immature children, we overly nurturing adults have let them get away with it. We were at fault as much as the students—a fact that became all too clear to me as time went on.

I forged ahead into the remainder of my first year, my idealism about teaching and education substantially intact, despite the many affronts to my sensibilities. For the most part, I figured that the problems I was having as a college instructor were my fault, due to my inexperience.

I decided to substantially alter the journalism course the following quarter, knowing that I basically had thrown together the course the previous quarter at the last minute. I didn't like the textbook and decided to get rid of it. Instead, I ordered several original softcover books that had scholarly or artistic merit. These included Noam Chomsky's and Edward Herman's *Manufacturing Consent;* Russell Neuman's *The Future of the Mass Audience;* Orwell's *1984; Brave New World* by Aldous Huxley; *Amusing Ourselves to Death* by Neil Postman; and Ben Bagdikian's *Media Monopoly.* This was a fun and stimulating set of books, I figured, which would give students an excellent overview of how mass communication works in our society, while encouraging students to think critically about the media. (I took this approach as a new instructor, unaware of the latest fad on many college campuses known as "critical thinking.") Recalling the reading demands I had in college, I asked the students to read approximately one book per week. For each book, we'd break into seminar groups to discuss it. I appointed a seminar leader and a note-taker for each session and asked the groups to discuss a list of seminar questions I had developed for each book.

After my experience the first quarter, I should have known better than to expect students to read these books. Their incentive to do so was that I counted participation in seminars as some 15 percent of the overall grade. To seminar leaders and note-takers, I would give an A for the day in participation. Otherwise, I found myself in the rather ridiculous position of actually counting how many times each student spoke during a given seminar. I was succumbing to the Skinnerian world! The clever students would soon figure out that it didn't really matter what they said as long as they talked. And they could do that without reading the books. I also resorted to silly, unsubstantial questions on the mid-term and final exams to assure that they read the books.

But the complaints I routinely received from students on the supposed difficulty of the readings is what really threw me off balance. One young woman who sat at the front of the class said, "These books are too hard!" One day, after hearing this complaint a few times, I said, "The readings might be hard for you, but that's okay. It's okay to struggle with your reading in a college class. That's how you learn." I told the class that I considered the reading list as being no more difficult than reading a good newspaper or magazine, such as *The New York Times* or *Newsweek,* and I figured that college freshmen and sophomores should be required to read books at that level. I said, "If you can't read at this level, maybe you don't belong in the course."

I was equally idealistic with a writing class I taught spring quarter of my first year. Knowing how dull most such writing classes could be, I allowed my students to pick a topic area they could stick with all quarter, such as the environment, medicine and health, geology, AIDS, or whatever interested them. This idea, quite different from how most writing instructors trained in English approached the course, came straight out of my experience at newspapers, in which writers developed and concentrated on areas of expertise.

As this was a second writing course for students, they entered the class not only with high school writing but also with at least one college writing course behind them. Some students came to my class with an exceedingly high opinion of their writing. Who was I to tell them they might need improvement? Still, much of the writing I received in this class was simply horrid. Even after passing basic college composition, many students continued to write incomplete sentences, comma splices, and run-on sentences. Many students tended to be overly wordy or to write muddled sentences as well.

One woman in the class was particularly prone to muddled writing. I discovered two types of muddled student writers: Apparently bright ones who harbored excessively high opinions of their writing but who'd always gotten away with doing poor work; and people who just had trouble thinking straight. The clever bad writers were far more difficult for me to deal with.

Joni was a poor writer of this latter variety. She chose to write about the environment for the quarter, and she seemed to have the seeds of interesting ideas, but her thoughts sort of turned to mud the minute she put them on paper. Joni was one of those ebullient people in class, orally very at ease. The C's I would give her on her papers clearly didn't match up with her self-concept, and she told me as much when she confronted me one day about the grades I gave her. "I've never gotten below a B in writing," she told me, strongly implying that I was the one, not she, who needed to improve. "It's just your opinion," she said.

Dealing with such people was worse than pulling teeth. There was nothing I could say to convince them that perhaps I had a bit more experience in writing than they and that maybe they ought to listen. Joni, for instance, was openly hostile to me in front of the class when I instructed on the subject of clarity and wordiness. I'd developed an exercise on this topic from a student's old paper about hemophilia, a disease of improper blood clotting which generally strikes males rather than females. I explained this to the class while showing them the original wordy passages. Then I compared the wordy passages to my rewritten passages to show students what I meant by concise writing. One day, Joni, in her smooth, confident voice, openly criticized my rewrites. "Why did you write 'he' so much? It seems rather redundant and besides that, it's sexist," she complained. Did I need to explain hemophilia again? Did I have to stand there and defend the obvious to this openly hostile woman? Again, my inexperience caught me in a bind, and I answered her with a sharp tone to my voice, certainly not as delicately as I now know I should have.

My idealism began to erode. That quarter I began to enforce an attendance policy, whereby I'd deduct 0.5 points (on a 4 point scale) from a student's final grade if he or she missed five classes. This formula was typical among instructors in my department. I also required written documentation from students to prove they had a legitimate excuse for being absent, such as a doctor's note or death notice. But even with such a stiff penalty, many students didn't show up for class. Then they'd cry foul at the end of the quarter when they learned their grade would suffer because they were absent so much.

Chad was fairly typical in this regard, except that he was brighter than most and tried to talk his way out of his fix. He was doing very well in the class, but I told him his final grade would suffer significantly as a result of his attendance problem. Chad told me he planned to attend law school and that he'd have to retake this class if he didn't get an A. "Maybe we can work something out," he said. I told Chad that there wasn't anything to work out, that the attendance policy was clearly spelled out in the syllabus and that he'd made his decision when he decided not to come to class, and now he'd have to live with it. I figured this was the usual, traditional approach to higher education whereby teachers assume students take responsibility for their decisions.

Maybe we can work something out. I would end up hearing that proposition more than once from students who didn't like the grade they were getting, and to whom standards were always something you could bend. This was a quintessential trait of Generation X. They had grown up in a world in which nearly everything else was negotiable, flexible, changeable; why not grades?

Consider also Hannah, a student in my journalism class one quarter. I was teaching the class about writing leads for news stories, the first paragraphs that normally consist of a single, straightforward sentence summarizing the story. I had assigned some lead-writing exercises that we were going over one day. I tried to make a practice of doing the same work as the students in order to show them how a professional might have approached the same story. So, as I was discussing a lead on the overhead projector, Hannah blurted out, "Isn't that kind of wordy?" The bluntness of her charge, ripping up my lead in front of the class, startled me. Defensively, I said, "No, it might be a bit on the long side, but I don't think it's wordy." The rest of the class looked on in silence, perhaps uncomfortable at my defensiveness with Hannah. That night, I took home the students' leads and graded them. I noticed that Hannah's were indeed succinct: They read more like terse story headlines, not weighted down by "the," "a," and other articles. She got a poor grade on that assignment, and she wasn't doing well in the course.

Hannah turned up at my office later that week to talk about her poor grade. I went over the assignment with her and pointed out what she was doing wrong.

I was in mid-sentence when she said, "Oh, God I feel stupid."

"What's that?" I said.

"You're not going to believe this, but I thought leads were the headlines."

"Well, that certainly explains why you thought my leads yesterday were wordy."

"God, I feel embarrassed. You must think I'm really dumb."

"No, I can understand why you made the mistake," I lied, trying to make her feel better. Then our conversation broadened to her performance over the quarter. She attended intermittently, and this incident with the leads was a sure sign that she just wasn't in the game.

"I'm feeling you aren't really committed to the class," I said. "At the rate you're going, you're probably going to fail the course."

"I feel really bad about that. But I want you to know I am committed. It's just that I'm supposed to be at work when this class meets, and sometimes it seems like I'm not going to miss much so I go to work instead," she said.

Ah, just the words a professor wants to hear, that she thinks she's not going to miss much by not attending my boring class.

Hannah explained that she worked at an upscale shoe store as a salesperson. I remember thinking to myself, "She looks the type, petite, athletic, attractive." Don't they earn bonuses by persuading people to buy things?

My thoughts almost anticipated her next words. "Well, maybe we can work something out," she said. Her large, attractive eyes seemed to have no trouble meeting mine head on. There was little doubt this young woman was confident with older men, and my inner voice whispered, "This is trouble, watch out." She moved closer and touched my arm. "How about if we talk about this over a drink," she suggested.

I could hear my real voice beginning to crack. I felt like she could see through me, watching the wheels practically churning in my head as I, for just the slightest moment too long, considered (perhaps that's too strong a word, toyed with, maybe?) her thinly disguised proposal. These were post–Anita Hill–Clarence Thomas days, and I was paranoid about a sexual harassment charge. In fact, I was so concerned about another female student being slightly off-balance in this regard, that I had gone to talk to Anita about the situation prior to that student's visit in my office. She suggested that somebody else be in the room with us. But now, I found myself alone in the room with Hannah. I didn't respond directly to her little gambit, and played it straight, trying to keep a straight face. It was, after all, sort of amusing for me, never having been in this position before.

"I think what you need to do is decide whether you're in this course or not," I said. "That means attending class and it means making a choice whether you want to be here or not. If you decide to be here, I'll help you as best I can."

Hannah came to class one or two more times. Then, as too many students seem to do, she sort of just vanished one day, and I never saw her again.

▰ ▰ ▰

Eventually, I reached a point during my first year of teaching when I almost quit. The crisis began with a student named Pete.

Pete at first seemed to be my ideal student. He was attentive and polite, rather unlike the guys with the backward baseball hats slumped in their chairs. Pete, in his late twenties, had returned to school after working a few years, and his real world experience had made him a quick study at figuring out the system at The College.

Pete had learned one of The College's key unwritten rules: The customer, namely, the student, is always right in disputes with a faculty member. And when he and the other students weren't getting the kind of grades from me they'd been used to getting from other instructors, Pete exploited this unwritten rule until I was confronted with a near mutiny.

From my perspective, Pete's main problem with my class was that he couldn't write at the college level. But he was outstanding at regurgitation; he did well on multiple-choice tests that came straight out of the book. Let me concede that I was probably a bit too tough a grader at first, coming from the professional world. But I was shocked and amazed at the poor quality of the papers I got. The journalism papers were often painful to read. All I was really looking for in the papers was some evidence of thinking and a decent presentation in terms of grammar and spelling. I would ask myself, "Is this college level work?" If not, I'd give a D or an F. I gave Pete average grades, and I considered those generous.

One day, after I returned the students' first papers analyzing a newspaper, Pete came to my office to talk to me and ask why he got such a poor grade. "I'm an A student," he said. "And I need an A in this course to graduate with honors."

That was a refrain I would hear often over the next several months from other students: "I *need* an A," or "I *need* a B." Sometimes it was "I need a 2.0" so he or she could remain qualified for financial aid. At first, I didn't know what to say when students confronted me with such objections and pleas. My instinct—which was wrong, of course—was to say, "Well, I'll do what I can," thus falling into their trap. The trap being that it was somehow my responsibility that they get their desired grade, or more to the point, my fault if they didn't. Being unused to handling this sort of manipulation, I probably fell into Pete's trap, and gave him the impression that his grades would soon improve. When he came to see me, I went over line by line why I gave him the grade. But his next paper was equally bad. I didn't hesitate to give him another grade well below his expectations.

Pete wasn't the only one in the class getting lower than expected grades on the assignments. What really threw me was that I was giving an abundance of such grades on straightforward multiple-choice tests. But it was little wonder. I noticed that during my lectures, many of the students just sat there staring at me, not even taking notes. This blew me away. It turned out that, like many aspects of school life, my students often needed to be told what to do. The educational culture they'd come from had trained them not to breathe without a specific instruction to do so, it seemed. One day, I got so irritated at this lack of note-taking that I told the class, "You'd be well advised to start taking notes, or you will fail the exam."

It also turned out that they weren't taking notes because they were waiting for The Review, for that's when they'd get down to some serious note-taking. Why waste the time scribbling if it's not going to be on the test? One day, as the mid-term exam was approaching, a woman in the front of the class raised her hand and asked, "When is the review?" "Yeah, when's the review?" a chorus of voices chimed in. My initial instinct would have been to say, "There's really no need to review because I'd just end up repeating what I've already said. Everything you've read and heard in lecture is fair game." That, anyway, was the sort of thing I used to hear from my college teachers. But even then, I sensed that would be a little too harsh, so I said, "Well, I hadn't thought about that, okay, let's have a review the day before the test."

On Review Day, the pens and pencils started flailing and the tongues wagging like excited puppies. My students showed the sort of enthusiasm and focus I had hoped for all along. As I was reviewing the material, I found myself being quite direct about what I considered important and would probably ask about on the test. Was that the nature of The Review, to spell out what was going to be on the test? Had I fallen into another trap?

When we had wrapped up The Review, a student asked, "Will we need Scantrons?" "Will you need what?" I said. "Scantrons. Computer grading forms." I'd never heard of these things, and knowing I was appearing to be ignorant of the ways of higher education, I said, "Oh, yeah, bring those."

The test was easy, consisting of some twenty-five multiple choice questions, taken directly from the book and my lectures. There wasn't much thinking or imagination involved. If you had read the book and taken notes, any notes, you'd ace this test. On test day, I was encouraged when many people finished in twenty minutes. After class, I compiled the completed Scantron forms into a neat deck, and fed them into this machine in the department office that automatically processed the forms then spit them back out with the number each student missed. It took me all of five minutes to grade the test. To my astonishment, many of the students missed half the answers. I was feeling guilty, until I figured that the average was about a C, or about a 2.0 on a 4 point scale. This was satisfying for me. I had grown up in the world of the bell-shaped curve, where the average was supposed to be a C; so the results of the test fit well into the way the world ought to work, or so I figured.

My students, however, had grown up with different notions of how the world ought to work. I wouldn't actually take this knowledge to heart until several months later when my student evaluations started coming in, and when I started asking around about grades at The College. But my students knew what I didn't: The *average* course grade at The College was a strong B. In the twisted logic of many students, a mere 2.0 was half of a 4 point, which in their minds means you flunked.

After I handed back the test, the muttering of complaints and dissatisfactions began. One of the big-haired young women said, "Do we get any extra credit?" Pete nodded his head and said politely, "It sure would be appreciated." I didn't know what to say. *Extra credit?* I thought, Wasn't that what they did in high school? This is what college students expected these days? I don't remember, but in my irritation I might have said something like, "I'll think about it. But you're not in high school any more, folks." The class stared silently, blankly back; Pete whispered something to the student next to him while shaking his head in feigned disgust. I sensed trouble ahead.

One day, I showed a film about the presidency and the mass media, focusing on the president's relationship with the press. It was fascinating stuff, but I felt uneasy. The poisonous relationship that had been developing between me and the class was palatable as the projector flickered away in the dark room. It was a Friday. The hour ended, and the lights remained low as I clicked off the projector in the back of the room. I then told the class of their next assignment, which I said was due Tuesday. "What?!" the chorus of voices screamed. "That's not fair!" I heard the word "weekend" several times. I was in the back of the room, feeling like a trapped animal, my head flushed with anxiety. I couldn't think. Why was it unfair? I was losing control of the class, and in my inexperience I didn't know what to do or say. I think I said something like, "What are you afraid of, a little work?" I gathered my book bag, made a prompt exit, ending that little scene. But the real battle had just begun.

"Hey, you have a minute?" came my (acting) department chairwoman's smooth, cool voice behind me as I was walking to my office. I slowly marched behind her upstairs to her spacious office, which occupied a good part of the second floor. Anita had served as chairwoman of the department on several previous occasions and had one of the larger offices on campus. The lights were low and cool. She was dressed in jeans, tennis shoes, pullover, and blazer, her usual work wear. She crossed her legs, and smiled. After a minute of small talk, Anita said, "One of your students has come to me with a complaint." She looked at a note in her hand over the tops of the rims of her glasses. The note was her summary of an apparently lengthy conversation in which Pete had taken the opportunity to give Anita a laundry list of complaints about me, everything from my lecturing style to my allegedly poor instruction. Anita handed me the note and said, "Maybe you ought to take the initiative to meet with Pete and try to resolve this." You can imagine how I felt. A new teacher, my first year at The College, and already I'm being reprimanded by my department chair.

A day later, I ran into Roger, who had been sort of a mentor of mine in the department. He said he'd talked to Anita and that we needed to try to handle this little problem as a department and try to keep it from going any further, meaning up the chain of command to some dean or vice president's office.

Next day in class I saw Pete and invited him to my office to discuss his complaint. "I understand you have a problem you'd like to talk about," I said. He grabbed his pack in a huff and said, "You bet I do."

In my office, Pete told me my expectations were unreasonable. "I'm not alone in feeling this way," Pete said, explaining that he'd talked to others in the class who have rallied behind him. He said he decided to be a spokesman of sorts for the class's complaints against me after the incident last Friday in which I "used abusive language" with the students in my little remark about the students being afraid of hard work. Pete added, "I thought this whole thing had gone too far when a guy in the class threatened to punch your lights out."

Shortly after this encounter, Pete, Anita, Roger, and I planned to meet. Our agenda, according to the plan Roger and Anita had worked out, was to do whatever it took to make Pete happy so he would "go away." At the time, I was more than happy to make Pete go away. I was having bad dreams about him and the class, and was seriously considering just walking away from the whole ugly situation and chalking up my attempt at teaching as a failure. Anita and

Roger said we could arrange a deal that would allow Pete to get what he wanted, even though the official deadline had passed to make such an arrangement. "I'll have a talk with the registrar's office," Roger said. I can't reveal what the deal was, but it was attractive for all parties, especially Pete.

So we met. Pete huffed and puffed, seeming to sense that he had the entire department at his beck and call. I tried to stay calm and not become entangled with Pete in an argument. I felt like strangling him because I could see him manipulating the system to get what he wanted, despite his protestations that he was acting on behalf of the entire class. We made Pete the offer, and he accepted. This blowup occurred with about a quarter of the course remaining. Pete would not attend any more of my classes.

Although I didn't know it at the time, I would learn later that my Pete affair was far from unusual. Though Roger and Anita had hinted as much in the midst of the crisis, they never came out and said it. But I would later discover that, at one time or another, virtually every instructor on campus had had their own Pete to deal with at some point.

I was glad to be rid if Pete; not seeing him glaring at me from his little perch in the corner was a great relief to me for the rest of the quarter. But privately I was bothered by the outcome. Roger and Anita would disagree, arguing that what we did was fair and ethical, but in my mind we had sort of bought him off, paid him what amounted to hush money to quit complaining and stop upsetting the happy life at The College. Was anybody else in the class offered the same deal to have the rules bent? Well, no. Pete got what he wanted, and he probably graduated with honors. I got a black eye. But it wouldn't be the last one resulting from my encounters with students. I learned about the very legal—and some would believe, ethical— pandering, usually in the form of grades, that we teachers engaged in every day out of habit or perhaps simply as a matter of professional survival.

After that fiasco, I began to wonder just how typical my experi- ence was at The College. Was there something unusual about stu- dents at my college compared to other colleges and universities? Did only students at my college refuse to read? Did only our students be- have so inappropriately during class? Did only ours look so bored and disengaged? Were twenty-year-olds at community colleges all that different from those at four-year schools? At first glance, a casual observer would very likely conclude that I was experiencing an ordinary generation gap, that I was witnessing what teachers had been experiencing throughout the ages. Or, this observer might say my experience was limited to community colleges, which continually battle the stereotype of being academically inferior to four-year colleges and universities. Indeed, I figured at first that my experience couldn't possibly be shared by professors at more prestigious institutions. Welcome to "A-Mart" College, I told myself. Welcome to teaching, period, I thought.

But my views soon changed.

One day, I was sitting in my office when Leah, a sales rep at a major textbook publisher, stopped by. As usual, she was trying to sell me textbooks, when the futility of my ordering books that students wouldn't read suddenly hit me.

"Are you looking for any new texts?" she asked. I looked at her and then I looked some more at her and then I said, "You know, sometimes I wonder why I should bother even ordering textbooks, because my students don't read them anyway." I had unwittingly struck a nerve in Leah, who suddenly became animated. For the next thirty minutes, Leah told me about a curious phenomenon textbook companies had been noticing in just the past few years at colleges and universities throughout her sales territory: Textbooks that instructors would require for classes would remain unsold at college and university bookstores for weeks or even months into a new term.

"Over the last two years, students have definitely changed," Leah said. "There is something different about this group of students. Now, unless the instructor specifically says, 'This is important and it's going to be on the test,' they don't seem to find that buying the books is an impending need."

I asked Leah if students could afford the books. She said, "Yes. It's not about economics. They're still buying other things like CD's and nice cars. There's even more of that than in the past. Bookstores are well stocked with expensive sweatshirts and T-shirts. No, it's not economics. I think students have changed. The value of a book and the value of learning hasn't been instilled in them. They've got less connection to the printed word. We're just noticing that a lot more books are just sitting there."

Perhaps Leah shouldn't have been so up-front with me. I ordered no new books on that visit.

About the same time, I called a friend at a large state university campus in California. Greg chaired a large department and also the faculty senate. Greg had been involved in higher education for many years, and I called him figuring that if any school was a fairly good barometer of recent trends at public four-year universities, his sprawling, highly diverse state university campus would be it. I told Greg some of what I'd been through and asked him if he could relate. Now in his fifties, Greg reflected back to his college days and told me that, even through the Vietnam era, student attitudes and traits had remained fairly constant but that something fundamentally changed after the mid-1980s.

"All, generations change," he told me. "The Vietnam generation was different than the others. For instance, everyone tried to break down the grading system, but that didn't catch on. I see real continuity all the way from my own generation of students up until maybe 1985 to 1988. At that point, there was a qualitative shift."

I asked him how he would characterize that shift. He said, "Over the past four or five years some of our students are less prepared, have more of a sense of entitlement, and they're not very deferential . . . . Some are outright hustlers and try to brow-beat professors into giving good grades."

Greg told me that nearly half of the freshmen on his campus at a given time were on academic probation for doing C-minus work, compared to 22 percent who earned that dubious honor just ten years ago.

Then there was my encounter with Madeline, providing further evidence to suggest that my experience at The College was in no way unique. Madeline had recently left her job as an administrator at a university to take a job at The College. One day, we were chatting and, prompted by my recent experience, I asked Madeline if our students were any different than students where she had come from. "Absolutely not," Madeline said. Then she told me something quite startling, which for the first time summed up for me the source of the profound shift that Greg and others were talking about. "You've heard of Generation X haven't you?" she said. "Well, it's a Generation X thing."

Thus went my first year of teaching. On some days I felt like walking out of the classroom in disgust, never to return. My students wanted it all: a Mercedes grade—even the Mercedes itself—but were often willing to give me only a Chevy's worth in terms of quality or effort. And I, trying to impose my own values in which hard work and talent still mattered, was determined not to give them an inch they didn't earn.

My students weren't going to change. They were the power now. They paid the bills and the salaries at The College, and it often seemed that teachers like me were tantamount to their public servants. My students were the coveted youth, the objects of desire in youth-worshipping America of the 1990s.

The only thing to change was me. While continuing on my journey to become a teacher, going through what every teacher went through to become a full-blown member of the academic club, I decided at that juncture to return to my roots as a reporter. I wanted to understand what it took to succeed teaching the X Generation. So I went undercover.

CHAPTER 3

The Castle, with Apologies to Franz Kafka

I came to The College with a cohort of several new full-time instructors, and for nearly three years we were treated not too differently from interns, expected to jump through the necessary hoops to reach that Kafkaesque Castle called Tenure, a state of being that people in academia consider to be next to godliness. This was because, in theory, a tenured member of the faculty couldn't be fired.

I need to explain the tenure process because tenure is the *raison d' être* for a great deal of what happens at colleges and universities. I was appointed what The College called a "tenure committee," composed of faculty members in my department who were supposed to watch me, critique me, and make a recommendation about my progress toward tenure to another, bigger tenure committee, that I will refer to as the Big Committee. This key committee would evaluate me and make a recommendation about tenure to the president of The College, and he in turn would give me a thumbs up or down to the Board of Trustees.

Tenure is the reason young assistant professors at major research universities are willing to publish or perish; and it's that state of nirvana called tenure for which people at smaller teaching-oriented institutions such as mine were also willing to jump through hoop after hoop.

Not the least of these hoops was allowing students to anonymously evaluate instructors, irrespective of whether students were in a position to know good teaching from bad. In coming into teaching, I had assumed that student evaluations of my teaching would be considered but that these would only be one of several factors, including my colleagues' evaluations, professional and research activities, work on faculty committees, and so on. But that assumption was just one of the many that turned out to be exactly wrong.

Before I tell you about my experiences with student evaluations, let me briefly explain the other ways that teachers were watched. They were watched when they knew they were being watched and watched even when they didn't know it. When I knew I was being observed, it was usually because some administrator or tenured faculty member had decided to come to my classes to watch me teach.

Beth, whom I've mentioned before, was on my tenure committee. So was Clark, an old hippie who, among all the committee members, took the most jaundiced view of the process. Finally there were Andy and Ken, the latter a gangling southerner, who chaired the group.

People on my tenure committee visited my classes, and they watched me teach. A Visit by a tenure committee member had the potential to be very demeaning—appropriate to my internship-like status—depending on what status games my visitors felt like playing. Ken was often the worst in this respect. Theoretically, the visits were supposed to be as non-intrusive as possible so the evaluator could get an accurate and objective reading on the class. But Ken didn't seem to know or care about the Heisenberg Principle, the law from physics which says that the very act of measuring something can alter what you're trying to measure. Ken seemed to go out of his way to make his presence known. He'd chat with students and generally give off vibes that he was there to watch lowly me. And let me tell you, it's not good classroom politics for college students to know you, the instructor, are being watched. In this case, knowledge truly is power, for it gives students a sense that they can push you; it gives them that imperceptible bit of leverage with which to wield power, and power for them means being able to extract what they want from the instructor, which usually boils down to getting a good grade.

One day during my first year, Ken came to visit my journalism class. I happened to be showing students that day's front page of the *New York Times* to illustrate some points about news judgment. Ken was a proud reader of the *Times,* and he seemed to like to show this off. Apparently that morning he'd read some minor story on the inside page. I don't recall what the story was about. But in the middle of our class discussion, Ken piped up, asking me an irrelevant question about this story that had no noticeable connection to our topic. "I don't believe he's doing this," I said to myself. I answered his question tersely and dismissively as possible, taking just about five seconds. Then I moved on to the point of my lecture.

Like Chauncy Gardner, The College liked to watch. Over the course of nearly three years, each of the four people on my committee would watch me teach a total of seven times, for a total of twenty-eight classroom visits. That didn't include additional visits by my department chair, and by a dean of some sort. After about ten visits, you'd ask yourself, What's the point? What are they going to see that they haven't seen before?

While I was mildly amused at the intrusive nature of The Visit, the committee members' write-ups of their visits to my classes were uniformly positive. According to my tenure committee members' written evaluations, it seemed clear that I was doing a good job in their eyes and was, to my mild surprise, performing well as a teacher.

In the meantime, I often discussed the tenure process with Chris, a colleague who was also being evaluated for tenure. Chris grew up in a totalitarian country. He had studied in Europe and in the United States, and had some teaching experience abroad. Especially during the culture shock of the first year, Chris and I would talk frequently about life at The College, and the challenges of teaching this generation of American college students.

One day, Chris and I were talking, and he said something I found profound and rather surprising. Chris said, "I grew up under a totalitarian government and worked as a teacher there, and never did anybody come to visit my classroom to make sure I was toeing the line." In that sense, Chris said, there was more "oppression" of teachers in the United States, a country that boasts the ideals of freedom of speech and thought, and that there was more pressure to conform to "acceptable" ideas in U.S. classrooms.

Chris and I got our own private chuckle out of that irony. Still, we both fared well under the particular form of scrutiny called The Visit. I of course didn't openly complain, not even about Ken's interference in my classroom. The visits were one of those things in life you couldn't do anything about, so why bother getting worked up?

In addition to being bombarded with uninvited visitors, I was watched not even knowing I was being watched, when, or by whom. But the paper trail from this form of watching came in a report the department chairwoman had prepared, summarizing the comments he'd received from other tenured faculty members about the tenure-track people. There were no rules of conduct pertaining to these comments; the other instructors were permitted to say whatever they wanted about the instructor whether or not they'd actually interacted with him or her. It was an odious exercise, subject to all manner of abuse. If you rubbed a tenured faculty member the wrong way, didn't smile and say hello in the hallway, that person could hit back, and hit hard. Then you had to trust that the department chairwoman's report was a fair and accurate summary of the comments he'd received.

Well, I got slammed. Anita, the acting chairwoman, wrote in her report that one member of the faculty, whom she did not identify, submitted her comments pertaining to a conversation this instructor had with one of my students, who also was unidentified. According to Anita's report, this instructor said the student had complained to this other instructor about my "harsh" feedback on her essays and my "rude" attitude. Nearly the whole report was devoted to describing this alleged incident. I didn't have a clue what he was talking about. And even if the incident happened, what kind of system was this that allowed this anonymous slander into my official record without any checks or balances? It was annoying that the student didn't talk to me first, and that the anonymous instructor didn't check his facts first.

The incident underscored for me one of the ways students could exercise their power in the hiring and firing of their instructors, and do so with very little accountability. For all I knew this anonymous student was Joni or some other student I'd crossed during my first year of teaching because I tried to maintain grading standards. Chris's comparisons to his totalitarian home swirled in my head as being truer to our situation than we dared to admit. I imagine what the headline might look like:

Probationer Jailed for Thought Crimes!
Unnamed Professor Says of Dupe Instructor:
"He Was Rude!"

Last, but certainly not least, I was watched by students.

And, after students watched you, they also made anonymous comments about you in something innocuously known as "student evaluations." As I said, I had figured that student evaluations were only part of the entire tenure evaluation process. After teaching a few quarters, I felt quite justified in this belief, because I figured an intelligent system would absolutely have to take the viewpoints of students with a grain of salt. After all, many of them had difficulty writing a complete sentence. I tried to be the best teacher possible and not cave in to what I considered to be unreasonable demands many of the students placed on me. I assumed that just being myself, and trying to make students think, and being as frank as I could be in my evaluation of their performance, would be enough. But I would learn that that wasn't enough.

When I got my first set of student evaluations, I was actually sort of pleased. There were some very harsh criticisms, some of which gave me things to think about and try to work on, but I received other comments that seemed so off the wall that I dismissed them out of hand. I also got some flattering comments, which suggested perhaps I was on the right track.

Here's a smattering of student comments from my first journalism class, the one that really initiated me into The College's culture and its students:

> *"He shows up for class."*
>
> *"I did not like one thing about this course."*
>
> *"I feel the instructor was very dry and boring. . . . Instructor needs to Liven Up!!!"*
>
> *"I sort of feel bad for the instructor because the students this quarter gave him alot (sic) of grief. I think he did very well at making us think which is what college should be for. I think kids expected him to baby them when in reality they needed to be taught . . . . I liked him alot (sic) and hope he does not get discouraged with the students at (The College). But personally I've been here for 2 years and he is the only teacher I've had who tries to make you think."*
>
> *"He did not make the class exciting, I always fell asleep and the papers were not fair. The way he presents himself is not very interesting."*
>
> *"Hair uncombed usually, clothes wrinkled. . . . Boring."*
>
> *"A challenging instructor who desires his students to think and act responsibly when taking in information about the class. He desires excellence."*

As I look back on those sentences from the clear perspective that one achieves with time in the Rocky Mountains, the meaning of my students' words is far clearer to me now than when I first received them. The comments spoke volumes about the stark dichotomy that existed among students I taught, a generation divided by the more serious ones who were going to college with purpose, and by those whose reasons for being in college weren't at all clear, who seemed more concerned about being entertained than by learning. I was pleased and flattered by the comments from those who said I taught students to think; but I would eventually learn that professional survival demanded that I pay less attention to them and more attention to the students for whom thinking was a painful and alien process.

The evaluations from my first writing classes fell along the same lines. A pattern developed immediately. It seemed students liked me a lot or else despised me with equally remarkable vigor. And at the time, that didn't seem so bad.

Here's how they loved me:

> *"This was probably the most informative writing class I've ever had."*
> *"I learned how to write a lot better than I did in high school."*
> *"I really have learned to enjoy writing!!"*

And how they loved me not:

> *"My last two papers have been destroyed with comments that are entirely your opinion."*

When I got those first evaluations and shared them with my partner, Sandy, I said, "Well it seems clear to me that I've got to teach to the serious students. They're the ones who are getting something from what I have to offer. Let the others flounder." She seemed to agree that that seemed like a good way to handle the unsettling fracture among students which showed up through the evaluations. But that approach would turn out to be a mistake. The unmotivated students who wanted things to be spelled out in black and white, who wanted you to spoon-feed them facts and information or to "teach them how to write" far out-numbered the students who understood that their education was a far more complicated process, who knew that as a teacher, I could only help them get on the right track, and that ultimately, they had to do it themselves.

My student evaluations only got worse.

The following quarter came the writing course I've previously mentioned, in which I told students to pick a general topic area, and stick to it all quarter with each paper they wrote. The students indeed seemed to like that idea, until they started to see how I graded their papers.

These comments from the student evaluations sort of summed up what they thought of my grading:

> "This may be just my opinion, but to me, the instructor expected far too much."
>
> "Overall, he's a great teacher, but I think his grading system is a little too hard."
>
> "Very critical grading—I think that the grading was far too tough."

And in the following comments, the students themselves noted how many of their peers wouldn't do the assigned work, unless they were somehow forced to:

> "Unfortunately, students don't do their assignments because they are not worth any points."
>
> "The class approach is good in principle. The problem arises when a large portion of the class is not very motivated."

And others slammed me for not being more friendly:

> "He antagonized students the first week of class with his demeanor. Should try to develop a rapport with his students. It would be nice if he would crack a smile once in a while."

Then there was this precious paragraph that seemed to capture everything students disliked about me as a teacher:

> "I have found nothing in this class productive or useful. I hated this class and found it hard to get up in the morning to get here. I would have dropped it except that I am graduating in June."

Okay. That doesn't look good, I thought when I saw this comment. Even if the evaluations weren't going to count for much—(I was still operating according to this grossly inaccurate assumption)—I figured very negative comments like that were going to raise eyebrows.

But there were still evaluations to come from my introductory journalism class, the one I was so idealistic about in trashing the boring textbook and bringing in the works of Chomsky, Postman, and other authors. I was hopeful.

The day the student evaluations came out, I eagerly opened the manilla envelope in my in-box and scanned the nearly four single-spaced typed pages of comments. I looked for some good stuff. I liked the one that said I dealt with the class in "real world terms" and didn't "sugar-coat things," and several others that said I knew what I was talking about. But there were also plenty of stinging remarks. I repeat those here because they became determinative in the minds of people on my committee and other authorities at The College who decided whether an instructor was competent or not. My students wrote:

> "The course had an overload of reading texts—by the time I finished one we were into the next."
>
> "The reading material was terrible, and hard to understand . . . . I wouldn't recommend this class to anyone!"
>
> "There wasn't one thing that I really liked best about the course. . . . I'm sure he's very competent in his professional field, but it's hot out and it needs to be more interesting to keep our attention."

Having received these poor evaluations from students, I would have truly taken them to heart if I hadn't received such praise from my committee members in their own written evaluations of my teaching. I began to wonder what could explain the fact that some students were seeing one thing in my teaching while professional teachers and even many of the students were seeing something entirely different. The disparity that emerged between what my colleagues thought of my teaching and what students said about me in their evaluations was odd. The disparity was in fact rather sharp, as if the faculty and the students were describing two different people.

The trouble was, it got worse. And ironically, the collective say-so of the most negative students—and quite likely the ones with the worst skills and motivation—would turn out to carry the most weight for the gatekeepers of this Castle.

MTV Generation Cries Foul!
Incompetent Boomer Hanged in Public!
"He Put Me to Sleep," Complains 'Bored' GenXer!

CHAPTER 4

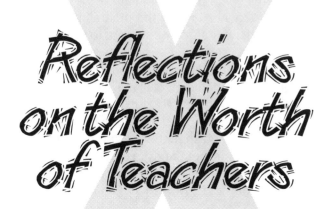

Reflections on the Worth of Teachers

So ended my first year teaching. I was bruised—and absolutely ready for the big payoff—summer vacation. Chris and Mike (other first-year teachers), stayed on campus to teach summer session. I couldn't fathom it. I was burned out and wanted rid of the feeling that I was some kind of energy source that students would constantly and mindlessly suck until there was nothing left of me. If I taught another minute, I might have murdered somebody. I think I felt like a mother of young children who needed a break before she snapped.

But that three months of freedom reminded me that I'd perhaps done the right thing going into teaching. First, Sandy and I drove out of state, camped out, and rode our mountain bikes in the wild, open, high desert. Then I flew to Copenhagen on the first stop of a two-month journey through northern Europe. I bicycled through the pretty meadows of Denmark, climbed mountains and trekked across vast expanses of open, empty country in Norway, drank beer in Amsterdam, and slept on sunny Swedish beaches. I flew home, caught a Grateful Dead show, then Sandy and I rented a convertible and drove eighty miles an hour to Yellowstone to camp out, hang out, and try to forget about my teaching and her medicine.

Yes, travelling was a big reason I had left newspapering. It helped me come to terms with my doubts that I had quit newspapering just as my career was beginning to pay off fairly handsomely. I knew I was a good reporter, that I thrived in that environment. But I wasn't sure I was a good teacher or had the mentality to ever be a good teacher, at least in the way students seemed to view good teaching. I began to doubt whether the negative aspects of the job itself—revolving principally around the students' incompetence, and sheer laziness—outweighed the benefits of teaching. Nor could I push from my mind dark thoughts about the profession of teaching itself, especially how poorly American society valued teachers relative to other professions. This latter thought haunted me perhaps more than other teachers. Watching my partner Sandy becoming a physician and seeing the dozens of very highly paid opportunities she commanded, I was reminded daily of the downwardly mobile nature of my journey into teaching.

During that first year, I would get into long discussions with Sandy about my anxieties. She was in no position to give much energy to my cause because she was in the middle of her own journey, trying to finish her first of three years of residency. We were quite a pair, constantly bitching to each other about our jobs. I'd complain about students who refused to take responsibility for their educations, and she'd complain to me about some welfare patients whose modus operandi was basically the same: "Take care of me." Here we were, both avowed liberals, I far more liberal than she, starting to sound at times like Newt.

Sometimes we'd talk about money and self-worth. I was still smarting some from the very hefty pay cut I'd taken to become a teacher. In episodes of self-pity, I would stew about the low value society placed on teachers. One night, on a drive back from a weekend vacation, I got into one of these existential funks. "It really annoys me," I said. "As a teacher I'll earn less than a third of what you will. Does that mean that I'm a third as valuable as you?" In a market economy, exchange value was as true as possible a reflection of what something was "worth." Many of us might wish that teachers, nurses, social workers, day-care employees and others in the so-called "helping" occupations earned as much as doctors and lawyers, but the mindless, collective decisions of the marketplace had concluded differently, I told Sandy. She answered, "You've got a very narrow definition of worth." I thought my economic logic was irrefutable. But when I would get into my funks and launch into my freemarket harangue, Sandy would remind me that I might not be making as much money as I did as a journalist or as a research consultant but that I was simply trying out a new path. Then she'd draw a little metaphorical graph in the air. "You were here, you did this, you accomplished all this, and now you're here, trying something else. You're willing to try new things."

These were comforting thoughts, but I would continue to struggle and entertain doubts. I wasn't even sure I valued what teachers did—or perhaps what I thought teachers did. Even as the product of pretty good schools, I had this notion implanted in my brain that those who couldn't "do" went into teaching. As a reporter, I saw myself as a doer. I was used to being judged by the quality of my work, which was open for all to see every day in the newspaper. I was used to being judged harshly if I missed a story or an important angle, or if I wrote something unclearly. I was used to a culture that demanded excellence.

As a teacher, I carried this old stigma about doers with me into my social life, sometimes ashamed to tell people at parties or wherever that I was a teacher. Saying so felt so soft, accommodative, nurturing—traits I had been taught not to value, especially as a man. Besides, I wasn't very good at those things. If that's what being a teacher meant, then maybe I was in the wrong place.

But having acknowledged that I had been programmed to think a certain way, I'm not going to tell you that I underwent some miraculous transformation to change my mind about the worth of teachers and the virtue of teaching. Maybe that's what society wants, to know that there are all these inspired, selfless teachers out there who somehow can transform our youth and our culture—and we only have to pay them $25,000 or $30,000 a year.

That's how it happens in Hollywood, with movies such as *Renaissance Man,* starring Danny DeVito. Maybe you've seen it. He plays an advertising professional who gets fired, forcing him to teach a group of deadbeat army recruits. After a period of high cynicism and just going through the motions, laying plans for his big move back into advertising, DeVito is transformed. And like all inspired teachers, he touches the lives of our young recruits who, because of DeVito, learn to love Shakespeare, learning, and knowledge.

Such plots make good fodder for Hollywood, and they help perpetuate what I now believe is, largely, a destructive mythology about teaching in America. This mythology was given life by the rise of middle-class fortunes and the idealism of the 1960s and 1970s, and was perpetuated in the multicultural orientation of the 1980s and 1990s, as higher education became vastly democratized, opened up to more classes of people than any society had ever done before. But this opening up hasn't come without costs. As an outsider to education looking in, the culture I encountered during my first year of teaching was a near perfect microcosm of our nation's obsession with a form of higher education in which virtually everybody is entitled to success. The "success model" pervades public schools, and as they have failed to produce competent and motivated students, the educational system's response has been to reproduce the same failed paradigm in higher learning. I saw the results of the success mythology in my students, the stories of whom I described in chapter 2. Many of these students were taught by teachers steeped in the ideology and rhetoric of the success model. I'm jumping ahead a bit in my story, but I eventually became involved with a small group of faculty members who were rebelling against the myth that all students deserved to succeed. We called ourselves the Save Our Standards Committee, and our mission was to try and restore academic rigor at The College. At one point, we posed the proposition to all members of the faculty that there was subtle pressure on teachers to ease up on academic standards in order to ensure student "success." The following response was typical of those who worshipped on the altar of success at any cost:

"I will always sacrifice the academic standard of the wealthy and educated elite class in favor of assisting underprepared and motivated students better succeed," this instructor said. "Maximizing the learning of all students, no matter their level of preparation, should be the top priority of all professional and compassionate educators."

It was wonderful sounding rhetoric, but I recoiled at the sound of it. Was it because I didn't have it in me to be the model teacher whom that teacher described? During the times that I reflected on my journey into teaching, I would rip myself apart for being a lousy teacher because I wasn't as compassionate and caring as I thought so many other teachers must be. Once, I was walking down the sidewalk on campus and overheard two students talking. "Oh, Joan is great. She really cares about her students," one said. Caring. That was the model teacher, and I could never see myself being jovial, effervescent, caring Joan.

But I kept returning to the thought that perhaps there was another way, perhaps a better way to be a good teacher. Was it really compassionate and caring to students to ease up on standards so all students might succeed? Were we educators really helping under-prepared students by bending over backwards to bring them up to speed in courses they weren't equipped for? I still wasn't convinced that to be a good teacher, I had to fit the mythical nurturing mold. I could be a good teacher in my own way, by being demanding, intellectually challenging, and by knowing what I was talking about, couldn't I? In my reflections on the worth of teaching and teachers, I thought, teachers aren't worth much if all they become are surrogate mothers who give and give to their students, unconditionally. As a teacher, I wasn't interested in that kind of compassion. My compassion was more one of passion. I was passionate about journalism and about writing. And I cared deeply that my students do both of them well.

CHAPTER 5

"We're Grownups Now"

Last night I dreamed about The College. The dream has been one of the few I've recalled since being in the Rockies because I've been sleeping so deeply and peacefully in the mountains. In the dream, I was talking to Roger, one of the tenured people in my department. Normally calm and cool, Roger was uncharacteristically very irritated, and he was irritated at me. It seems that all The College's students that day for some reason couldn't get a ride to school, and Roger was imploring me—or browbeating is more like it—to personally go and pick up "our students" so they could get to class! It seemed that I was the one instructor being asked to do this, and I refused. "You've got to be kidding," I said. "We can't go around and pick up every student who needs a ride to school! This is college, not kindergarten."

But my position was weak. I knew I didn't have tenure yet, and I would be hard-pressed to resist doing the politically correct thing. I argued with Roger. My selfish reason, I recall, was that I simply didn't want to go around and pick up all the students; I had better things to do. My other reason was more philosophical. I told Roger that our bringing the students to school was wrong and paternalistic, and really wouldn't do them any good in the long run because they had to learn to take responsibility for themselves.

"But we owe this to our students," Roger said. "They depend on us." He kept referring to them as "our students." "If we don't help them, they might drop out of school and we can't allow that," Roger said. We went back and forth, both of us getting angrier and angrier. The dream ended there. I didn't give in. I stuck to my principles.

Had I dreamed this during my first few months at The College, I probably wouldn't have realized what it meant. But I know now that the dream spoke volumes about the prevailing culture of accommodation at The College and how I met with that culture, resisting it because its values were so alien to those I'd become accustomed to before coming to academia. Coming into teaching, I was a firm believer in what I considered traditional notions of self-reliance, initiative, effort, and learning how to think and reason — to provide just enough guidance to allow students to succeed or to fail on their own. But interestingly, students would distrust me for trying to resist the culture of accommodation. Although gaining tenure was not to be my own motivation, I would discover that college instructors, at least those at teaching-oriented institutions who are pursuing tenure, had better give their students that proverbial ride to school.

As my second year began and though my doubts about teaching still lingered, I was fresh from summer break and ready for battle again. I would be teaching two general writing courses, which had been going relatively well in past quarters, and at last, a newswriting course. I'd be rid of that awful introductory journalism class, which seemed to attract more than its share of flaky students who figured it would be an easy A; it didn't take a management genius to figure that I was the wrong teacher for such a match up. The previous spring, I had approached Anita, the acting department chairwoman, one day and said, "So when am I going to get to teach newswriting? After all, that's what you probably hired me for." We agreed. The following fall, I'd take over one of the newswriting sections.

When I was working as a journalist and sometimes imagined being a teacher, I saw myself teaching young, eager students about the art of being a reporter. I remembered back to my own journalism training and thought there was so much more I could teach students about the craft of journalism that Ph.D.'s in mass communications neither knew nor cared about. In having the chance to teach newswriting, I knew that I'd at last be completely in my element.

If there were lessons to be learned from my first year of teaching, about grading and how best to deal with students in order to make them happy, I certainly didn't heed them going into my second year. With a year of classes under my belt, I was more comfortable simply being up there, exposed to the students. The combination of that plus my comfort level with the subject matter of newswriting made me somewhat supercilious as I told the class the first day what to expect for the quarter. And to be honest, added to all that was my recent nomination for a Pulitzer Prize, which seemed to fuel in me this quasi "boot camp" attitude that I was going to shape young people into real journalists. I began the quarter telling my students about my professional background and warned the students that the class wasn't going to be easy, in what amounted to a vain attempt to weed out immediately the students who didn't know a comma from a period.

In the first week a teacher sets the tone for the entire quarter, and it didn't take long for me to get on the class's bad side. The first blowup came with a young woman, who I noticed looked awfully bored by nearly everything I had to say. Once while I was lecturing, I looked up and saw her reading *USA Today.* After class ended that day, I said, "I'd like to talk to you a minute." I told her, "Please don't read while I'm talking to the class." I then asked her a few questions about herself, why she had signed up for the class and so on. She said she'd had taken journalism in high school and worked on the high school paper. "I'm taking the class for the credit," she said. I tried to hold in check my my disdain for the superior attitude she oozed, like she was under consideration for a job at the *Times* or something. "I still might have a thing or two I can teach you," I said.

A day or two later, I was discussing some topic with the class, and this same young woman simply got up and left as I was in mid-sentence. Call it a quirk of mine, but I found this to be plain rudeness. So I confronted her on the spot. "Are you in this class or not?" I asked, purposely trying to make her commit or drop the class. I couldn't tolerate the smirks and her know-it-all attitude. She responded as she stomped out of the room, "Not any more, I'm not." "Good," I said, and then turned to the class to resume the discussion, hoping the other students had gotten my point. But I could see that the atmosphere was poisoned, heavy with resentment. Of course, what I did was professionally unacceptable. In addition, it was uncool to show any emotion or passion with these students, many of whom would stare at you with blase, disengaged looks.

At the time, I didn't understand the psychology of students well enough to figure out why things happened the way they did in that class from then on, but now I realize that when the students saw me demanding their respect and attention, they simply did the opposite and shut down on me, so alien was my behavior from what they were accustomed to from other teachers at The College and from their past experience in high school. From that moment on, I then understood, I'd lost the class, and nothing I could do would win them back.

In the meantime, I forged ahead trying to teach newswriting. Apparently I was a tough grader, but it didn't seem so to me at the time. I told the class that I would grade as if I were an editor on a small paper. In theory, the best grades would go to those stories that required the least amount of work to get them into our hypothetical little paper. And I told them that I'd fail papers that couldn't run even with major re-working. Still, I found that in practice I had to relax those standards. I ended up giving what I thought were decent grades to stuff that could never in a million years see their way into print. I didn't tell the class this, but let them play along with the fiction. I didn't want to belittle their efforts. At the same time, I would critique their stories with comments about how they could improve; and I gave everybody a shot at re-writing their stories for a better grade—against my better judgment.

I found that this sort of tough approach was paying off. Students bitched and complained and often didn't look like they were having much fun, but at key times they were bearing down, concentrating on the work. And in small increments, the quality of their work was improving. They were actually starting to write leads that made sense, to organize their ideas into a sensible order, and write without scores of grammatical and spelling errors.

Shortly before the end of the quarter, I complimented the class for their efforts. I said, "I've noticed some dramatic improvement in the work of many of you, and I appreciate all your hard work. Give yourselves a pat on the back." I didn't give such praise easily, and I had hoped that they would appreciate what I said because I honestly meant it. As I was saying this, I detected a softening in the features of some of the students, like perhaps we had mended our differences and were together again as a class.

Not long after that, Ken and the gang (my department tenure committee) wanted to do my class evaluations in time for the tenure meeting with the Big Committee. That meant doing the student evaluations well before the end of the quarter, which could skew the results, but it had to be done. Things were beginning to feel right in the journalism class, so I had high hopes for the evaluations.

A week after the evaluations were taken, I met with Ken and the gang to discuss the results. On the afternoon we met, I hadn't yet seen that quarter's evaluations. Our meeting was held in a large lecture hall where Ken team-taught an interdisciplinary course on European history with some historians. I walked into the cavernous, dimly lit room and noticed the Nazi flags and paraphernalia adorning its walls, the apparent results of a class project. I wondered privately how unknowing members of the public would take these symbols of fascism if they were to walk into the room. Ken and I engaged in small talk about his course, waiting for Beth, Clark, and Andy to show up.

As the meeting began, Ken passed out the compiled evaluations from my three classes. I quickly scanned the two writing sections, and they seemed fine. Then I turned to the journalism evaluations. As I read them, I could hear the silence, the members of my committee also reading them over. Staring at the students' words, summarized into neatly bureaucratic typed reports, I felt powerful jolts of betrayal vibrate my body.

> *His arrogance far outweighs his helpfulness,*
> *A very hard grader,*
> *Allows questions to be raised*
> *As to why*
> *He is teaching.*
>
> *He presents himself as God,*
> *Extremely sarcastic,*
> *And the class has no destination.*
>
> *Ought to be eliminated.*
>
> *We should get some credit.*
> *Expects us to be great,*
> *He grades*

Very hard,
He snaps
At people.

Considering what I spent
For this class.

We are grown-ups now,
He grades too hard,
He presents himself
As God.

You cannot leave class
Without Him
Getting mad.

I am extremely disappointed
With the instructor
Of this class.

Ought to be eliminated.

We are grownups now.

There, in this surreal situation, surrounded by Nazi flags and the silence of the members of my committee, I didn't hide my reaction, which spurted out like blood. "I can't believe this," I said. "This isn't the same class I thought I was teaching. I feel betrayed by this."

My reaction to the evaluations turned out to be a major tactical error, because I allowed the floodgates of criticism to open wide. Ken, who turned out to be a true believer in student evaluations, expressed his grave doubts. Beth reacted with dismay. Clark, as usual, made light of the evaluations, because he always figured the worse they were, the better you were teaching (Need I say that his views were in the distinct minority at The College?).

I offered an impromptu analysis.

"I think it boils down to a matter of expectations on the part of the students," I said. "I believed I was teaching a rigorous course in newswriting, but they had something entirely different in mind, something less demanding."

"I think that's probably right," Clark said. "Who's this jerk, 'He presents himself as God?'"

Saying very little was Beth. What must have been her sense of complacency was palatable because I could almost see a smirk on her face. I had visited her classes and had concluded they were much less rigorous than mine. Hers appeared to be an intentionally "more fun" approach. Once, when I visited her class, I was struck at how much like high school it was. Whereas I had students using the *New York Times* as a model for editorials, she asked students to write a letter to the editor. Nothing in her approach seemed too simple or too condescending. I think I had been positioning myself counter to the whole dumb-downed approach that I saw in Beth's classes; but it was becoming clear that her approach to teaching was winning. What's more, I discovered when I would visit other classes that Beth's soft approach was favored among many instructors. In trying to be rigorous and demanding, I seemed to be in a distinct minority.

I continued talking, still on the defensive. "I mean, an analogy might be like accounting or math. If I'm going to prepare people to go on to the next course or to work on the college paper, they need to take one step at a time; they need to learn the fundamentals."

"I hear you're a tough grader," Beth said, in one of her rare statements of opinion. "I wouldn't want to be in your class."

"What do you think about the evaluations?" Ken asked Beth.

"It's a major concern because newswriting is his area of expertise."

Andy took my explanation and ran with its implications. "Maybe if you made some adjustments and taught in a way that might be slightly less demanding but more inclusive, to try to bring in those students who are kind of shopping around, who aren't yet sure if journalism is something they want to pursue," he said.

"I suppose that's possible," I allowed. "It's all a matter of what approach you decide to take."

Ken hadn't said much until now. But his silence was telling. "I think we're burying our heads in the sand here," he said. "I think we have a real problem here."

Suddenly, I thought, all the good things my committee had said up till now about my teaching didn't matter any more. I was now encountering a powerful institutional belief in the sanctity of student evaluations, especially students' comments that focused on my demanding, not-so-entertaining traits as a teacher. And I was startled that the pretty good comments I received from students in my other writing classes were virtually ignored; there was nothing I could say to get Ken and Beth to see things differently.

"This must make you feel pretty rotten," Andy said. "It sure doesn't represent the class I visited. I think you were talking about interviewing and sources or something and it was absolutely clear that you were in your element, you were in control." Then he turns to Ken. "He comes here as an accomplished journalist, he was nominated for The Prize . . ."

At that point, Ken cut Andy off. Ken said, "Yeah, but he's at The College now."

Of course, Ken's comment carried the quite vivid connotation that I'd left the world of working journalism behind, and that that world was now effectively irrelevant. As of now, I belonged to Ken, to this committee, to the acting chairperson, to my colleagues and their anonymous evaluations, to the keepers of the Tenure Castle and its secretive deliberations. And most of all, I belonged to student opinion—however well founded—of what defined good teaching.

And with that terse statement, Ken put an end to the meeting, and he also made it perfectly clear that he would have major reservations about my future at The College.

My tenure meeting the following week with the Big Committee was therefore predictable. If members of your own department committee are entertaining second thoughts about you, you don't have much chance with the Big Committee.

My quasi-trial before the Big Committee began with a bit of small talk and a few questions. But everyone at the table knew we were putting off the inevitable. Finally, the chairman got down to business. "Of course, we have a major concern about the student evaluations," he said. "Yes, I realize that," I said. I knew that at this juncture my disagreeing would have been futile. After a bit, the chairman came up with the idea that I might consider taking an acting course in order to improve my class presentation skills. Were they suggesting I needed to be more entertaining? I wondered. Of course, the word "entertaining" would never cross anybody's lips, but that seemed to be the unstated implication.

Then I was asked to leave the meeting and wait outside the conference room while Ken stayed behind for the deliberations. Some fifteen minutes later, Ken emerged from the meeting. He lit a cigarette, took a long drag, and said in his southern drawl, "Well, they voted to continue your contract another year. But it *waaas* close, four yes, one no and one abstained."

"What did they say?" I asked.

"They want to see a major improvement in the student evaluations. They left little doubt about that."

I wanted Ken to be explicit about exactly how important student evaluations were in this whole process. "Meaning I don't get tenure unless the student evaluations improve?" I asked.

"I'd say that's a fair conclusion."

So there it was, out on the table. I was now on notice. If matters weren't clear enough, the Big Committee put it all in a memo, informing me that its favorable recommendation for tenure would be impossible unless there was significant improvement in my student evaluations. I actually was quite impressed with the clarity of their position. One normally didn't expect such clarity from government bureaucracies. But they'd played their hand, telling me in no uncertain terms what I had to do.

A few days later, as the quarter was coming to an end, something else happened that would wake me up. It seemed that my colleague Roger (the one who figured prominently in the dream) was opening my eyes in more ways than one about teaching in the 1990s. Only this time, it wasn't in a dream.

I stopped Roger on the way to class one day, and we chatted a moment. The subject of grades came up, and it occurred to me to ask him what for some reason I had not yet asked anybody else.

"So what *is* the average grade at The College, anyway?" I asked Roger.

"It's a B, about a 3.0." Roger said this quite matter of factly, repeating what was obviously common knowledge on campus. In that instant, asking that simple question and receiving a simple answer, the past year and a half of trial and error at The College suddenly came into sharp focus. The proverbial light bulb went off; I think I also even uttered something like, "Aha!" I had been in my own fictitious world, operating under the false assumption that a C was average. I felt like Rip Van Winkle; since I had last been in an undergraduate classroom in the 1970s, the rest of the world had inflated the average to a B.

Of course, I felt a bit naive, not being fully aware of what was really going on in the collegiate culture in the 1990s. But looking back to when some students were destroying me in their evaluations, I'm not sure my not knowing this open secret about grades would have really changed things. I wasn't completely idiotic, though many readers by now must be wondering what rock I had buried myself under not to know about the cultural phenomenon called grade inflation. I wasn't unaware of grade inflation; being a newspaper and information junkie, of course I was aware that grade inflation was out there. But I suppose I just didn't give it that much thought. I *was* idealistic about teaching, and I was determined to give grades according to my professional judgment of quality, not according to the distorted norms of the college culture. I had been too idealistic.

But things were now getting interesting. My students were slamming me. The College was threatening to kick me out if the students didn't start liking me more. And my curiosity about just what it took to succeed as a teacher was certainly aroused.

CHAPTER 6

Where All the Kids Are (Way) Above Average

It began out of mere curiosity. My encounters with college students of the nineties made me want to find out more precisely what they thought about. One day, I experimented with letting my writing students jot down on the back of their essays the grade they thought they deserved. I guess you might call it market research. One student wrote this:

> "For my writting [sic] skills this was a great paper. Since this was the first essay, I think it deserves a 4.0."

Other students wrote similar remarks, revealing to me a value system of theirs that placed a high priority on how hard you tried relative to where you started, rather than what you knew relative to what you were supposed to learn. I decided to find out more. One of my first steps was to develop an attitude survey. Over a period of several months, I asked about 150 students to anonymously answer some questions about their attitudes toward college. The results were further confirmation of many of my suspicions, underscoring how off base I had been when I first arrived at The College, having approached teaching with assumptions about students that were no longer true.

Having been through periods of hell with my students, at times feeling quite inadequate, I was particularly interested in what personal characteristics students really valued in a college teacher. So I asked the multiple choice question shown in table 1.

TABLE 1 *The Most Important Quality of an Instructor*

In addition to being knowledgeable, please circle your first and second choices for qualities of an instructor that are the most important to you:

		1st Choice	2nd Choice
1.	Entertaining	41%	4%
2.	Friendly and warm	37%	6%
3.	Easy grader	2%	6%
4.	Challenges students	16%	24%
5.	Accommodates individual learning styles and abilities	4%	56%
6.	Demanding	0%	4%

I had suspected that college students these days, who more likely than not grew up with *Sesame Street* and MTV, placed a high value on being entertained. I figured that because Generation X, in particular, had been engulfed by entertaining images since birth that they would also value it highly in college. Indeed, nearly half the students picked entertainment as the trait they valued most in a college teacher. The next most valued trait was being friendly and warm.

In fact, there was the strong tendency for students to place a high value on what I call "soft" traits in an instructor. Fully eight out of ten students said the most important trait of a college instructor was either to be entertaining, friendly and warm, an easy grader, or accommodating of "individual learning styles and abilities."

Also on this question, there emerged an interesting schism among students. Note their choice of traits of secondary importance. Nearly a quarter of the students said they wanted a teacher who challenged them, a "hard" trait I'd consider the traditional role of the college teacher. But far more students, nearly 60 percent, said they wanted a teacher to accommodate their individual learning styles, a thoroughly recent development in higher education derived from recent trends in high school, junior high, and grade schools.

This same schism showed up in another question, this one about grades; a gap between students occurred along traditional versus non-traditional lines. The multiple choice question, as shown in table 2, concerned the issue of what grades should be based on.

TABLE 2 *What Grades Should Be Based On*

Grades should primarily be based on:

1.	How hard you try	16%
2.	Your knowledge and performance in subject	52%
3.	How much you improve compared to where you started	26%
4.	Your attitude	1.5%

The idea that college students should be graded according to what they know and how well they perform is the commonly perceived ideal of the American meritocracy. But just barely half of the students in my survey said that should be so. The other half said grades should not be based on performance at all, but on such subjective factors as attitude and effort. It seemed, then, that students themselves had come to believe deeply in the "success" model of higher education, based on the well intended, egalitarian notion that achievement should be based on how hard one tries.

And the students had very high expectations. In my survey, I asked students what they think should be a reasonable average grade. (See table 3.)

TABLE 3 *Reasonable Average Grade*

What do you think should be a reasonable average grade among students in a college-level course?

1.	2.0 (C)	10%
2.	2.5 (B–)	35%
3.	3.0 (B)	51%
4.	3.5 (A–)	2.2%

At this point in my story, it should come as no surprise, but fully 90 percent of this modest survey of college students thought the average grade in a college-level course should be a B minus or greater. Half of them thought the average grade should be at least a B. Just one out of ten students believed that a C should be average. Remember Garrison Keilor's *A Prairie Home Companion,* about the mythical Lake Wobegon, where all the children were above average? Although students at The College had probably never heard of Lake Wobegon, they were taking its myth to heart.

But how much were students willing to work to get those high grades? I asked them about that. (See table 4.)

TABLE 4 *Time Spent Studying*

Realistically, how much do you study per day for all your classes?

1.	1–2 hours	34%
2.	2–3 hours	27%
3.	4–5 hours	3%
4.	less than 1 hour	21%
5.	hardly at all	14%

This shows that some 70 percent of the students studied less than two hours a day for their entire class load. That compares to a rule of thumb among educators that one should study at least 3 hours a week for each college credit, or about 45 hours a week for a full class load.

And yet, the students thought they deserved high achievement no matter how hard they tried, as shown in table 5.

TABLE 5 *The Right to Succeed at College*

Please respond: "Because students have a basic right to succeed, achievement should not be made difficult at college." Circle one.

1. Strongly agree	2. Agree	3. Disagree	4. Strongly disagree
4.4%	17.7%	59%	16%

To be sure, the assertion that college students are actually entitled to succeed was rather radical to my way of thinking, and in fact some three-quarters of the students disagreed with the premise. But nearly a quarter of the students agreed or even strongly agreed with the statement, suggesting that a significant portion of students harbored a disproportionate sense of entitlement.

I was also interested in how students perceived their role in the educational system. From what I had ascertained, it seemed that most students these days saw themselves as consumers and the teacher taking the role of their employee or service provider. In my experience, students seemed to be rebelling against the traditional view that students are really clients of professional teachers who historically have had undisputed authority in the classroom. I sought to pursue this by getting the students' responses to the statement shown in table 6.

TABLE 6 *Responsibility for Learning*

Please respond to the following statement: "I'm the consumer who pays the bills, and so my instructor should be mostly responsible for making sure that I learn and receive my money's worth." Circle one.

1. Strongly agree	2. Agree	3. Disagree	4. Strongly disagree
15%	37%	37%	9.6%

Indeed, well more than half the students thought of themselves as consumers, placing most of the responsibility on instructors for getting "their money's worth." Still, there was a significant split among students on this point.

A few points became immediately clear from my survey. A lot of my students had very high expectations for themselves but weren't working very hard—at school, anyway—to achieve their high goals. Viewing themselves as consumers of college in the same way they bought other goods and services, students seemed willing to put most of the burden for their success on me as their teacher, and on the system itself, rather than on their own knowledge, skills, and performance.

In my follow-ups to the questionnaire, many students sensed that their attitudes stemmed from peculiarities of their generation.

For instance, Liz was one of my better students one quarter. I could tell she was clearly torn as to whether she wanted to really commit to her academic work or blow it off. "Maybe it's my age," she said. "A phase. It seems others my age are lazy too. We are all just going through a stage, and the motivation will come back after we play a while. Or maybe our whole generation has lost the will-power to succeed. We don't want to try any more. There are plenty of students who don't have goals. They feel it's no use to have goals, society will keep them from those goals anyway."

Others admitted that they and their peers had blamed their teachers when they didn't perform well. "Kids today do have extremely high expectations," one student told me. "And if they receive a D or an F, it always winds up being the teacher's fault somehow."

What was going on here? So many students on the one hand were *behaving* irresponsibly and were so disengaged, but others were as cognizant as I was that their peers at school weren't holding up their end of the educational bargain. There were two possible explanations: One was that I was somehow capturing only the views of the responsible students; but I don't think so. Some of my students did but many others did not have their heads in the game. I came to conclude that many of my students were torn about these matters of responsibility, expectations, grades, and so on, reflecting the confusion of a changing culture. On one hand, they knew that their generation was profoundly ill at ease with the rules of the game they'd been taught, because, like Liz suggested, they'd seen that following the rules guaranteed nothing in the America they grew up in. And yet following those rules remained the only way they still knew to the "good life" as the dominant society had defined it. As a result, many students tried but half-heartedly to follow what they believed were outmoded rules of the game. Indeed, they weren't sure they wanted to play the game at all, but they saw it as the only game in town.

CHAPTER 7

Hooked on Hand-holding

Amanda was like any number of young female college students. This day, she wore a dark dress with straps that covered a bright white T-shirt, and she carried a large cloth shoulder bag full of papers and books. She looked like she had her act together. And in an out-of-whack way, she did.

As I walked to the front of the class, I looked around to see who was absent. Amanda had been gone three times this week and missed a quiz. She got up from her chair and walked toward me. Her smile was mixed with sweetness and guilt. She said, "I had to go to my grandmother's funeral this week, can I make up the quiz?" I considered this a moment, thinking about my policy of no make-ups, except for "valid" excuses. "Sure, okay," I said.

It wasn't until much later in the quarter that I became wise to Amanda's game, and just how cynical Amanda was when it came to playing at college. Amanda had a very impressive grade point average but knew she really didn't deserve the high grades she got. She was frequently absent, turned in assignments late, and rarely got marked down for missing deadlines. Amanda found that instructors would frequently cave in to her requests for a second or third chance by smiling and acting even somewhat interested. Learning this about Amanda, I recalled once how she brought me articles and other tidbits about journalism. I was flattered by her interest in the subject. Amanda knew well that she was getting good grades for lousy work. She confessed, "If no one is going to stop me, how can I stop myself?"

Amanda was hooked on hand-holding. If the system and its success model of education wanted to hold students' hands, spoon-feed them information, and bend over backwards to ensure their success, neither Amanda nor scores of others like her were going to argue. In Amanda's world, there was little learning and a lot of game-playing going on. Nobody was willing to draw the proverbial line in the sand with this young woman, and she was smart enough to figure that out, and so she got what she wanted: very high grades with a minimum of effort.

I came to believe that Amanda's game-playing was a rational response to a corrupt, or at least malfunctioning, environment. The system had endowed her with tremendous power and legitimacy, while asking virtually nothing in return. The system was willing to go to great lengths to make sure that such people were satisfied customers—and students took advantage of that.

And that irked Marissa and Carol to no end.

They were two young women I got to know one quarter. Both were in their late twenties. They had worked at jobs for a few years before returning to school, and they had plenty to tell me about their fellow students *and* their instructors. After talking to Marissa and Carol, I discovered how the good students were cheated worst of all by the hand-holding and attention paid to the bored and unmotivated students. As very good students, the views of Marissa and Carol were virtually excluded by The College in order to accommodate the whiners and complainers. Marissa and Carol were angered by this because their own educations were being cheapened as a result.

We decided to meet one day after class for lunch at a local coffeehouse. I asked the two young women to give me specific examples of the hand-holding that so bothered them. Marissa went first, and she picked on me. "Should I bring you into it?" she asked. "Sure, go right ahead," I said, warily.

Marissa reminded me of one time I was pulling teeth to get students to turn in drafts of their stories, and about two-thirds of the class just wouldn't do the work. "I didn't turn in my draft and you reminded me in a generic sense, actually the whole class, that they were worth 15 percent of the whole grade," Marissa said. "I was very well aware of that and I was very upset that I didn't have it done—that would be an example of hand-holding. You see students slipping and instructors want to help them, they want to remind them, that 'Hey, people, wake up, your grade is going to suffer,' but they should know that; they're responsible adults, they're in college and they shouldn't expect people to keep them in line."

Marissa told me about her history class. Apparently, students had come to expect as routine so-called "study guides"—summaries of the course material offered in bite-sized chunks easily digested for student consumption. I had never heard of these things, and I didn't use them. Marissa said the guides typically "cover topics you can expect to be on the test. So instead of doing the assignments and the readings, you look up definitions, dates, and easily pass the test." This was quintessential "hand-holding," and not appropriate for college-level work, in Marissa's view. In her history class, "students were terribly upset because they weren't provided study guides," she said.

In Marissa's speech class, the instructor went so far as to ask questions on the test that weren't covered in the study guide. "All hell broke loose," Marissa said. "Oh, did students complain to the teacher. In one case, they took it to the administration. They were terribly upset."

Marissa told me how spoon-feeding students is so seductive, but over the long run destructive of one's self-esteem and sense of accomplishment. Her illustration of this also came from her history class. The class had been co-taught by two instructors, and intentionally or not, they took sort of a good cop, bad cop approach. One professor was a tough teacher and grader, while the other had a reputation for being mellow and easy (traits students ranked highest of instructor qualities in my own student survey). The tough teacher was retiring right smack in the middle of the quarter, a rather unusual move. (Hearing rumors that the students had complained about him mightily because he was a hard grader raised my suspicions, but I was never able to confirm that this contributed to his early retirement.) With just two weeks before the end of the quarter, the tough guy left the country, the easy instructor took over, and he immediately gave the entire class fifteen bonus points, in order to raise the overall average, eliminate the "damage" wrought by the tough guy, and generally get the class to shut up, Marissa told me. Meantime, Marissa said that with hard work, she'd been earning a

B–, and suddenly she saw her grade rocket to a B+. "I was shocked that fifteen points were given out for free," she said. "Of course, I'm glad I'm getting a better grade, but I want to and expect to work for my grade, not have it handed out for free."

Why did Marissa's history professor give out the fifteen points? His explanation revealed that he was uncertain about the decision, and his story says to me anyway that he just wanted the students to shut up, quit thinking so much about grades, and focus on U.S. history. After listening to the students' loud complaints, he explained that he "was just at a place where I had to make a decision, whether it was right or wrong, I possibly will never know," he said. "Grades can do a lot of damage. Students seem to lose focus on what they are trying to accomplish in college. They can be too concerned with getting a high grade and not about learning, so I gave them the points in hopes that they would focus again on learning."

Carol had a similar story. She said that in her philosophy class the instructor expected students to participate in class and he supposedly weighted it heavily in the grade. Students were expected to come prepared each day to defend their positions. And every day, Carol said, she put herself on the line, taking risks with unpopular positions on social and political issues. She became unpopular with other students, not only because of her views, but because of her work ethic that surpassed many of the other students. "I don't know of anybody who felt comfortable speaking out in class. I didn't feel comfortable speaking out in class, but I did every single solitary day. Yeah, because it was part of the grade and also because I wanted to grow and be challenged to learn," Carol said. But she said the disparity in class participation among the students didn't ultimately seem to matter when it came to the final grade. One day, the instructor passed out a sheet of paper with the final grades next to social security numbers. "So I'm sitting alongside twenty other students who refused to speak, and they were getting A's. . . . I was amazed that most of the class, probably 75 percent or better, got A's. I was angry. It was not fair. If I was going to get an A in the end anyway without having to risk all that exposure of myself, then I wouldn't have done it."

But students like Marissa and Carol suffered not only educationally because their instructors were holding the hands of the less motivated students. The slackers couldn't stand them.

Marissa and Carol were just slightly older than the average student at The College, but their work ethic was far better than most.

The difference in the way they acted toward me compared to most other students was like night and day. Instead of bored, superior stares, their demeanor was attentive and polite. Indeed, their eyes met mine when I talked, and they seemed genuinely interested in what I had to say. In a very real sense, Marissa and Carol were a bridge between me and the younger students with whom I struggled to make meaningful contact. My conversations with these two young women helped to explain a lot of what I was seeing in my classroom.

But Marissa and Carol told me that they paid a heavy price for breaking with the pack and paying as much attention to their instructors as to their peers. While I had been oblivious to this, Marissa told me that one group of young students in my class would often make snide remarks about her and others in the class, laughing about the way they dressed or the questions they asked. Marissa explained that it was simply considered cool by the younger students to be aloof from the entire process.

"The younger students are very angry with us," Marissa said. "We're serious about our schooling, we go the extra mile, we do what's needed, and we don't cop out. I think we're a representation of the teacher, of higher authority, and the cool thing is to chat right along with everybody else or to slack off with everybody else. If you actually study your brains out and prepare for the next class, and do what is expected, then you're looked upon by a lot of the students like a nerd, a geek."

These insights were immensely interesting to me because the women were my means of discovering what students were saying and doing when *my* back was turned. As I had suspected from my own experience, both Marissa and Carol told me that many of their peers were contemptuous of their instructors, ridiculing them for the way they dressed or how they wore their hair. Carol said students in her math and philosophy classes seemed to get special joy out of slamming their instructors, for rather spurious reasons. Carol told me:

"'Oh, god, look at what he's wearing today,' this other student, Dora, says to me one day. Our philosophy teacher doesn't dress great, but so what? Today he's got a checked short-sleeved shirt and one of those cloth teacher's ties with the square ends. It was green and rather unfashionable, to say the least. Dennis was about fifty, and balding. He sort of was nerdish. We were talking about ethics and he was really excited about something. It was interesting. When

Dora said that for the umpteenth time that quarter, I just had to say something. Where did she get off? 'Hey, he's just a guy,' I told her. He's got some good things to say. He's smart.' Dora sort of stares at me and rolls her eyes then looks away. And now I'm a bad person because I've stuck up for the teacher."

Carol continued, "My math instructor was also sort of a geek, at least in the eyes of most of the students. He had long hair, a pony tail, sort of an old hippie. He was different looking. This was basic algebra, so it was often just basic boring formulas and stuff, but he made an effort to make it interesting by showing us special problems on the board that were advanced for us, but they showed us how math could be used in the real world. One day he was doing this and started writing formulas on the board. Then people in the class started snickering and rolling their eyes. It was like junior high school! It's not cool to want to learn, to laugh at the teacher's jokes, to be accepting of your teacher."

By the end of the quarter, I had my final encounter with Amanda.

And again, she was looking for special favors. I had told the students they would flunk their last assignment if they didn't show up for the oral presentations. On the last day of class, everybody was able to finish their presentations, and when the time came for Amanda's she wasn't prepared. "I'm not ready yet," she said, appropriately embarrassed. I would have flunked her, but I realized that in the now-legalistic world of higher education, she had an out that she could take to the administration which I hadn't anticipated. I had allocated the final exam day to finishing up any presentations that we didn't get to the last week of classes, and Amanda could argue that she was ready by the day of the final. After class that day I talked to Amanda. "I could flunk you," I lied, "but I'll give you another chance. Come prepared to give your presentation on the day of the final." She nodded contritely, almost in tears. Amanda showed up on the day of the final, presented her mediocre work, and I gave her a passing grade. To be honest, it was either that, or be prepared to do battle with Amanda—and, as I would learn next, with an administration quite willing to back her up.

CHAPTER 8

"Hey Dad, Put It on Pause!"

I became somewhat close to my colleague Chris. I felt he was one of the few people to whom I could really talk to. It was especially interesting for me to hear his perspective about goings on at The College. As a foreigner, Chris had a fairly objective and sensible view of The College and its larger social context. He could look at America and its people without being blinded by all the ideology about Freedom, Democracy, Individualism, Capitalism, and so on and so forth that had been drummed into our heads since childhood. As I was completing my attitude survey of students at The College, I told Chris about the results. He wasn't surprised.

"This is a totally different world, this and the outside world," he told me one day. "Different values, different people. Instructors get three months off, work half days, they take life easy. So, if you can smile at your students, and be happy, you can have all that too."

In a way, I agreed with him. This was a different world from the daily grind of many work places. But sadly, what took place within the confines of this world also reflected something fundamental about the outside world in a way I hadn't yet really thought through or explored. But to suggest that there was little connection between this world and the outside world, I felt in my gut, was untrue. We as instructors, The College as an institution, were fed by the larger culture in which we operated, and something about that culture was creating the strange world that we found inside.

Despite the campus-wide rhetoric holding that everyone, especially students, ought to be, above all, happy, one of the real ironies about The College was that few of the faculty members were smiling in their private moments. I opened my eyes and ears to talk around the campus, trying to pick up what other faculty members were saying to each other for clues to help me explain what was going on here. I was surprised to discover that many other instructors were feeling many of the same things I was, and that in the views of many experienced college teachers, we were in the midst of a profound cultural upheaval that had completely changed students and the collegiate enterprise from just ten years earlier.

Indeed, other instructors told me about the same sort of disengaged rudeness in their students that I had discovered myself. And my colleagues also told me how students were playing out their angers, stresses, hatreds, and general frustrations with life while in the classroom. Students were breaking the traditional social contract in college and the working world that said, "Leave your personal problems behind when you walk through the door." Instructors were becoming increasingly frustrated that they were having to deal with such non-academic matters, as if The College were less an institution of higher learning than a social service agency. After all, professors would tell me, as teachers they were trained as biologists, economists, or journalists—not as social workers for their students.

I would hear anecdotes from other teachers on campus walkways, over lunch, or waiting at the coffee bar. One reliable source for a good story was my colleague Howard. He was a good guy and he was always quite frank with me. Howard was a slight man, with a doctorate from back East. He had an unmistakable midwestern twang when he talked. While I was careful what I'd say to Howard, he didn't seem all that concerned about what heresies he'd utter in my presence.

After teaching at The College for several years, Howard seemed to be growing increasingly frustrated, and he vented his frustrations when he'd stop between classes to sit on a bench and have a smoke. One day he told me about an incident in which two male students had exchanged sharp words in class, and then later one of the young men physically threatened the other in the college's parking lot.

Howard said he learned what had happened through campus security when an officer asked him for information about the incident. "Nobody prepared me for this in graduate school," he told me in that twangy voice, taking a long drag on his smoke. "I just wasn't trained for this."

Howard also told me about a student in his writing class who one day was just staring blankly into space, a rather disturbing sight. After class, Howard said he asked the student, "'Can I see you outside for a minute?'" After they went outside, Howard said the student told him, "'I'm a psychiatric patient, and I can tell that you have lost control. If you'd like, I'll give you back control now.'" Howard kept his cool and told the student, "'No, I haven't lost control, but if you have a problem with your illness or your medication for your illness, you should get professional help.' I just wasn't prepared for this," Howard said. "That really floored me."

One day at the coffee bar, Howard must have told that story to Barbara, another instructor. I saw Howard starting to walk away as Barbara began talking to a student. The student said to Barbara, "That looked like frustration on his face," referring to Howard. Barbara answered, "Yes. Students are so different today. I've been here longer than almost anyone, and the faculty are just very frustrated. They're like a bunch of doctors with their gallows humor. It's really how we release our frustrations."

My colleague Mike also talked to me at length about his frustrations. He had a Ph.D. from a prestigious university in the East. One day he was on a rant, talking about the "criminal element" that had invaded his classroom. He was especially disdainful of the "guys with baseball hats," whom I was also so fond of. "I turn on a video, turn off the lights, and hope that there's no blood on the floor when I turn them back on," he said.

If I had any doubts that there was something profoundly wrong and that I wasn't simply hearing unreliable tidbits from various teachers, or that my own experiences with students were unusual, such doubts were soon put to rest. One day, tacked up on the bulletin board in our department office I saw a flyer announcing an upcoming faculty seminar, a regular if sparsely attended event in which teachers from throughout the campus would get together to talk about various educational topics. The vast majority of these seminars were uninteresting to me, typically on arcane issues of educational pedagogy, and since I didn't consider myself an "educator" by training or by sentiment, I rarely attended these sessions.

But this particular flyer startled me, because it was another clue that many other instructors were cognizant of the cultural changes in students, and that other teachers might be as frustrated with teaching Generation X as I was. Teaching college was turning into a whole new game, because the people teachers were now dealing with seemed to be such fundamentally different human beings than students a decade ago.

One professor, the one who wrote the flyer, was willing to go public with his politically sensitive views about changes in student culture in recent years. The flyer tacked onto the bulletin board in our building was provocative, raising questions about such influences as consumerism and the mass media's impact on college students in the nineties. The instructor, who had been teaching for many years, complained that he found himself working harder and harder to engage students in learning but that nothing seemed to work any more to counter the consumerism and entertainment young people were accustomed to in the outside world. He said that, as a teacher, he was tired of bending over backwards for students who weren't willing to work. Maybe it's time to point the finger at the real cause of deteriorating standards—the students themselves, his flyer seemed to suggest.

And so there it was. Here was somebody at The College, a tenured faculty member with far more experience and legitimacy as an educator than me, who had gone public with his frustrations and condemnations. He was practically pleading for some kind of answer. I wasn't going to miss this faculty seminar for anything, and I would have my reporter's notebook and tape recorder in hand.

As I said, these faculty seminars were usually rather thinly attended. But when I arrived, the crowd of instructors and administrators waiting to enter the room was strung out the door. By the time the instructor who was leading the seminar was ready to begin talking, a standing-room-only crowd had gathered to see what this was going to be all about. The turnout among faculty and administrators was staggering, and people I spoke to said the attendance was unprecedented.

The seminar leader began to speak. He said, "Somebody was just saying to me, 'I guess you struck a nerve.' I said, 'Looking at the 99 percent turnout, I think you're right.'"

As the words came out of his mouth, I kept thinking, "My god, I'm not alone." He said, "Student culture has changed dramatically. I think students would like to switch us off and on like channels on a television set. I think that's what the video generation is all about—they're not reacting to us in the same way we reacted to our teachers a generation ago."

Then, he reported the results of his own informal survey of students, confirming many of my own discoveries. On average, his students worked about twenty hours a week at part-time jobs; took about fifteen college credits; said they would be "satisfied" with an average grade of 3.3 (a high B); that 14 percent didn't like to read; 7.4 percent didn't read books; and 3.3 percent had trouble even reading the survey form.

"For most of you, that's nothing new, that's what you know," the seminar leader told the gathering of faculty and administrators. "I think a lot of faculty have already jumped through a lot of hoops; how many hoops do we have to jump through?"

Then the deluge began.

"I absolutely agree," said one teacher. "That's what I'm doing in my job every day. The first message is that we have to deal with grade inflation, across the board. We have to tell students, 'Either you measure up or these will be the grades you will get.' It's a hard-nosed position, but it goes back to expectations . . . . Let's make it a real community issue, because it's a real community problem."

The seminar leader said, "For a vast number of students, they think they can pay their money, open the top of their head, and I fill it up. Then they close their heads and walk out."

A math professor said, "Students know in high school that they don't have to learn anything and they can still get to college. Students don't take individual responsibility for doing extra work outside of class, that's the problem."

"It's a very pervasive problem," another instructor said.

One instructor objected: "But we're not the Ivy League. We're not taking the chosen few."

A psychology instructor said, "Let's take a look at the cultural issues. We need to socialize the students—or maybe ourselves."

This tirade went on for about an hour, and it was clear that a collective nerve had indeed been struck. The faculty were frustrated and fed up, and this meeting had opened up the floodgates for their ill feelings. It was suggested that the seminar leader, who had lit the match igniting this fury, would at that point pursue the formation of a special committee. The group would explore what small steps the faculty and administration of this one college, a minor player in the larger academic world, might take to counter these ominous cultural trends. I didn't personally know the seminar leader, but I was determined to meet him and try to become part of that committee.

Immediately after the faculty seminar, I was chatting with my colleague Roger. He had an especially interesting and useful perspective on educational matters because in a former life he had taught in public high schools and could compare what was happening there to trends beginning to take hold at colleges and universities. He was concerned that matters were only going to get worse for college teachers, because high school students were being trained not to think, analyze, and solve problems, but to excel at performing small, measurable tasks. This approach stemmed from politicians in state legislatures, for whom educational "reform" meant being able to quantify learning. "The frustration I heard in that meeting—it's real and it's serious," Roger said. "It would benefit all of us to go back to high school and junior high to see what's going on there. It's only going to get worse. It's all worksheets. It's all task oriented. We've got to get even more used to rote learning because the students are even less able to think critically. It's all 'measurable objectives,' like identifying a noun or an adverb. Those are measurable, bite-sized, and state legislatures are promoting this."

Eventually, I called Steve, the professor who led the seminar, and told him I was interested in being on the new committee. I told him that I shared in his concerns. A few days later, he and I met in the cafeteria. He was a trim, well-dressed man in his late fifties, about six feet two inches, with black rimmed glasses and neatly cropped graying hair. He had a pleasant, warm smile.

I asked Steve how he became interested in this whole issue of student culture. Compared to the standard rhetoric one finds these days in higher education, his answer bordered on heresy. "I decided that I wasn't the problem," he told me. "Students were the problem." He said he was increasingly bothered by the "consumer mentality" college students seemed to harbor nowadays and told me a story about a business professor who in his own way was trying to counter this consumerism. Apparently, this instructor would tell his students, "'I'm the employer and you are the employee, and I pay you in the form of grades.' That made students very uncomfortable," Steve said. "They didn't like hearing that."

We also talked about students' demands to be entertained, another source of irritation for him as a teacher. "My own kids'll sometimes tell me, 'Hey dad, put it on pause,'" he said. "As teachers, we've become just another video image to be turned on and off. I teach anthropology, and if anything would be easy to keep them entertained, it would be that subject. The other day I had a gay couple come and speak to the class. Later, a guy in the class piped up and said, 'You should have brought in a straight couple,' as if he wasn't getting his money's worth hearing what a gay couple had to say about sexuality."

It was clear that we agreed on many points. While Steve probably wouldn't put it in these terms, I believe he was, in essence, rebelling against the entitlement paradigm of higher education that had become so dominant in the past ten or fifteen years. Then I raised an obvious objection to the whole undertaking of the new committee. "We're talking about fundamental cultural changes, the influence of the mass media, about the innermost existential life of young people. Maybe there's really nothing we can really do about it," I said. But listening to myself, I thought I might hurt my chance to get on the inside of this committee, so I quickly added, "Still, I'd like to join up, and see what happens." A few days later, Steve called me and left a message telling me about the committee's first meeting. I would be on it along with half a dozen other faculty members from throughout The College.

So, here I was. The irony was worth savoring. In truth, I was on the verge of being an outcast at The College because I had tried to maintain college standards, taking a lot of flack from both students and my tenure crew as a result. And now I was on an important campus committee. Like a gnat on an elephant's ass, our little committee would try to single-handedly stem the rising tide of mediocrity.

◢ ◢ ◢

We would call it, somewhat tongue in cheek, the Save Our Standards Committee, or SOS for short. Before long, we were meeting once a week, and I found that I actually looked forward to our sessions. Being undercover at these meetings felt awkward for me, particularly when I wanted to take notes. As a reporter, whipping out my notebook and being the neutral observer was always the most natural thing for me. But now, I wasn't just a reporter; I was also on the inside. Eventually, I became a respected, contributing member of the group. I learned what it must be like to be a double-agent, being of two minds at all times, one devoted to the group I'd infiltrated and the other devoted to a cause, and all the while keeping a poker face. At times, I felt ashamed at my duplicity. But I felt that, in the end, they might forgive me. I was advancing a larger agenda telling what needed to be told. And, while these people seemed to have strong attachments to The College and no inclination to expose to the outside world what was going wrong with higher education, I had no such attachments.

As a group, we were sometimes not all that well directed. Steve was really too nice a guy to keep the group well on track. Often, we would get into lengthy bull sessions, trading war stories about our students that we'd apparently been itching to share in some way. So these meetings often became therapeutic. This was gallows humor at its best, and I must admit that it was sort of fun and heart warming to share our stories. I didn't feel so alone. It was at one of our meetings that my colleague Jill told us about her portable TV watching student, who, when told to put the thing away, responded that he'd seen the show anyway.

One day, as we were planning activities SOS could do for an upcoming week of faculty seminars, one member told us about his David Letterman "top 10" idea. "How you know it's going to be a long quarter": 1. You recognize one of your students on "America's Most Wanted"; 2. You ask to see a student's class-entry test scores and he says, "Talk to my lawyer"; 3. You mark down a student for poor spelling, and she says that's illegal because she's got a learning disability, and so on. Such were the grim but unfortunately true things that made us laugh about teaching in the 1990s.

After SOS floundered for several weeks, we came up with a list of several assertions, reflecting our collective observations. Our statement was tantamount to a widely cast indictment of modern undergraduate education, particularly at public, teaching (read: consumer) oriented institutions like ours. The statement was blunt, except that Steve toned down the document by inserting "some" instead of "most," as an adjective preceding "students," "faculty," or "administrators," in order to make the wording less inflammatory. Then we distributed the list of assertions to get written comments from other faculty members.

Judging by the responses we received from other teachers, there was little disagreement that instructors were facing profound problems teaching today's college students, and the problems had been festering for years. Some instructors wrote lengthy memos analyzing the problem. One instructor clipped copies of Doonesbury comic strips that took aim at the modern college student and at the untenable position into which colleges and universities had placed their teachers.

For example, SOS asserted that "some" students lacked appropriate skills for college work, and we received comments such as these:

> *"Basic English communication skills seem the most glaringly absent."*
> *"I agree 100%!"*
> *"Many can't read at the college level and therefore can't effectively prepare for class. The problem is compounded because they work and don't even expect to have time to read."*
> *"Not some. Lots!"*

Our SOS group asserted that students expected to be entertained rather than challenged. The faculty responded with comments such as these:

> *"I always tell my students that I am an educated and responsible professional, not Michael Jackson or Madonna."*
> *"The TV generation expects to be entertained. With an attention span that is equal to the material between commercials, that is not surprising."*
> *"Send them back to high school!"*
> *"Some students don't want an education—they just want a dry warm place while their parents pay the expenses."*
> *"They prefer TV."*

Still, many faculty understood that they themselves had to take part of the blame for the shortcomings they found in students. Our committee asserted that faculty took too much responsibility for students' learning—in other words, that instructors did too much spoon-feeding and hand-holding. We received comments such as these from members of the faculty:

"You mean I shouldn't tap dance any more?"

"Students will always whine and complain as a means of testing the instructor's limits."

"Yes, but those who spoon feed students make many students antagonistic toward faculty who don't."

"I present, encourage, and work my full and responsible 50% of the teaching/learning experience. The rest is up to them. My drop rate is high."

"Students often complain about 'boring' teachers. Part-time instructors who must be evaluated each quarter want to ensure they have good reputations. It's scary to look at a sea of sleeping faces."

"When you challenge, they drop the class."

The latter comments were especially interesting to me. Teachers were actually *afraid* to challenge students, because they'd *drop the class.* In the era of unrelenting budget cuts for higher education, there was no greater perceived threat to a teacher's job security than he or she not holding up a full-time teaching load because students were dropping her classes or not enrolling in them. Thus, for reasons of economics, for reasons of job security, faculty members were reluctant to uphold grading standards because they believed they wouldn't be supported by administrators when push came to shove.

For example, when our committee suggested that the prevailing campus atmosphere didn't support faculty when enforcing college-level grading standards, we received these comments from instructors:

"Very true. Atmosphere on campus seems to be to keep student fees/tuition flowing in without regard to standards. The higher the enrollment, the more money. Obviously, this is being done at the sacrifice of any academic standards."

"Yes. Too much placating of students and parents. Administration is not the staunch advocate of/for educational excellence."

"We pay too much attention to 'at risk' while our academic stars are falling through the cracks."

The anger and frustration in the instructors' comments were palpable. Indeed, this was nothing less than an unarticulated, undeclared culture war going on between the college faculty and the mass of twentysomething students. There may have been anecdotal evidence of conflict that I would hear about in conversations over lunch or on campus walkways, but SOS, for the first time, had unwittingly unearthed hard evidence of this culture war.

Months passed, and I continued my work on Save Our Standards. To be sure, being a member would look good politically, for purposes of the tenure game. But mainly I wanted to be on the committee as a way of going deeply undercover, to be closer to the psyches of other tenured instructors, and to the higher-ups in the administration, and to collect more information about the peculiar subculture of academic life. I wasn't sanguine that SOS might actually change student culture. It seemed that students' way of approaching the world, and the institution's response, were too entrenched and institutionalized. Fundamental change would be tantamount to changing the genetic code of The College, and the chances of that happening seemed infinitesimal. Everybody had too much at stake in the present system, which revolved around high enrollment and good grades. Instructors used grades to evaluate students, and The College as employer, like scores of other colleges, used students to evaluate instructors. The combination, I would discover, was a formula for rather cynical manipulations.

Indeed, this point was driven home to me one day when an academic dean called the faculty to an "emergency" meeting. The emergency? Scott, the dean, told us that our enrollment had fallen below budget, and he outlined several steps that The College needed to enact immediately in order to turn things around. His central message was that The College needed to act more like a business in order to attract and keep students, and that faculty would play a central role as "salespeople" in this endeavor.

"We need to better appeal to our constituencies," Scott told the faculty. "We need to take a customer-service oriented role with our students."

Of course, as an academician, the dean felt obliged to add, "I'm not talking about lowering standards." But, reading between the lines, the message seemed quite clear for many of the faculty: Priority No. 1 at our newly discovered quasi-corporate enterprise would be to maximize sales, that is, enrollment. And doing that had the potential of playing fast and loose with standards. What teacher who cared about job security would be willing to bet otherwise?

My fears were borne out. Soon after Scott's speech, The College circulated a memo informing the faculty that rules for entry into The College's classes would be altered to be less restrictive to new students. The move was a blow to the work of the standards committee because establishing stiffer class prerequisites and entry requirements had been one of our top priorities for beefing up academic standards.

The enrollment problem and Scott's marching orders created a sort of fear around the campus. From then on, the message was clear that everybody who dealt with students in any fashion, from the phone operators to the physics professors, would be watched more closely than ever. If the cultural climate at The College had been overly nurturing and accommodating before the enrollment problem, it became doubly so after Scott's speech. Teachers wondered, Where would the line be drawn between simply upholding academic standards on one hand and general friendliness to the student-consumers on the other?

For example, our SOS committee was in the middle of pushing hard for a mandatory freshman orientation course that would, among other things, inform students about appropriate classroom behavior. In my mind, the course meant students would learn that they couldn't watch TV during class, ask instructors for Kleenex, and that they just might have to read the assigned books to do well in college. In essence, the course would amount to a "re-education camp," with older generations of instructors attempting to teach GenXers how to go to college. In a survey of the faculty conducted by the SOS group, the vast majority agreed that a mandatory class was sorely needed. But our high hopes for such a required class were dashed when the enrollment problem surfaced. Although the fear was never openly discussed, teachers whispered that we would simply drive away students who saw a mandatory class as just another hassle they didn't have to put up with as paying customers. Students would just go someplace else that took a friendlier approach.

One day, Steve and I were waiting for other SOS committee members to show up for a meeting. He confided his concerns to me about our work in the wake of the enrollment problems and our dean's orders to become more "customer friendly"—the very attribute we were afraid had already become overemphasized in academia. I could see then just how deeply Steve felt about his self-imposed mission to try to deal with the cultural changes in students.

"I'm very concerned," he told me, a note of frustration in his usually upbeat manner. "I mean, I still feel the same, and what we're doing is right and the way to go. But I'm afraid that other teachers on campus are going to say, 'Hey let's hold on here. We've got this enrollment problem, why make it worse by getting tough on standards?"

Indeed, from the perspective of a given faculty member, what conceivable incentive was there to, for example, fight grade inflation? To uphold one's professional ethics? That really was the only reason any teacher would try to maintain grading and academic standards. In fact, there were numerous *disincentives* to holding the line on grades. Being a tough grader often meant being singled out for unwanted and unflattering attention. You risked the wrath of students who complained about you in their student evaluations or complained about you to administrators; you risked low enrollments in your classes as word got out that you graded hard; you risked being called in to some administrator's office to defend your low grades and your low enrollments. You risked your job. For many faculty, it was simply easier, indeed, rational, to look the other way.

After floundering for several more months regarding how to get a handle on the problem and how to fix it at The College, our SOS committee kept coming back to this issue: Did the faculty face subtle or not so subtle pressure to ease up on standards in order to ensure student "success?" Again, we decided to ask our colleagues what they thought. Overwhelmingly, our colleagues told us they were watering down their standards in order to accommodate a generation of students who had become increasingly disengaged from anything resembling an intellectual life.

"So far this quarter," one colleague told us, "I have had these inquiries from my students:

> *"Do we have to read the text? Why are the chapters so long?"*
> *"I won't be in class for three days this week and two days the next week; will I miss anything important?"*

This instructor also described the following remarkable scene: "Upon awakening, a loudly slumbering student who was asked if he was tired replied, 'My coach says I have to be in class every day, but he didn't say I had to be awake the whole time.'" The professor continued, "When discussing a controversial subject and presenting scientific research to support that point of view a student remarked,

'Why are colleges trying to force this stuff down our throats and try-ing to make us think when our minds and opinions are already formed?'"

To be sure, this teacher added, "there are some very good, atten-tive, thoughtful, and challenging students in my classes, but if I don't make assignments easier, act as an entertainer, 'dummy-down' ex-ams, and give points for every little thing, a good portion of the stu-dents will not succeed."

She signed herself, "Musings of a teacher after a long day in the trenches."

One colleague answered our question this way: "I'm curious where this 'subtle' pressure comes from. "Students? Administrators? Dominant society? It's definitely there."

Another teacher summed up the varied nature of the problem, saying: "Yes, the pressure is there when you realize that the grades you give are tied to students' financial aid status (passing grades are required to receive aid); when your students show you their grade reports with nothing less than 3.5 averages; when you want to be spared the hassle of elaborately explaining to one student why she/he doesn't deserve a passing grade; or when you are not sure if en-couragement in the form of an inflated grade is exactly what some students should have."

A number of our colleagues returned again and again to this point: Their willingness to weaken standards meant more satisfied student customers, which meant higher enrollments—which meant a smaller chance of ever losing their jobs.

One instructor said, bluntly: "The enrollment crisis creates a cli-mate of pressure to get people who wish to follow the line of least resistance. Our department chairperson is so intimidated by her stu-dents that she gives extra testing time to those who want it. . . . How many of the rest of us buy student approval with test re-takes, large amounts of extra credit, and pre-test handouts that deal specifically with test topics only?"

A part-time instructor said, "We (part-timers) are under conflict-ing pressures. One, maintain collegiate standards as we remembered them from our college days. Two, keep these students happy enough not to trash us on evaluation forms. Job security would help!"

Another colleague said, "I certainly feel more pressure than in the past not to let people fail."

"Absolutely," yet another instructor said in response to our question, "and my enrollment is still soft. I'll need to get easier yet! And, lobby to get my classes required for *all* degrees."

Finally, one professor offered this scary experience: "The pressure I have had was not subtle. It has ranged from the administration changing my grades to the threat of a lawsuit."

For my part, such comments were painful reminders of my culture shock coming into teaching. I remembered encounters with my own students like Pete, Joni, Caitlin, and the rest. And, ironically, despite my work on the standards committee and the fact that so many other faculty members were feeling exactly as I did, my teaching days were numbered. It had become clear that if I kept heading on my same hardcore path with respect to academic standards and grading, I'd be fired. If anything, my experience on SOS and my conversations with other members of the faculty convinced me that I, too, would have to give in to the pressures all faculty faced if I wanted to succeed at teaching in 1990s America.

CHAPTER 9

The Sandbox Experiment

Having been given my ultimatum by those who held the key to The Castle as to how I might become a permanent fixture there myself (had I been so inclined), I had a good long talk with Sandy. We talked the evening after my tenure meeting with the Big Committee, after they told me my student evaluations must significantly improve, or else. My conversation with Sandy that night ultimately inspired me to keep going in my journey into teaching, rather than simply write off the whole experience. The actual possibility of Failure—yes, Failure with a capital F—was haunting me, and my self-confidence was waning. "People who can't do, teach, and I can't even succeed as a teacher." That was the demon in my head. And for a driven Boomer who had learned how to compete adequately in a world with millions of other Boomers, steering clear of Failure was probably what kept me going in my experiment at teaching. I still wanted to know exactly what one had to do to succeed—or survive, perhaps—teaching the MTV generation. In one of those classic moments in life, Sandy and I landed upon the perfect solution.

I was in my study when she got home. She plopped on the floor in my study. "So, what happened?" she asked, referring to my meeting that day with the Big Committee.

"Well, it's pretty simple. Either my student evaluations improve or I'm out."

"So that's what it takes to be a good teacher? Just make the students happy?"

"I suppose so. Otherwise, I'm gone. Oh, yeah, and they want me to take an *acting* course," I said, my voice dripping with sarcasm. "I'm not entertaining enough for the MTV crowd."

"I wouldn't blame you if you quit," Sandy said.

"Well it is interesting. I mean, now they want me to change my personality. Apparently, quiet people can't be teachers. Maybe I ought to go on Prozac."

It was an amusing thought—me on Prozac and changing my personality from quiet and thoughtful to Mr. Entertainment. We traded silly jokes about it for a few minutes, and then it dawned on me that *I could go on Prozac!* What an amazing social experiment that would be!

At the time, I had just finished reading the book, *Listening to Prozac* by psychoanalyst Peter Kramer. I was fascinated by his account of this antidepressant that could actually alter one's personality to be more socially appropriate. As I understood his argument, shy people like me might not become extroverts, but they could become more like the people who seem most prized in our culture, which seems to place greater value on outgoing, vibrant, dynamic personality types than more quiet and subtle personalities. I was reminded of what Harvard psychologist Jerome Kagan was quoted saying in the September 1994 *Atlantic Monthly*: "The cultural ideal now is Bill Clinton. If you happen to have an unfashionable personality, you suffer the consequences."

And so Sandy and I discussed the Prozac scenario. It wasn't that far-fetched. I could go to a doctor and complain about depression. The thought of formulating such a clear-cut social experiment fascinated her as much as it did me, but she was ultimately against the idea. (She said she liked me the way I was.) Though in a way I wanted to experiment with this personality-designing drug just to see what would happen, I was annoyed to think that The College, as a vanguard of the educational establishment, would just as well have preferred that I do so. Indeed, the institution obviously valued a certain bubbliness in its teachers, and my going on Prozac would have been no skin off its bureaucratic back. I got down on myself for seriously considering the notion of "fixing" my personality in order to fit in the "proper" mold. The Prozac idea was neat as social experimentation, but I couldn't, I wouldn't go that far.

I don't recall exactly how the idea came to me, but after I rejected Prozac as the means to become a successful teacher of Generation X, I got another idea. If one option was to chemically change my personality with a drug to be more outgoing, entertaining, and nurturing, then the opposite approach would be to consciously alter my behavior and actually *manipulate my environment.* There seemed little doubt that the system was actually pushing me in that direction. It suddenly became clear to me that being a good teacher didn't seem to really matter in the system of rewards and punishments teachers faced; excellence wasn't really the point. It was becoming increasingly clear that the real point was whether you kept students sufficiently amused and entertained.

Like the Prozac idea, the scheme I would simply call "the Sandbox Experiment" started out as something of a joke. As Sandy and I sat there on the carpet in my little study, I said, "What I should do is to become like a kindergarten teacher and do everything possible to make my classes like playtime. I'll call class the Sandbox. And we'll play all kinds of games and just have fun, and I'll give all my students good grades, and everyone will be happy. Students will get what they want — whether they learn anything or not doesn't matter. The College will get what it wants, which are lots of happy students. And I'll get good evaluations, because students are happy and contented."

From that seed, we then brainstormed what my new classes ought to be like, and sitting there on the carpet (in our sandbox positions) we came up with the essential outline of my new syllabus. To hell with the fundamentals; my little sandbox would emphasize amusement. We'd do restaurant and movie reviews, write about sports, have lots of guest speakers, write advertising copy (which I knew next to nothing about)—I would shamelessly plug into popular culture and the demands of this generation to be amused.

But that wasn't all. I'd have to alter my whole attitude toward people who hated me because they thought I was passing myself off as somehow superior to them. But that's an overstatement of the problem. Hints of one of the most important yet subtle characteristics of these students had been emerging in my evaluations for months, and it had something to do with their revolting against the traditional balance of power between the teacher and themselves. Sure, by most measures I was somewhat accomplished as a journalist who undoubtedly knew far more about the subject I was teaching than students did. But many students were still uncomfortable with the idea that my knowledge and skills were important or even relevant. They seemed far more comfortable with what some educators might call a "collaborative approach." That's a fancy sounding phrase, but it boiled down to mean that students felt what they knew about a subject was just as valuable as what I knew. And who was I, trying to shove my version of the world down their throats? I'll admit, I did come across as if I knew more—a lot more—about journalism than my students. And in doing so I violated this seemingly unwritten code: Don't *act* as if you know more than the students, even though you do.

And so I devised a few techniques to cope with this peculiar attitude. First, I would tell students on the first day of class to call me Peter; that would help break down barriers and assure them that I thought of myself as their equal. Second, I vowed not to tell them anything about my background in journalism. Doing so seemed only to intimidate them and draw attention to our inequality. Psychologists probably have a term for it, but I could see how disoriented students would be if faced with the contradiction of thinking they are both my equal and my inferior in the classroom at the same time. Something would have to give, and it would probably take the form of irrational behavior, sullenness, or other behaviors that were unproductive for me and them. So, from then on, I would be a blank slate, and they'd call me by my first name, simply a "resource" for students to "facilitate" their learning. In the fashionable jargon of some educators, we would be "partners" in the "learning process."

Welcome to teaching in collaborative, multicultural, multivalued, postmodern America, I thought. Form, method, and style had triumphed over substance. For, in the end, it really didn't seem to matter what I knew about my field when it came to teaching. I remember talking to my brother, who was trained as an actor, about my teaching job. At thirty, he was at the older end of Generation X and had recently finished a graduate degree in drama. I said, "My students would probably consider you a better journalism teacher than me, because you know how to act; with just enough knowledge, you could simply play that role." He thought about what I said a minute, then slowly nodded his head and said, "Unfortunately, I think you're probably right." The irony, of course, was that The College hired me over people who had far more teaching experience than I had because of my journalism experience, and yet I had to play down my expertise in order to become a successful teacher. This truly was a strange world, I thought.

Finally, there was the question of grades. It is here that I made what is surely the most important decision about my little Sandbox Experiment, and the one loaded with ethical dilemmas. I decided that, just to see what would happen, I would consciously give what, in my own estimation, were outrageously good grades. I hypothesized that when students were receiving poor grades, they would blow out of proportion characteristics about a teacher that bothered them. But if students were content with their grades, they wouldn't make such a fuss out of other things about a class, such as the difficulty of the readings or my speaking style, which students said wasn't sufficiently entertaining.

And so, in my mind, I became a teaching teddy bear. In the metaphorical sandbox I created, students could do no wrong, and I did almost anything possible to keep all of them happy, all of the time, no matter how childish or rude their behavior, no matter how poorly they performed in the course, no matter how little effort they gave. If they wanted their hands held, I would hold them. If they wanted a stapler (or a Kleenex) and I didn't have one, I'd apologize. If they wanted to read the newspaper while I was addressing the class or if they wanted to get up and leave in the middle of a lecture, go for it. Call me spineless. I confess. But in the excessively accommodative culture that I found myself in, "our students" as many of my colleagues called them, had too much power for me to afford irritating them with demands and challenges I had previously thought were part and parcel of the collegiate experience. Metaphorically speaking, if they needed that ride to school I refused to give them in my dream in the mountains, now I'd give them a ride, and then I'd ask if there was anything else I could do to please. But to be sure, it wasn't always easy for me.

But you're probably thinking, "That's unethical. You're buying off students with high grades." You readers who are also parents of college-aged students might well be adding, "We're paying tuition for you to teach, regardless of how students behave."

I do understand the sentiment. But I believe that my Sandbox Experiment was defensible. First, grades are relative, and the grades I gave out during my experiment were in fact more equal to what was common at The College than the grades I'd been giving before the experiment. As I explained in an earlier chapter, I stumbled into the realization that the average grade at The College, as for most colleges and universities, was a solid B. That's compared to the C average I tried to maintain before the experiment, which I believe compelled many students to evaluate me so harshly. As a result, I brought down my standards to match those of the rest of The College, and it was professionally suicidal to try to do otherwise. As I shall describe below, in often subtle and occasionally quite overt ways, I was in fact strongly encouraged by college administrators and colleagues to do just that. In short, I had to get real. Second, as I explained in in an earlier chapter, it became clear to me from my work on the Save Our Standards committee that one way or another most other instructors were watering down standards, essentially buying off students with lots of spoon-feeding and undeserved grades.

Is it a valid defense to say that "everybody was doing it?" Well, as far as I could tell, everybody *was* doing it, this pandering to students. And they weren't doing so for selfish gain—as opposed to Bill Clinton and Newt Gingrich trying to outdo each other on tax breaks for middle-class voters. The teachers at my college, rather, were going easy on students because they were afraid for their jobs. That's how grade inflation had become institutionalized, and virtually nobody was willing to acknowledge this. Given the incentives of benefits and punishments teachers faced, pandering became quite rational and justifiable, however unfortunate its collective results.

Still, I remained troubled in my choice to relax my personal standards in order to determine just what kinds of behavior the educational system rewarded. As a social experiment, I felt, my one true justification was that the end would justify the means. In an absolute sense, I might have been wrong to act in the way the system was compelling me to act; but now, I am confessing, and hoping that the virtue of my act lies in exposing the corruption that has enveloped much of higher education.

⬛   ⬛   ⬛

My Sandbox Experiment was to get its first key test in my journalism class. I was fortunate to get a pretty good group of students with which to deploy my new methods. There were Steve and Holly, both a bit older students with whom I could easily engage in small talk. There was just one hard-core grunger who had pieces of metal

protruding from her nose and ears, but she was bright and a pretty
fair writer and I got along well with her. There were several Asian
students, including Japanese and Koreans who almost always made
life easier for a teacher because they worked hard, listened well, and
didn't give you a lot of crap. But there was also Caitlin. Remember
her? She was the one who didn't have any tastebuds because of a
cold and wondered if she still had to complete her restaurant review.

Did I change? Let me show you the ways.

I became a master of hand-holding and spoon-feeding. Take
Daniel, for instance, a student of mine who was an official of some
sort in student government. He was outspoken, often absent—and
potentially dangerous to a teacher who might demand too much of
him. For one assignment, I showed a videotape of a speech so students could write a speech story. Daniel missed that day but didn't
tell me he'd be absent. Nevertheless, I agreed to give him a written
copy of the speech so he could do the assignment anyway. Before my
Sandbox Experiment, I wouldn't have allowed him to make up the
assignment. Still, I couldn't suppress saying when handing him the
speech, "If this were a real job, you'd be fired by now." I sort of
winced to myself as I said it, but I couldn't help it. Another time,
Daniel hadn't attended class for a few days and he did the wrong
assignment for a story. Instead of flunking the paper, as I would have
done before, I let him do the correct assignment—and gave him extra
credit for the wrong assignment.

When I used to take attendance, if somebody came in late I'd
mark them absent anyway. Now I would go out of my way to erase
the little 0 (absent) and write in an X (present) if a student walked in
after I'd taken attendance. Whereas in the past I'd demand some sort
of proof to document an absence, now I'd simply take a student's
word. And nearly any excuse would do. If they cared enough to lie,
then I didn't care.

Indeed, my self-inflicted lobotomy was very hard to live with at
times, especially toward the end of the quarter when my nerves and
patience wore thin. Sometimes when students were being real jerks,
I'd say things I'd later regret and then try to figure out a way to make
it up to the student I might have offended.

Caitlin, for instance, was the sort of student I might have flunked
or given D's before, but now I indulged her incompetency, figuring
that she was potentially one more happy student who would say

good things about me come evaluation time. One day she came to me with another excuse (besides nonfunctioning tastebuds) about why she hadn't done an assignment. This was toward the end of the quarter, and I could only keep up this little act of mine for so long. I gave her the same line I laid on Daniel: "You know, if this were a job, you'd be fired by now." Whereas Daniel could handle my criticism, Caitlin couldn't. She started crying and then left the room to compose herself. I felt bad about coming down on her—and I envisioned Caitlin's retaliation on her evaluation of me: *"What a jerk! He treats us like he's the boss and this were a job or something! He has no compassion."* And I imagined how the Big Committee would respond to such words. So, when Caitlin returned to the classroom, at the end of the hour, I walked up to her desk and said, "Caitlin, are you okay? I'm sorry if I came down on you too hard. You're doing fine," I lied.

I also took to plain old bullshitting with students, going out of my way to be informal with them whenever I could, and it was working well in my new journalism class. I talked with Rick about skiing, Tanya about jogging. "How was your weekend?" I'd say. When Heather, the grunger, took time off from in the middle of the quarter to take a vacation in New Orleans, rather than get irritated that she had missed so much class, I asked her, "So how was your vacation? Did you enjoy Mardi gras?"

Of course, my newfound happy-face approach to being a college instructor would have meant nothing if I didn't follow through on the grading end. It's one thing to try to be a nice guy; there's nothing wrong in trying to communicate better with your students. But when it came to my new grading system, I was a shameless lush, handing out mostly A's and B's, often for work that I would have given C's before. But while I felt shameless, I had to remind myself that nearly nine of ten students got A's and B's at The College—and the same went for top schools like Stanford.

I recall one news story a student wrote, containing so much muddled language that it was nearly impossible to follow. According to my theoretical grading system, the story should have gotten a D because it required so much work to whip it into shape. This is what the new me wrote on the student's paper: "Okay. Some unclear spots that don't make sense, mechanical problems, style errors (use your stylebook)."

And I gave the paper a warm and friendly B minus.

Over the entire quarter, that journalism class "earned" an average grade of 3.5, equivalent to an A minus. Compare that to the 2.3 average (a C) in the introductory journalism class that got on my case so hard during my first quarter at The College.

And so went the first phase of my grand experiment.

If there was any question that my plot was on target, all doubts were alleviated in a series of encounters I had with colleagues on campus. Of course, they had no idea that I was being so utterly cynical, but as they became convinced that I sincerely wanted to change and "improve" as a teacher, they increasingly opened up to me and revealed their own (shall I say cynical?) secrets about teaching. These encounters were enlightening, if disgusting, in their message about what it took to succeed as a teacher.

One day, I called everybody on my tenure committee and told them I thought it would be a good idea for us to get together informally to talk. "Great idea," everyone said, and we met over beers at a nearby cafe. We started off talking about the best ways to deal with students who disrupt class, the ones who read newspapers while you're trying to talk, and other problems. "Never single anybody out during class," I was advised, against my inclinations to do otherwise. Take the student aside after class and remind him or her of proper conduct.

Then we talked about ways to improve the general "atmosphere of learning" in my classes, which translated from educationese meant how to tone down my hard edge and be a nice guy. Beth and Ken especially thought I came across as too strong and tough-minded for college students in the 1990s.

Beth offered this advice: "The first week of class I tell students, 'I have some expertise, and you all have some expertise. My job is to facilitate this process. And please call me Beth.'" Throughout the quarter, give praise easily, Beth added. "Tell them they've improved," because that makes students feel good about themselves, and they feel good about you, too.

As our little soiree continued and the beer flowed, Ken showed himself to be a big fan of extracurricular activities, such as field trips and guest speakers, anything to be more "glitzy and sexy," as he put it. That's what students thrived on and made them think well of you, Ken said. In a virtuoso display of getting wrapped around the axle,

Ken and Andy must have argued without the slightest bit of humor or irony for a good five minutes about which local media outlet would best achieve the proper level of sex and glitz, the large metro daily or a much smaller local paper or even a well known TV station. Ken also offered this tip: After the field trip, meet the class for a pizza dinner. "They'll love it, and they'll love you," he said. "You'd be amazed what a difference it can make seeing you relaxed in a different environment."

"Bring donuts," Beth said. "That's what I do." She was obviously amused by the image of me bringing my students Mr. Donuts some morning. The thought amused me, too, because it was so clearly not something I would ever feel comfortable doing, and she knew it. "You can get away with bringing donuts, Beth," I said. "I never could."

"Play the game," Andy said, embarrassing me with his frankness in front of everybody. "That's right," Ken said. I simply nodded, not responding directly to this advice. Within moments we were talking about something else. I wanted to ask them, "What do you mean exactly?" But I didn't, leery of pursuing this line of thinking further. I sensed that in spite of this little bit of openness being expressed by Ken especially, this was a dangerous subject to be speaking out loud. I knew that Ken was really very serious about his role in the tenure review process, and this might be the beer talking, and the last thing you wanted Ken to think was that you're "just playing the game."

A few weeks after our "sex and glitz" talk, I had a conversation with the department chairwoman. On the surface, Anita was the nicest, most capable person you could imagine meeting; but there was something about her, perhaps her very unflappable coolness, combined with a great deal of power, that did not inspire my trust. One day, she asked in her usual way, "Hey, you got a minute?" and we proceeded up the stairs to her office. "We haven't talked in a while, and I was wondering how things were going." After we chatted a few minutes, I told her that I was taking an acting class to improve my class presentation skills. (When Ken *et al.* had suggested it would be a "good idea" for me to take such a course, I at first was repulsed at the idea. But I ended up finding an improvisation course for non-actors that actually turned out to be sort of fun. The instructor, a Brit, was especially enlightening on the subject of "status games" that people play in their daily lives, in which they engage in certain behaviors according to their relative social status. I found this knowledge to be useful in professional situations. I doubt that taking the class actually influenced my classroom behavior, but the six-week workshop turned out to be good material in encounters with authority figures at The College.)

When I mentioned the drama class, Anita, who was usually fairly low-key, absolutely lit up. "I took a dance class once. It changed the way I teach," she told me. She said that after taking dance, she became much more animated, spontaneous, and free with her body while in front of the classroom.

Then, this cerebral woman said, "We are really just performers up there." Teaching, she said, "is just a performance."

I also had several impromptu discussions with Richard, an acquaintance of mine on campus who gave me political counsel, even though I never asked for it. He had this maddening habit of beginning these conversations with the word, "Confidentially," then he'd go on to tell me things I thought should have been openly discussed in my committee meetings but never were. I wasn't sure how much I could trust him. One day Richard said, "Confidentially, I'm feeling that we're throwing you to the wolves and letting you hang out to dry." Richard said he was concerned that I was brought in to The College without significant teaching experience, was given no training or orientation about what to expect from students nowadays, and then was held up to the same expectations as instructors who'd taught twenty years or more.

But most revealing, every time we chatted Richard would say to me: "You're just going to have to teach to the evaluations."

I would simply nod and not say anything or pursue Richard's line of thought further by talking about the implications of what he was suggesting. Little did he know just how enthusiastically and aggressively I was heeding this advice.

◢ ◢ ◢

But the student evaluations to follow would be the real test of whether my rather cynical hypothesis behind the experiment—that students would respond positively to good grades and a happy face.

A week or so before we took the evaluations, Ken followed his usual procedure of making sure that he or one of the others on my tenure committee were scheduled to show up ten minutes before the end of each of my classes to conduct the evaluations, while I left the room. The subtle power games imbedded in the procedure still bothered me. But this time, I did my best to work the situation to my advantage. A day or two before the evaluations, I told my classes that somebody was planning to come in and do them. I took a light-hearted tone, and Heather, the grunger in my journalism class, picked up on this, saying, "So Big Brother's coming to visit." "Yeah, that's right," I said. I suppose the groundwork I'd done all quarter to get the students on my side had helped as well.

Andy, a member of my tenure committee, was designated to do the evaluations in my journalism class. On the day he showed up, I was still running the class, and I kept talking and showing overheads for about five minutes about writing magazine headlines, leaving Andy standing a bit awkwardly in the back of the room. Before, I would have just interrupted my talk in order not to be rude to our guest, but this time I figured the more control I exerted in the situation, the better. Taking up extra time was another good move, because that would leave the students less time to write lengthy and potentially negative comments. (That was a tip I got from my colleague Chris, the bureaucracy master.) When I could delay no more, it was show time.

"Okay folks, it's evaluation time," I said, beginning to pass out the forms, careful at this point not to let Andy lift a finger or utter a word. All I wanted him to do was to collect the forms, a job that anybody could do, and I figured the students would pick up on this. In this performance, I would be the magician, and Andy my handy assistant.

I told the class, "Go ahead and fill these out please; I'd like a little feedback from you about the course. When you're finished, just hand them to my colleague here." I then pointed to my "assistant," Andy, and he didn't say a word because there was nothing left to say.

One day a few weeks later, I saw Ken at the department office. The recent evaluations were tabulated, and he had copies for me. "You're going to like these," he said. "They look pretty good." He handed me the manilla envelope. But Ken was bothered by something. Though the the numerical rankings were good, the students in all the classes had written very few comments on the forms. "That's really weird," Ken said. "I don't know what they're going say about that," he added, referring to the Big Committee. Shit, I thought. Ken will find any excuse not to be happy with my student evaluations. I said, "I think it's a sign of contentment. Students slam you when they're not happy." Ken had nothing to say about that.

Indeed, the evaluations looked good. One comment I got in the journalism class said, "The instructor was fun. Somehow he made this class go quickly without seeming to lag. It was fast-paced and interesting. He made it fun." Good, the Fun word, I thought. Ken will like that. On the bottom-line question, "Would you recommend this class to other students?" I prevailed with a score of 9 Yes and 2 No.

My writing classes were even better because there were high numbers responding. Bottom line in writing class one: 16 Yes and 2 No. Score in class two: 15 Yes, 1 No. And such poetry came from the students' formerly poisoned pens:

> *A great instructor:*
> *I'd heard, before taking this class,*
> *That he was a really tough teacher,*
> *Which he is,*
> *But in being tough*
> *He encourages you*
> *To work harder.*
>
> *The class was fun.*
> *I have learned a lot*
> *From this class.*
> *A great instructor:*
> *The class was fun!*

Still, Ken was right. This was good stuff, and the "scores" looked good, but the Big Committee might be bothered by the paucity of student comments. The results of Phase One of my Jekyll and Hyde experiment were indeed promising, but there still could be doubts; those few evaluations from a single quarter might have been a fluke; and besides, I remained under the cloud of having another quarter to go in which to convince my little corner of Generation X that this Boomer was a cool guy.

As the quarter came to a close, I ran into Richard, my self-appointed political confidant, at the office where I was turning in my grades. For some reason, he was standing next to the desk belonging to the clerk who proofed the grade sheets. Then he got started on one of his little "confidential" lectures.

"Confidentially, you're just going to have to teach to the evaluations, if that's the political thing to do," Richard said. And I did my usual sort of noncommittal nod, still not knowing whether to trust him, as I said, "I guess so," and handed the clerk my grades, which were in Richard's full view as she checked them for legibility. It was disconcerting. Just a glance and Richard would be able to see that the class average was very high. I was sure that he saw them, and that my little secret was now out.

■   ■   ■

The following quarter was the make or break time for me, the one that would resolve one way or another my fate as a college teacher. Since my Machiavellian formula seemed to be achieving the desired results, I tried hard not to change anything about my courses or my rather calculated behavior. The danger, however, was that I was becoming more confident, and students could interpret confidence as superciliousness, which I wanted to avoid. There was potentially great danger for an instructor trying to cope with students. Whenever they'd act childish, rude, or bored, a teacher might have to pinch himself real hard to keep from blowing up, walking out of the room, and telling them to all go back to high school or whatever Neverneverland they'd come out from.

My journalism class, as usually seemed to be the case, put me to the greatest test. It seemed that there was something about the journalism sequence at The College that attracted more than its share of difficult students. We had no professional school of journalism, and so most of the students had no interest at all in going into journalism or mass communications but were taking the course to satisfy a writing requirement.

This particular class was a special dog. Whereas my "turnaround" class the previous term had included some motivated students, by whom I was generally viewed favorably—this class had several quintessential members of Generation X who tested the limits of my patience.

As with all my writing classes, I had students first do drafts that they would then revise before turning in a final draft. I'd let them work on drafts during class time and allow them to get feedback from their peers. I'd also try to look at the drafts to give the students an idea whether they were on the right track. Doing the drafts was so important that I made them worth 15 percent of the final grade. As I've mentioned before, students at The College as a general rule would not do anything if it didn't directly affect their grade in a significant way. But in this class, I had a core of people who didn't do drafts, week after week after week, 15 percent of their grade be damned.

If my journalism class were a movie, it would have looked something like this:

Camera: *Long shot from the back of a good-sized classroom, as college students file in to take their chairs. Sounds of tables and chairs being shuffled, voices in small talk. Zoom to teacher at the head of the class, smiling and casually talking to a student about skiing conditions over the weekend. After a few minutes at 11 A.M. sharp, he removes his rear end from the table (posing in a very casual, friendly way), stands up, and starts talking to the whole class.*

Teacher: *"Okay, folks, go ahead and pass me up a copy of your drafts due today. Then break up into your groups. Remember, today we're working on leads."*

Camera: *Scan back to students. Little movement detected. Two or three people take their assignments from folders and pass them to the student ahead. The rest of the class stares at the teacher, expressionless.*

Teacher (incredulous): *"Do I have everyone's draft? Is this it?"*

Camera: *Seeing no further movement from the inert students, the teacher moves back to his power position in the front of the podium, adjusts his body uncomfortably a second, then speaks.*

Teacher: *"Let me remind everyone that the drafts are worth 15 percent of your grade. If you don't come prepared, there's not any productive work we can do during class."*

Camera: *Scan back to class, still inert and silent, zoom in on two young men in the back sitting together at a table. Both have long hair. Not hippie long. More grunge or metal anti-hippie long, both in their early twenties. One sports a baseball hat and a goatee. The other has no baseball hat. He's a grunge-metal cross: long-sleeved checkered work shirt unbuttoned to his chest, showing a black T-shirt with the name of a metal band blasted across it. Slumped in their chairs, they stare alternatively at the teacher and down to their desk, obviously bored.*

Narrator Voice-over (teacher staring back at class):
> *"Look at these idiots. I've got three drafts. What the hell am I going to do today? I have a notion to just cancel class and send them home. How would Tom Hanks or Harrison Ford say it if this were a movie? 'You people make me sick. Get the hell out of here, come back when you've done the work. You're wasting my time.' . . . Yeah, right. In my dreams."*

Teacher: *"Okay, tell you what. Break up into your groups, give feedback to the ones who've done their drafts and the rest of you go over your outlines with each other and try to come up with an interesting angle for your leads."*

And so I caved, and I caved over and over that quarter as I tried to please in the midst of mindlessness, to my students' deep sense of entitlement, and to the inordinate amount of power the system had given them.

Another incident from that class brought into sharp focus the chasm that existed between me and my students, no matter how hard I tried to bridge it, underscoring for me that perhaps my teaching wasn't the problem at all but that there was something else going wrong here. We were discussing feature stories, and one day I decided to read a model story from a collection of prize-winning features. My selection was called "Fat Albert," by David Finkel, a story that appeared in the *St. Petersburg Times* in 1985. The story was a wonderful model of a personality profile, delving into the life and character of an 891-pound man known as Fat Albert, who was a side-show in a circus in the South. What made the piece particularly strong was its empathy toward its character, its sense of humor and its vivid descriptions, bringing Fat Albert to life. I wanted to read the piece just to give the students a sense of the magic that was possible in good feature writing, beyond the how-to stories they were accustomed to reading in *Cosmopolitan* or the lifestyle page of many local newspapers. But I also thought the story would be entertaining. To be honest, to be entertaining was probably my chief motive for reading the piece.

When I finished reading the story, I looked up and took the pulse of the class's sentiments. I judged their expressions. I focused in particular on Justin, a young man who sat in the back of the room. He had longish hair, a goatee, and advertised himself as a sports fan by always wearing a baseball hat bearing the name of a professional basketball team. Somehow, for me, Justin *was* Generation X staring back at me. His work was usually pretty good, but I always felt very distant from him. For some odd reason, I sensed that if I could reach him through this story, I could reach his entire generation. I figured that "Fat Albert" was universal in its appeal. Who wouldn't be amused by a story of an 800-pound man? (True, the story was about a fat guy, but the writer avoided any danger of political incorrectness by emphasizing Fat Albert's own explanation of his obesity: he was fat because of genetic metabolism, pure and simple.)

But when I looked at Justin, all I saw was blankness. I must have looked at him for several seconds, searching for an expression, a smile, a sign, a movement of his eyebrows, something to indicate that, Yeah, that's good stuff and I'm glad this teacher turned me on to it. But I saw nothing. Justin's eyes met mine, and in those eyes I saw boredom and contempt. Those eyes said, "You don't amuse me with your brand of so-called good writing. There's nothing you can do or say to impress me."

I looked around the class and met other eyes and most all those eyes said the same thing as Justin's, and I then concluded that the Fat Albert story fell flat. But while the vast majority of the class responded as Justin had, there were two or three students whose eyes were lit up. One was Perry, who was one of the brightest students I'd encountered at The College. When I asked the class a few questions about the piece, Perry had thoughtful things to say. But nobody else joined in, and when it became clear that Perry and I were engaged in our own little conversation, I had to stop, fearing that horrible pressure of Let's Move On from the rest of the bored class. The tragedy is that Perry deserved to have his say. He was among the few in the class who had any potential to get anything meaningful from what I had to offer, and yet he was being deprived by the tyranny of the majority who demanded something else at the moment. For them, it was time to change the channel, and so with regrets and feelings of awkwardness, I changed it. Justin and the mediocre majority won. And Perry, the thoughtful one, was the loser, and there was nothing I could do about it short of alienating the rest of the class.

Indeed, a core group of about half a dozen fairly hard-core, angst-filled suburban GenXers in the class, who sat together in the back of the classroom, formed sort of an impregnable fortress with each other. In my effort to win them over, I really dropped a lead balloon one day.

They were a tough group to crack, and I should have known better. Their collective body language seemed to suggest that their allegiance lay with the group and little else, not even their own educations. Other than being part of the class, some of the people in this group seemed to have little else in common except that they belonged to the same generation. They stood in this fortress against me as a Boomer, and even against their peers whose energies seemed more traditionally self-directed, and who were interested primarily in doing what was best for themselves rather than seeing themselves primarily as one of a group. The core group included Justin; Lance the music guru and grunge king; Marjorie, the Doc Marten grunge queen; Jane the airhead; and Mark, a just-released army veteran whose military experience seemed to have addicted him to groups, and so he always seemed to be just hanging on to this group for the hell of it.

To be sure, I probably cultivated their group identity because it was my intention to promote Sandboxdom, and I had the students work in groups as much as possible (I would later discover that while I cynically called this method the Sandbox, other college instructors were using such group work extensively and enthusiastically, and calling it "critical thinking," one of the educational establishment's newest fads and buzz words.) For one assignment in particular, to produce a legitimate magazine ad on a product or a spoof ad, I thought it fitting for the students to work together in groups. The hard-core group, of course, clung together from the first moment, and they wanted badly to do a spoof. (There was method in these spoofs. I figured that giving the students a chance to slam established commercial products would provide an outlet for their general anger toward established institutions, and at the same time see me as being on their side as a slammer rather than a slammee.)

One day, I sat down with the hard-core group a few moments while they were brainstorming ideas. The atmosphere in the class was relaxed and people were talkative. Marjorie said she had just seen the movie *Reality Bites,* and thought maybe she could do a spoof ad on the film. I hadn't seen the movie but I'd heard it was sort of a funny but realistic look at the aimless angst of a few twentysomethings. Marjorie, in fact, reminded me of a taller, skinnier version of Winona Rider. "Great idea," I told Marjorie. I thought she was really on to something here; the ad could make light of the Generation X stereotypes, and I figured that's exactly where Marjorie was going with this—why else do a spoof ad on this particular film? So, without thinking, after she suggested the idea, I came up with a concept for the spoof: "Yeah, you might call it *Reality Brats,*" I said smiling, figuring we were on the same ironic wavelength. But as soon as the words left my mouth, they plummeted to the floor, and you could almost hear the *kerplunk* as they hit the tile. Marjorie's faced assumed that same blankness as Justin's had several days earlier with the Fat Albert story. Marjorie's expression said, "You've gone too far, Boomer. Don't make fun of us." Nobody else in the small group thought my concept was funny either. Afterward, my only thought was how pitiful that these people had no sense of irony, and how seriously they took themselves. But I learned that I would always have to keep my generational distance with them, that I could never really be a good guy with people who ultimately didn't trust me.

Eventually, the time came for the quarter's student evaluations. The drill was the same: Ken, or somebody else from my tenure committee, would come to my classes to collect the filled-out evaluation forms while I'd put my little tail between my legs and leave the room. I'd do my best to retain control over the hearts and minds of the students while trying to keep from being humiliated by the institution's exercise of power. In just a few weeks I would go before the Big Committee, and its members would undoubtedly give me some sign as to whether students' views of my teaching had improved sufficiently.

Thus, my little experiment, my test of the Sandbox theory, had come down to whether some seventy-five mostly eighteen- to twenty-two-year-olds liked me or didn't like me; to whether they thought I was sufficiently entertaining; to whether the grades I gave them had met with their B+ expectations; to whether I presented myself as their equal who "facilitated" their learning and held their hands at every turn, or as their superior who demanded too damned much.

How well did the Sandbox Experiment work? In a word, it succeeded fabulously. That term's evaluations were the best I'd ever received at The College. In fact, they were sterling. The score in my writing class—when students were asked whether they would "recommend this class to other students"—18 Yes and 0 No; average grade I gave the class: 3.0. How about this comment: "I found (the instructor) was always willing to help me if I had any questions on my papers. I found his style of writing refreshing, and not like other stale writing classes I've had." And the final score in that problematic journalism class: 10 Yes and 1 No; average final grade I gave in the class: 3.0.

Still, I couldn't help but be amused at one of the comments a student wrote about the journalism class: "The teacher did not seem to have a good grasp of the material. I don't think he is qualified to teach this course." Apparently, at least for this particular student, I'd gone a bit overboard in striving for the humble approach and playing the role of teacher as facilitator. Either that, or he didn't have a clue about about anything that went on in the class, and believe me, that's a distinct possibility.

With these student evaluations in hand, I was left with one more task before the meeting with the Big Committee. I was supposed to submit a report, summarizing my progress and essentially stating my case for being granted tenure. In my report, I confessed my past sins, telling the keepers of the Castle that I had begun my career at The College without a clear idea what to expect of students in the 1990s. I said that I had completely revamped my approach, and that the results as shown in the student evaluations were "indeed encouraging." Continuing in this quasi-religious atonement, I then told the committee of my being transformed—Danny DeVito-like as in the movie *Renaissance Man*—by having the privilege to be a teacher of such deserving students. I wrote: "I've made these changes from a better understanding of our students . . . No, our students probably aren't Harvard-bound. . . . But many are eager to learn and are hungry to improve their lives. They aren't spoiled or privileged, and when you find them, they make teaching great."

Writing this statement didn't really ring true for me. It seemed an idealistic stretch. But the statement represented the great sustaining myth at The College, truly a matter of religious belief among some of the faculty and administration. Somehow I sensed this. Here and there, I would pick up references to this "success" mythology of higher education; it was pervasive, always laying between the cracks in the brick and mortar. Although an increasing number of faculty members no longer believed in its validity, the myth remained powerful and institutionalized. I decided to exploit it.

I saw Ken a few days after I gave him a copy of my statement to the Big Committee, and he ate up my atonement and conversion. "That statement was neat, *extremely* neat," he said in that drawl of his. "I think we're going to have fun this time" with the Big Committee, he said.

Then came the day of judgment. After an awkward few minutes everybody got down to business, and the chairman of the Big Committee spoke. "I'm very pleased," he said. "I see you've made a 180-degree turnaround," and then he lavished praise on my report. As he spoke, I looked around the table at the other members of the committee, and many were nodding their heads in agreement.

They continued to lob me some softball questions for a few minutes. Then one Big Committee member asked me a tough question. "In making these changes you've described in your statement, have you compromised your standards at all?" he asked. Of course, it was an obvious question, but I hadn't anticipated it. After fumbling a second or two, I came up with what was sounding to me to be a convincing answer as the words came out of my mouth. Basically, I told them that whether one compromises standards all depends on where your students are coming from. I said that I had "adjusted" the level of my course to meet the students' "abilities and needs."

As I think about what I said, it seems to me absurd that such a response could even be considered legitimate, and yet for this group of people that was exactly the right answer. Before the Sandbox Experiment, my mentality was such that if you asked students to perform at a reasonable approximation of college level work, then it was their job to rise up to your level, not the other way around. I still don't think I was ever expecting too much of my students; and in a less corrupt system in which students themselves were not empowered, by virtue of their own mediocrity, to essentially define their own standards and curriculum, there would have never been a problem; they would have performed at the college level, or would have been forced to find something else to do with their lives. As matters stood, students were getting away with inferior work, getting good grades to boot, then sent away under the illusion that that's how the real world worked.

As I made up my answer for the Big Committee, the cynicism (or utter naivete) underlying the one member's difficult question was almost palpable. Having been at The College for several terms, talking to other instructors and also many students, I knew that compromising standards in order to accommodate students had become a way of life at the institution. Everyone knew it, but nobody would ever publicly admit it. I could almost see the subtle winks and nods from the committee members as I was talking.

I left the meeting feeling . . . is *good* the right word? No, I think it was more a feeling of satisfaction that I had figured out how to unlock the gates to the metaphorical Castle. I had figured out what it took, according to the system, to be considered a "good" teacher.

I left the room, and Ken stayed behind the closed doors while the Big Committee discussed my case. Ten minutes later, he emerged. The first sign that everything had gone well was the relaxed, pleased look spread across Ken's face as he walked toward me. We started walking back to our office building, and he said, "They *looovved* you in there. They didn't miss a thing. They were extremely pleased with your mannerisms; you connected well with everyone. I think we're home free. Congratulations." And he patted me on the back.

A few days later, I ran into Richard. "How'd the meeting go?" he asked. "I'm golden," I said. "They loved my statement, and they loved me. They said I've made a 180-degree turnaround." Richard again told me his concern that I'd been "thrown to the wolves" without receiving a proper orientation. But this veteran of The College couldn't help but feel satisfied with the outcome. "Still, the system works," he said, and then began vigorously patting me on the back, and he suggested that everything that had transpired to that point had been right and true. "This is a real triumph!" Richard said.

If only he knew, I thought. But maybe he did. Richard had been there at the clerk's desk when I turned in my grades. He had to have seen those grades. He knew the secret to success—and he kept telling me how to play the game: "Teach to the evaluations, teach to the evaluations," he would say, like a mantra.

And thus, my little Sandbox Experiment worked just as Sandy and I had hypothesized. That was how the system worked. Teachers like me dished out high grades for students' mediocre work. That is what I saw. That is what I did.

A few months later, I was awarded tenure.

▰ ▰ ▰

In the mountains, alone, one does see clearly. But being in the mountains, in a place vast and unpeopled, reflecting on these past few years of my journey into teaching, it's easy to forget the time and place I came from. Perhaps like going off in a spaceship, you have to keep up on what was happening back on Earth in order to keep feeling connected to it. I came to the mountains from a city in America. Back there, masses of people were plugged in. They were glued to the televised surrealism of a former football hero in a white Ford

Bronco on an L.A. freeway, methodically pursued by a procession of police cars. Virtually the entire culture was worshipping Forrest Gump. Books about angels, near-death experiences, and satanic cults filled bookstores and topped best seller lists.

I had experienced teaching the X Generation, often in a state of bewilderment. Now I needed to explain them, to finally come to terms with them and with my journey into teaching. I knew I wouldn't find the answer in the purity of the mountains or in the academic subculture. I would find the explanation in the city, and in the postmodern society that had born and bred what we've come to call Generation X.

PART II

Education in Postmodern America

CHAPTER 10

The Postmodern Revolt

The Elliott Bay Book Company in the heart of Seattle's old Pioneer Square is a book lover's paradise. It is quintessential Seattle, a city of many bright, educated people. In some ways it is the antithesis of the easy, breezy mega-bookstores one finds nowadays in fashionable shopping malls. Elliott Bay is old and compact, its space brimming with books, its customers squeezing by each other through thinly spaced aisles on their browsing adventures. Elliott Bay is to Seattle what City Lights Books is to San Francisco, where poets read their latest works and intellectual types gather. You get the feeling that even Elliott Bay's clerks have doctorates or are published poets or essayists.

And so, after leaving the Rocky mountains in September on a visit to Seattle, I was left a bit breathless by the sight before me as I browsed the Elliott Bay shelves. Spanning an entire 20 or 30 foot length of wall, reaching nearly to the top of the store's high ceiling, was Elliott Bay's prominent offering of popular culture: a vast section of books, perhaps the largest single section in the entire store, consisting of best-selling works on angels, UFO's, paranormal phenomena and other titles reflecting Americans' obsession with such topics. I stood for a while before this altar, admiring both its completeness and the effort involved to assemble such a collection. Then I meandered further into the bowels of the bookstore and came across the Science section. In contrast to the store's devotion to Angels, Science looked unloved and unappreciated, with minimal offerings in one or two short rows inconspicuously surrounded by a sea of books.

Not long after my visit to Elliott Bay, I was talking to Marie, an acquaintance, about my not-so-excellent adventures teaching Generation X. I told her that so many Xers seemed disengaged, passive, and bored with college, and how I seemed compelled as their instructor to amuse them and dish out high grades. "Well, whose fault is it?" Marie asked. "We can't blame the kids. Half of them were latchkey kids from broken families." As a parent to a couple of college students herself, Marie became quite defensive of Xers—"kids," she called them—and was far more willing to place blame for shortcomings in the educational system on parents and teachers, who she said often "don't care about the kids." She concluded: "Seems to me like what you're talking about is just a generation gap."

Was that all there was to it? Latchkey kids, divorced parents, and generation gaps? To be sure, these might be obvious explanations for what I observed over the course of three years in the trenches of higher education in the 1990s. But while obvious, Marie's explanations were also just partially true. I believe this because, as my visit to the Elliott Bay Book Company reinforced for me, the apparent revolt against reason and thoughtfulness, and the overwhelming dominance of America's amusement culture, weren't limited to the habits of twenty-year-olds. Some Generation X watchers are saying the very notion of Generation X is dead because Xism, they argue, is a "state of mind." While part of this argument stems from the X culture's seemingly genetic need to be on the cutting cultural edge of anything, the argument seems valid in the sense that all of us are now Xers, to some degree. To be an American in the 1990s, a time when one can almost feel the world quaking into something that's at once scary, new, highly technological, and profoundly uncertain, is to be "Generation X." Consider the following additional, seemingly unconnected, signs of our times:

- In the wake of the 1995 bombing of the Oklahoma City federal building that killed 169 people, conspiracy-crazed anti-government militia leaders say they are in fact the "victims," and they blame the government itself for planting the bomb.

The militias say the government is trying to deprive freedom lovers of their right to bear arms, and believe the government is trying to keep tabs on Americans via secret codes implanted in dollar bills and stop signs.

- A movie about a good natured idiot is the most beloved film in America, becoming the third-highest grossing film in history. *Forrest Gump* turns actor Tom Hanks into a cultural icon, earning him at least $31 million, while the man who creates the character and writes the book and screenplay earns just 1 percent of Hanks's take on the film.

- The Evergreen State College in Olympia, Washington, known as one of the best small public liberal arts colleges in the country, offers a two-quarter course on *Star Trek,* and the class is in such demand that, according to the Associated Press, parents are calling the college to get their sons and daughters enrolled, and dozens of students who want to sign up are turned away.

- In a *Time* magazine poll, nearly seven in every ten adults believe angels exist. More than half say angels are an important force in their lives.

- An organization searching America Online for examples of "innovative" teaching cites the example of one teacher who dresses up in a chicken costume "to the delight of his students."

Marie, my acquaintance, was of course right—in a sense. The X Generation surely can't be blamed for who they are and how they see the world. But neither are parents, latchkeys, and generation gaps to blame. There seemed to be something larger at work, encompassing not just college students disengaged from intellectual life, but educators seeing innovation in chicken costumes, the embracing of Forrest Gump, and the magnificent Angels section at Elliott Bay. It seemed that each was a manifestation of Modernism itself in its death-throes.

The Modern Era has been arguably the greatest force of social change—but also for many the greatest source of disappointment—for more than two centuries. Now, the signs were everywhere that the epoch was dying, its beliefs in reason, sober analysis, and appropriate standards and authorities being overwhelmed by something

new, an "anything goes," postmodern way of being. My students—
who they were, what they valued, and how they behaved—seemed to
be one product of this profound cultural revolt that has occurred in
Western, postindustrial societies. Thus, what has come to be known
as Generation X, perhaps for lack of a better term, might be more
aptly called the Postmodern Generation. Whatever term you want to
use, Generation X is arguably the first fully postmodern cohort of
Americans, and they are the product of their culture and of their
place in history. And yet, Generation X is the progeny of the very
same transformation of society toward the postmodern that has
changed not just young people, but virtually the entire culture.

Indeed, the revolution from the modern to the postmodern worlds
represents perhaps *the* fundamental intellectual and cultural clash of
our times. The sphere of higher education has become an important
cauldron for this conflict for the very reason that, for generations,
education has been synonymous with the very notion of modernity.
But higher education isn't alone in being torn asunder. Debates
within academia over multiculturalism, academic standards, and the
like are mere skirmishes taking place within the real and much larger
battle between modernity and postmodernity that is occurring on
many cultural fronts besides higher education. You'll find evidence of
the modern-postmodern clash in such far-ranging aspects of life as
electoral politics, journalism, even religion. But the culture clash I'm
referring to isn't about good guys and bad guys. It's raging within
each of us to some extent as the modern and postmodern parts of
ourselves vie for dominance. To some degree, we are all
postmodernists now.

Although postmodernity is quietly transforming American culture, most people probably don't realize it, let alone think about it,
because the changes are rarely explicitly acknowledged in the ways
that our culture transmits knowledge about itself. Consider one regional newspaper, the *Seattle Times.* While visiting the city, I typed
"postmodern" into a database and found just a handful of articles
that mentioned the term. But there were thousands of articles that
referred to "modern" or "modernism." My point is that, for most
people, the language of our ordinary culture suggests that we still see
ourselves in terms of the ideology of modernism, even though many
people sense implicitly that the modern paradigm is being eclipsed
by a new age. What about the nation's most prestigious newspaper,
the *New York Times,* which with its huge information-gathering re-

sources is, of all news organizations, most firmly connected to the pulse of the American temperament? How explicitly does the *Times* account for the postmodern? Except for the rare instances when postmodern ideas are explored and explained, most explicit references to the postmodern in the *New York Times* are no more than glib allusions (*postmodern* this or *postmodern* that) in articles about real estate, books, or art. The articles assume that readers really know what postmodernism means. Given that scholars of the subject go to great lengths and difficulty trying to describe what postmodernism really means, I'd say the *Times*'s implicit assumption is unfounded. Here, for example, was one such casual reference to the "postmodern" in the *Times,* in an article about a real-estate development: "The first, London Woods, at Routes 132 and 6, was started in 1985 and has sold 100 of its 119 four-bedroom postmodern homes at $306,000 to $425,000." I could be wrong, but I am doubtful that even New York City real estate agents have a clue what this writer was referring to.

To be sure, many educated people have encountered passing references to postmodern notions—as in the *Times,* or perhaps in graduate courses in sociology, philosophy, or literature. Until I decided to find out more about postmodernism for myself, I would place myself in that category. But I would argue that most people, even highly educated ones, are unfamiliar with postmodern notions. The concept has mostly been used in esoteric academic circles or bandied about by art and film critics. I would speculate that many educated people, who haven't studied a lot of humanities or social sciences, have only a vague idea what postmodernism is supposed to mean. Take my partner, Sandy. She was educated in science at UC-Berkeley, went through medical school, and for years she's been an avid reader of the *New York Times, Harper's,* and other such elite publications that make passing references to postmodern this or that. Still, she'd always ask me whenever the subject came up in our conversations, "Tell me again, exactly what *is* postmodernism anyway?"

In my view, for the sake of clarity and pragmatism (and for the sake of people like Sandy), postmodernism needs to be brought out from the cloistered, elite worlds of artistic criticism, architecture, philosophy, and the humanities. The concept can be a useful, popularly understood tool for interpreting postindustrial societies and the people who inhabit them, not just a literary device for academics and art critics.

Ironically, the arena in which postmodernism is perhaps most discussed as an abstraction, higher education, is also among the places that could most use some clarity about just what postmodernity means for the effective *practice* of education. Educators, whose methods are rooted in the Age of Modernism, need to explicitly acknowledge, if nothing else, that many of the people they are trying to teach are, through and through, the children of a postmodern age. Postmodern writer Andreas Huyssen has discussed the pragmatic importance of understanding the consequences of the postmodern era. He says that by the early 1980s, the modernism/postmodernism question "had become one of the most contested terrains in the intellectual life of Western societies." He adds: "And the terrain is contested precisely because there is so much more at stake than the existence or non-existence of a new artistic style, so much more also than just the 'correct' theoretical line."

As you might guess, as a journalist I'm not much interested in theoretical abstractions here. And, unfortunately, much that has been written about postmodernism is abstract and out of the reach of nonspecialists, a world of "grand narratives" and "meta-discourses." Ironically, such obscurities have occurred despite one supposed key feature of postmodern thought being the eradication of the barriers between so-called "high" and "mass" culture, and between specialization and popularization. Let me confess now that, in the same way I don't think of myself as an educator as such, I'm emphatically *not* a postmodernist scholar. But, in the same way that in the first part of this book I tried to report my own experiences as an outsider to the academic subculture, I'll try in this second part to pry open the esoteric, often impenetrable world of postmodern philosophy and connect it to the world of higher education I experienced. My premise throughout is that we can't understand Generation X nor higher education's current upheavals without first looking to the transformation in larger culture that is shaping them. But before I try to answer Sandy's question about the nature of postmodernism, bear with me while I briefly touch on the rise and fall of the Great Modern Hope.

Modernism and Its Demise

In 1992, Czechoslovakian President Vaclav Havel gave a speech to the World Economic Forum in Switzerland titled, "The End of the Modern Era." A writer himself, Havel's speech was far different from the political addresses that Americans have grown accustomed to in congressional and presidential politics. Of all things, Havel was discussing *philosophy.* Disclosing his own postmodern predilections, Havel proclaimed that the time had arrived to finally put modernism in its coffin and bury it for good, so damaging has it been to the human condition. In stark terms, equating the end of modernism with the fall of Communism in eastern Europe, Havel said the now-discredited modern era "gave rise to the proud belief that man, as the pinnacle of everything that exists, was capable of objectively describing, explaining and controlling everything that exists, and of possessing the one and only truth about the world. It was an era in which there was a cult of depersonalized objectivity, an era in which objective knowledge was amassed and technologically exploited, an era of belief in automatic progress brokered by the scientific method."

Such is the fashion in which modernism is now demonized. Writers like Havel mark its demise in the elevated language of literature, rhetoric, and persuasion. But these anti-modernist ideas, I would argue, don't require a writer and scholar like Havel to legitimize. Postmodern, or anti-modern, thinking and practice have wended their way into everyday life; you'll find signs of postmodernism in such diverse places as classrooms, workplaces, newspapers, and even churches. You'll hear echoes of postmodernism in the language of plain people doing ordinary things. Scholars theorize about postmodernism, but as I shall explore, ordinary folks live it; they drink it, read it, and watch it. They talk the talk, and they don't even realize they're doing it, so accustomed are they becoming to the fragmented, uncertain epoch of postmodernity, and so thoroughly have postmodern thought and ways of being been woven into the everyday experience of Western societies.

It seems mildly ironic that, as Havel would have it, modernism, the fountainhead of Western thought and progress for more than two hundred years, including the foundations of American democracy, would now be seen in the same light as failed authoritarian Communism. What happened? What happened to modernism, which had once—and to many still does—held such hope and promise for the human condition?

In fact, the roots of modernism reside in the Age of Enlightenment that swept Europe during the 1700s, through the popular writings of the likes of Voltaire, Rousseau, Montesquieu, and Diderot. The Enlightenment established the dominant belief systems of secular Western civilization that included a trust in reason, science, progress, and individual freedom.

Historians Will and Ariel Durant describe the kind of backward world that muckraking troublemakers like Voltaire sought to reform:

> *A thousand superstitions survived side by side with the rising enlightenment. Highborn ladies trembled at unfavorable horoscopes, or believed that a drowned child could be revived if a poor woman would light a candle and set it afloat in a cup to set fire to a bridge on the Seine. . . . Julie de Lespinasse, after living for years with the skeptical scientist d'Alembert, kept her faith in lucky and unlucky days. Fortunetellers lived on the credit given to their clairvoyance; so Mme. de Pompadour, the Abbe de Bernis, and the Duc de Choiseul secretly consulted Mme. Bontemps, who read the future in coffee grounds. . . . Paris swarmed with magicians and other impostors who offered to ensure worldly success or eternal youth.*

But by the late 1700s, even royalty throughout Europe were declaring victory over the forces of tradition, backwardness, and superstition of the pre-modern age. Frederick the Great once said that "the edifice (of superstition) is sapped to its foundations," and he heaped praise on Voltaire as the promoter of the "revolution . . . in the human spirit." Voltaire also declared the triumph of reason in human affairs over the former society "founded upon fraud on one side and stupidity on the other." From the Age of Enlightenment onward, modernity became synonymous with the "victorious struggle of reason" over animal instincts and magic, truth over prejudice, and reflection over mere existence, says Z. Bauman, who writes frequently on postmodernism.

I like to think that the dawn of modernism was symbolically captured in the recent film, *The Madness of King George,* by its depiction of a doctor taking the unprecedented step of placing the mentally disturbed king in restraining straps against His Majesty's will. That metaphorical moment marked the complete transformation of society, in which a hired hand had triumphed over a king, science over royalty, and reason over tradition.

To be sure, perhaps the hopes for modernity were misplaced, given what then transpired in Europe and the United States over the next few centuries. Maybe Havel's accusation of technological rationality running amok was true: World wars were killing tens of millions; the rise of Nazi fascism was systematically murdering six million Jews alone in the most "rational" killing machine ever conceived; and the Cold War was sapping the Eastern and Western economies of trillions of dollars worth of lost opportunities—not to mention nuclear bombs or environmental disasters incinerating the people of Hiroshima and later threatening to annihilate all life on Earth. Thus, the sweep of history itself became modernism's own indictment, many scholars would argue. Indeed, modernism has become the "focus of increasing critical reflection in the course of the twentieth century," writes Barry Smart, a leading student of postmodernism at the University of Auckland in New Zealand. "The benefits and securities assumed to be a corollary of the development of modernity have become matters of doubt."

But What *Is* Postmodernism?

Exactly when the postmodern break from the tenets of modernism occurred is a matter of uncertainty, as are most things concerning the postmodern question. David Harvey, an Oxford geographer, pinpoints the "sea-change" at around 1972. But dating the postmodern moment probably isn't as important as recognizing that there is something profoundly changed and changing in American society. A rather disjointed, wholly unorganized break from the past has occurred, and observers in diverse endeavors, including art, architecture, philosophy, and literary criticism have called this phenomenon "postmodernism." It is a reaction to, and questioning of, modernism and its perceived limitations and failings. Paolo Portoghesi, a professor of architecture in Rome, has called the postmodern break "a trial against the Modern and its consequences," and a recognition that "everything has changed" in society and economics. While stopping short of labeling the postmodern split from modernism a "wholesale paradigm shift," Columbia University's Andreas Huyssen calls the break "a noticeable shift in sensibility, practices and discourse."

Okay, skeptics might say. Postmodernism is a breaking away, a rebellion of sorts, from modernism and all its trappings of science, reason, progress, and so on. But what *is* postmodernism? One would be hard pressed to find a concise, dictionary definition of it, despite casual references to postmodernism in real estate articles in the *New York Times.* My 1992 version of the *American Heritage Dictionary* has no entry for postmodern, postmodernism, or anything close. There's "postmistress" and "postmortem," but no postmodern. (Of course, my dictionary does define "modernism," sort of, and lest you think my dictionary isn't tapped into what's happening, it does define "modem," the computer hardware device that serves as everyone's on-ramp to the Information Superhighway.)

Indeed, various scholars who have carved out careers studying the postmodern question have noted that the concept is deep in definitional mud. Linda Hutcheon of the University of Toronto says, "Of all the terms bandied about in both current cultural theory and contemporary writing on the arts, postmodernism must be the most over- and under-defined."

Postmodernism defies definition because we're right in the middle of a cultural phenomenon still unfolding before us—it's a moving target. Robin Usher and Richard Edwards suggest that "all we can say with any degree of safety is what (postmodernism) is *not*. Certainly, it is not a term that designates a systematic theory or comprehensive philosophy. Neither does it refer to a 'system' of ideas or concepts in the conventional sense, nor is it the name denoting a unified social or cultural movement. All one can say is that it is complex and multiform, resisting reductive and simplistic explanation."

Postmodernism, then, isn't anything approaching the solidity of an organized social movement like the Christian Coalition; can't be described as a singular political force like Ralph Nader's Common Cause; and isn't a well developed theory such as Einstein's relativity or Darwin's natural selection. What's more, we can't conclude that the Modern Era has in fact run completely out of gas, or been bowled over by postmodern forces. "What we can say positively, is that the postmodern is, at the very least, *contested* terrain," Usher and Edwards argue.

Yet, there does appear to be at least one fundamental characteristic of the postmodern phenomenon that most analyses of the concept have in common. If nothing else, postmodernism is tantamount to a sweeping *delegitimation* of modernism. The indictment is cast along two key fault lines: delegitimation of modernity's sources of political and economic *power* and the closely intertwined delegitimation of its sources of *knowledge*. The cultural implications of these attacks on modernism are enormous, for higher education and teaching in particular, as we shall see.

In the table below, I have assembled an admittedly oversimplified schematic of the modern/postmodern split in order to contrast the two views of the world. I'll explore these topics in much greater depth as I go on in the book, but for now let me run down a few points about my chart.

TABLE 7
A Quick Guide to the Modern/Postmodern Split

	TRAITS OF MODERNISM	TRAITS OF POSTMODERNISM
Nature of Knowledge	Trust in reason, objective reality, and scientific method	Tendency toward relativism, subjectivism
Media and Society	Belief in progress, perfection of society, the Protestant ethic, and an emancipatory press	Spectacle of mass produced images; dominance of entertainment values
Authorities	Trust in democratic institutions, hegemony of producers and elites	Delegitimation of institutions, sanctity of pop-culturalism and popular entitlements; hyperconsumerism; dreams and heroes dead
Defining Metaphor in Film	Triumph of the professional, as depicted in *Madness of King George,* when the hired psychotherapist puts the king in shackles.	Triumph of the image, as in *Crimson Tide,* when the fate of the world depends on a twentysomething technician fixing the sub's communication system; to make the situation "real" Executive Officer Denzel Washington tells the technician to think of him as *Star Trek's* Captain Kirk.
Slogan of the Age	"All the News That's Fit to Print" (*New York Times*)	"Here we are now/ Entertain us" (Nirvana) "Trust No One" (*The X-Files*)

Consider the nature of knowledge, for instance. While the modernist believes that reality is knowable with the use of reason and scientific method, the postmodernist would just as soon put his faith in subjective experience. For the postmodernist, modernism's reliance on facts, truth, and objectivity no longer seems to work in a world in which many people seem to think of reality as being invented anew every day on the TV tube.

As for my schematic's take on authority, institutions such as universities, government, the press, and corporations have dominated in the Modern Era; but postmodernism, a force that brushes aside traditional political orientations of left and right, has wreaked havoc with this order of things, calling into question the legitimacy of modernism's traditional sources of trust and authority. As opposed to these delegitimated institutions, cultural populism—not the muckraking, ornery, and agrarian sort of the Oklahoma and Texas variety in decades past, but the 1990s opinion-poll and focus-group version—is virtually deified in the postmodern world.

Let's now look at the slogans for modernity and postmodernity in my rough guide. "Anything goes" has been used by various writers to describe the postmodern age's absence of rules, boundaries, criteria or authorities, and to be sure the slogan has a certain fit. Another candidate for the postmodern slogan that also seems fitting is the line from the immensely popular TV show, *The X-Files,* which asks its viewers to remember to "Trust No One." This suggests the postmodern collapse of authority and of a society riddled with government conspiracies trying to cover up the real truth about aliens from other planets and such. But perhaps the best candidate for postmodernity's byword is given to us by Nirvana and Kurt Cobain, the grunge rockers many observers might contend are emblematic of Generation X culture: "Here we are now/Entertain us," says a line from "Smells Like Teen Spirit," a lyric that hits upon the domination of entertainment values in contemporary culture, spanning politics, education, and even religious institutions. Indeed, one might modify Nirvana's lyric along the lines of Descartes to say, "I am entertained, therefore I am."

Ironically, I had a harder time thinking up a slogan for modernity than for postmodernity in my schematic. It's ironic because postmodernism supposedly defies the simplistic "totality" and uniformity that critics say has characterized modernity. As for modernism's slogan, modernism and the very notion of appropriate standards and acceptable criteria go hand in hand. Thus, my schematic shows the slogan of the the *New York Times,* which arguably remains a vanguard for modernity, despite even its attempts in recent years to respond to the demands of popular culture.

I've already described what I believe is the defining metaphor for modernity, depicted in the film *The Madness of King George.* As shown in my schematic, postmodernity's defining metaphor was illustrated in a much different kind of movie, *Crimson Tide,* targeted toward those viewers who might long for the nail-biting days of imminent nuclear confrontation with the Soviets. Picture this: the fate of the Earth depends on a young radio technician re-establishing the submarine's communication with the outside world. Denzel Washington (the sub's heroic executive officer who challenges the authority of "This is the Captain" Gene Hackman), employs the following, quintessential postmodern tactic: In order to make the consequences of not fixing the radio "real" for the technician, Denzel tells the young man to think of him (Denzel) as Captain Kirk of the Starship *Enterprise,* and pretend that Kirk has given him an order to fix the radio, or else billions of people will die. Of course, the young man who watched *Star Trek* growing up can fully relate to the fictional image of Captain Kirk a lot more than to his own executive officer and the all-too-real consequences of failure. And so the technician hops to it, sweating profusely, gets that damned radio fixed, and the world is saved. Like the young radio guy, we viewers could also relate to an order from James T. Kirk a lot better than an order from any executive officer of a nuclear submarine, even if he is Denzel.

Similarly, we've seen characters on TV such as Murphy Brown slugging it out about family values with Dan Quayle, and somehow Murphy seems just as real as the vice president, himself just a TV image for most of us. We watch Bill Clinton give Apollo 13 astronaut Jim Lovell an award in the presence of Tom Hanks, who played Lovell in the movie. (Or, was that an image of Forrest Gump, played by Hanks, being digitized into real history?) I'll confess, for me the flesh and blood hero, Lovell, somehow paled in comparison to Hanks standing in the background. Hanks was the real Jim Lovell. And the real Jim Lovell? Well, he was just some guy who showed up for an awards ceremony. It almost seemed that Hanks himself sensed the ridiculousness of it all, looking a bit uncomfortable. And so we've reached the point where we are more profoundly engaged by faked images than reality itself, a postmodern phenomenon I encountered frequently as a teacher, as I shall explore in a later chapter.

Just as the Modern Era has had both an enlightened and dark side, so have various writers taken positions on postmodernity as either Western civilization's hopeful new beginning with the coming of the millennium, or as something possibly far more sinister. Like Havel, optimists seem to envision postmodernity as some kind of liberating force from the alleged evils of modernity. They see it as the wake-up call America needs to escape obliteration, or at least to keep people from being enslaved by an Orwellian-like state. Charles Jencks, an architectural scholar and author of numerous books on modernism and postmodernism, says, "Post-modernism means the end of a single world view, and by extension, a 'war on totality', a resistance to single explanations, a respect for difference and a celebration of the regional, local and particular." Postmodern scholar Z. Bauman says postmodernity is "no more (but no less either) than the modern mind taking a long, attentive and sober look at itself" and "not fully liking what it sees."

But there is a dark side to postmodernity as well, and that's the one I seemed to encounter a lot in my teaching experience. As a revolt against modernity, the implications of postmodernism are indeed scary if you're the kind of person who would prefer the rock solid foundations of modernity's belief in reason, science, and progress.

Seeming to address postmodernity's less enlightened aspects, the French philosopher Jean-François Lyotard has said: "Eclecticism is the degree zero of contemporary general culture. [O]ne listens to reggae, watches a Western, eats McDonald's food for lunch and local cuisine for dinner, wears Paris perfume in Tokyo and 'retro' clothes in Hong Kong; knowledge is a matter for TV games. . . . Artists, gallery owners, critics and public wallow together in 'anything goes', and the epoch is one of slackening."

Indeed, as Lyotard has explored in his highly regarded writings on the subject, the world of higher education, the child of modernity, has not been immune to the "epoch . . . of slackening." In my view, we seem to be witnessing the "postmodernization" of America's entire educational enterprise, a revolution—or perhaps, devolution—into something that increasingly bears little resemblance to its past. As I discovered being on the front lines of college teaching, notions of standards, criteria, and measurements of quality have come to mean less and less, pushed aside by a powerful and pervasive popularization of academia. As I will explore in detail, the increasingly dominant and exclusive values of an increasingly postmodern larger culture, such as consumerism, entertainment, and entitlement—have seeped into the ivory tower. The delegitimation of modernism's perspective of knowledge and power are changing America so profoundly that no institution is immune, nor hardly any person unaffected.

CHAPTER 11

The Balkanization of Knowledge and Power

One day when walking down a sidewalk at the college where I was teaching, I ran into one of my students, a young woman of the sort I seemed to be encountering with some frequency in my teaching. She was a slightly older than average student, in her mid-twenties, seemingly bright and orally articulate. However, her writing just wasn't good, and she seemed to refuse to believe me when I told her she had a lot of room for improvement. When I passed her on the sidewalk, she had just received a B– on her paper. We glanced at each other and I nodded a cursory hello, and then she stopped me to talk. "I'd like to talk with you to talk about my paper," she said. "Sure, what's up?" I asked. "Well, I didn't get a very good grade on this, and it's frustrating because it's *just your opinion,*" she told me.

Another time, a student said in his course evaluation at the end of the term: "My last two papers have been destroyed with comments that are entirely your opinion. 'Awkward, unclear.' Those are some of the comments that I received from you. Yet, the people that I had peer edit them understood what I was saying. Sometimes I like to write awkwardly. It livens up the material and doesn't make it boring."

Later, I talked to a young woman named Marsha, a twenty-year-old student at another college in the region. I asked her to explain to me why students often seemed so distrustful of what their professors had to say, even about their field of expertise. As she sat across the table from me in a local coffee house, Marsha thought a moment about the question. She acknowledged that the phenomenon was very real. She said: "I've noticed that, but I don't really know why. Everywhere you go people are questioning authority and questioning what is supposed to be going on, like teachers, and what teachers say. . . . Even the importance of a homework assignment. An instructor will give some project for something and you wonder, 'Why should I be bothering to do this? What will I gain?' Not that you're consciously questioning, it's kind of a knee-jerk reaction. I find myself doing it. Yeah, it does occur, but I don't know why. I never really thought about it before."

I think Marsha hit the postmodern nail on the head. *"Everywhere you go people are questioning authority and questioning what is supposed to be going on."* That is one manifestation of the crisis of postmodernity, an epoch of widespread distrust and fragmentation of nearly anything or anyone presuming to be a source of knowledge, truth, facts, and authority, which are symbolized by such modern institutions as colleges and universities, state and federal governments, corporations and the press. The defiance cuts across traditional ideological lines of liberal and conservative. The delegitimation of knowledge and power is sweeping in scope, affecting everything from politics to economics to education. In my view, the manifestations of the postmodern revolt range from the relatively harmless cynicism of mainstream American political discourse to potentially dangerous paranoia of right-wing extremists. They range from a college student questioning the legitimacy of her instructor's homework assignment to a forty-year-old guy with a potbelly running around the backcountry in army fatigues, toting a semi-automatic weapon in preparation for the onslaught of one-world government and the pitch-black United Nations military helicopters that would impose it.

You Make Your World, I'll Make Mine
What the above examples illustrate is that the very notion of "truth" is in crisis, a state of affairs that obviously bears heavily upon higher education. The postmodern condition for Western societies is a profound "legitimation crisis," to borrow the German thinker Jürgen Habermas's phrase. We're faced with a crisis in knowing how to dis-

tinguish truth from falsity, the legitimate from the illegitimate, and reality from make-believe—or even caring about the difference. My conversations with members of Generation X suggest that such notions as truth, reality, and authority are especially problematic for them. But while the legitimation crisis seems to be a general cultural trend, belonging to more than just the X Generation, Xers were born at such a time that they know no other value system. As children of postmodernity, they seem implicitly to distrust anything that purports to be a source of knowledge and authority.

Born between 1965 and 1980, ranging in ages 15 to 30, GenXers have grown up in a world in which "truth" and "reality" are what Coke or Connie Chung or the American Medical Association might have invented through persuasion and technique. Reality for GenXers is an image created on a video screen, or how you employ digital technology to alter that image into a completely new reality. Remember that bumper sticker, "Question Authority"? Now, add to that a new bumper sticker that has cropped up recently, called "Question Reality." Members of Generation X are cynical and sophisticated, and their reality is not objective, measurable, or fixed. In the postmodern world, reality and truth are a fiction. This represents a profound break from modernity's belief that reason and science can discover what's real and what's true.

When George Orwell wrote *1984*, many critics presumed that his attack was aimed at Soviet-style communism in which truth and reality were questions only for Stalin, his central planners, and the state police to decide. But as Erich Fromm suggested in the afterword to the book, Orwell actually was warning us about a more subtle but equally dangerous trait of Western societies. Rather than authoritarian regimes telling citizens what was true, people in Western societies were faced with the danger of truth being subject to the whims of marketing managers and public relations flacks. In the afterword, Fromm recounted the experiences of one corporate executive, Alan Harrington, author of *Life in the Crystal Palace,* who wrote that truth for him depended on which corporation he happened to be working for at the time.

That was in 1960. Such attitudes might have seemed like a revelation then. By the mid-1990s, hasn't this notion become second nature, something most of us were almost born believing? It now appears that Orwell's warning not only has come to pass, but that modernity's whole notion of truth as something that is knowable is

under attack. "We have for millennia accepted the distinction between fact and fiction, reality and myth, truth and falsity," says philosopher Hilary Lawson. He says that postmodernism "poses a threat
to this distinction, and in doing so threatens facts, reality, and truth,
but so does it also threaten fiction, myth and falsity."

Science and reason have taken the brunt of the postmodern criticism of modernity. In the minds of many observers, the methods and
criteria that science has come to rely on for sorting out reality from
fiction and truth from falsehood have no more legitimacy than any
other way of doing so. One manifestation of this denial has been a
sweeping anti-rationalism. Of course I exaggerate, but at times the
postmodern critics seem to view scientists in almost conspiratorial
terms; it is as if scientists were a cabal of middle-aged white males
using their esoteric magic as a means of maintaining political power
and control over the world's spiritualists and non-linearists, including women, third-world peoples, and the poor.

Susan Haack, a professor of philosophy at the University of Miami, points to "radical sociologists, radical feminists and
Afrocentrists, and radical followers of the latest Paris fashions in
rhetoric and semiotics," who have been leading critics questioning
the legitimacy of science. "Now it is commonplace to hear that science is largely or even wholly a matter of social interests, negotia-
tion, myth-making, the production of inscriptions; that 'objectivity'
and 'rationality' are nothing but ideological constructs disguising the
exclusion of the perspective of this or that oppressed group," says
Haack.

In the face of this onslaught, one defender of scientific method
has gone so far as to suggest that, in today's climate of relativism and
anti-rationality, Galileo himself, in supporting the Copernican theory
that the Earth orbited the Sun, would get no better treatment now
than he did from the Roman Catholic Church in 1632. James F. Harris,
a philosopher at the College of William and Mary, contends that in
today's anti-rational climate, Galileo's observations would be viewed
as no more true than the Church's view, because all views and theories are considered to be equally valid. Says Harris: "Galileo could
easily find himself as out of step with many contemporary philosophers of science as he was with the Catholic Church in the sixteenth
and seventeen centuries, and Galileo's attribution of truth to his scientific theories would be as alien to much of contemporary philosophy of science as it was to the Catholic Church of the time."

Harris points to the influence that contemporary philosophers such as Nelson Goodman have had on the philosophy of science. According to Goodman, no theory or view of the world is uniquely true. "There are many different equally true descriptions of the world, and their truth is the only standard of their faithfulness," Goodman has written. "And when we say of them that they all involve conventionalizations, we are saying that no one of these different descriptions is *exclusively* true, since the others are also true. None of them tells us *the* way the world is, but each of them tells us *a* way the world is."

Have my students been reading Nelson Goodman behind my back? Does this explain why truth was so relative to them, why my judgment of the quality of their work was simply "my opinion," with no firmer basis for validity than that of a freshman writing student who might well have difficulty creating a coherent paragraph?

I doubt, of course, that my students were reading Goodman. In fact, the theoretical critique of modern science and epistemology served up in academic circles by Goodman, some academic feminists, and other critics pales in comparison to what's happening in the real world, the actual *behavior* that is unconsciously played out each day in classrooms, in voting booths, and on Main Street. As I suggested earlier, we are all postmodernists now, to one degree or another. Even avowed modernists like James Harris, I would submit, have large pinches of postmodernism thrown into their world views. One can hardly exist otherwise in today's society. It's now time to look at some specific postmodern trends in the larger culture that are shaping the attitudes of everyone in it, not the least of whom are members of the X Generation.

The Knowledge Crisis: A Spectrum of Postmodern Responses

The various indications of the crisis of knowledge and authority are so enmeshed in the larger society as to seem quite disconnected. We see, for example, an acute case of collective cynicism in the realm of mainstream politics; a proliferation of a belief in angels, Bigfoot, and satanic cults; and a ubiquitous mistrust in authorities, bordering at times on absurd and dangerous paranoia.

For the most part, social observers have taken note of these trends as isolated, disconnected phenomena. In my view, all of them may be manifestations of, and a spectrum of responses to, the culture's abandonment of modernity as the Western world enters uncertain and fragmented postmodern terrain.

Indeed, the pervasiveness of cynicism in our culture is probably the most common response to the legitimation crisis, represented in the following fashionable but increasingly dominant points of view being etched into the American landscape and mind set:

1. All (fill in the blank) is corrupt

It has become commonplace nowadays for journalists and mass media institutions to flog themselves for being too cynical. It's been painful to watch how so many organizations, from the *Columbia Journalism Review* to the *New York Times,* are wringing their desperate hands about how the press is at fault for replacing healthy skepticism of institutions with a sharp and unrelenting cynicism of public officials, corporations, and just about anybody else in a position of power or authority. But is the press really that cynical or really simply two-stepping on the heels of the real source of their cynicism: the public at large?

Fearful of alienating people, what the press almost never does is suggest that readers, taxpayers, and voters are the real cynics. Indeed, my experience as a newspaper journalist was that public sentiment was a profound and powerful force behind our writing and reporting. Journalists tended to take what they perceived to be public sentiment, and then amplify it and exploit it as an in-your-face assault on corrupt politicians, *et al.* It seemed to me that we journalists more often reflected public opinion than we were out front shaping it. In that sense we were rather shy and timid. In fact, a public opinion poll conducted by the Times Mirror Center for the People and the Press in the spring of 1995 seemed to bear this out, indicating that the public at large was far more cynical toward government and other American institutions than were journalists. For instance, while 53 percent of journalists rated officials highly for honesty and integrity, just 18 percent of ordinary citizens did so.

To be sure, the press gives the public some credit for being cynical. But it seems that what is typically framed as the public's cynicism toward politics and government is in essence the public's knee-jerk negativism toward almost anything at any level with any power and authority in the traditional, modern sense. Forget public opinion polls—the responses of ordinary citizens to questions of "Who Do You Trust?" have become utterly predictable, regardless of particular circumstances or complexities. For example, the *New York Times* did a piece eliciting public reaction to the Republicans' "Contract with

America." The reporter talked to a couple of construction workers at Stacy's Diner in Pittsboro, North Carolina. "They're all a bunch of damned liars," one worker said. "It's the same thing on TV every week." The story then quoted another guy at the diner, saying to the first guy, "You must be talking about the O.J. trial." The first guy responded, laughing, "Might as well be."

From my experience as a reporter, I'd say that you can give me a question about some topic in the public arena, and I can predict what 90 percent of the people asked about it on the street or in a diner are likely to generally say. It's fill in the blanks time, with angry, ordinary Person X knee-jerking against: A) government or politicians; B) the media; C) big business.

Now, add to that list: D) The O.J. ('but I watched it anyway') Simpson Trial.

2. Somebody in power is trying to hide the real truth

Possibly the best example of how deeply this sentiment resonates with the American public can be found in the TV show, *The X-Files.* This upstart on the Fox network has found an immensely faithful following, including many members of Generation X. The show, for any of you uninitiated readers, revolves around two very attractive FBI agents who team up to investigate UFOs and all manner of weird paranormal stuff in the FBI's "X-Files." But the show's subtext is that higher-ups in the FBI and possibly even higher in the U.S. government are part of a shadowy conspiracy to hide the real truth from the public about space aliens. Of course, "The Truth is Out There," or so says the show's slogan, implying that answers to the conspiracy lie not with the self-serving FBI and U.S. government, but with impartial (pseudo-scientific) investigation that will lead to evidence for the unexplained beyond the Earth's physical boundaries. "It's this ominous mix of the paranormal and the paranoid that gives *The X-Files* its edge and has fueled its popularity," says science writer Gene Emery.

Of course, *The X-Files* is just fiction, and everybody understands that. But you could easily argue that shows like *The X-Files* are popular because they exploit Americans' deeply felt cynicism about anyone or any institution that holds itself in a position of authority. Consider a full-page advertisement in the *New York Times* for a new information newsletter called "Bottom Line Personal: Incorporating Privileged Information." "WHAT THE AIRLINES WON'T TELL YOU. WHAT THE PHONE COMPANY WON'T TELL YOU . . . WHAT THE IRS WON'T TELL YOU," the ad blares, purporting to unveil the real truth about seemingly every major American institution. Of course, the newsletter probably offers its readers many valuable tidbits of information. But my point is that good information apparently isn't enough. The newsletter sees that it must advertise its launch into the marketplace with a full-page ad in the *Times* exploiting Americans' sense of distrust and cynicism.

In my own profession of journalism, too, a related trend has been at work. It has become the fashion to disavow the once-cherished notion of objectivity—a doctrine rooted in Enlightenment's faith in the truth-seeking scientific method—as tantamount to journalists being slaves to the government. Critics of objectivity accuse practitioners of such reporting as being mere stenographers and press agents for government officials, who set the agenda and manipulate the truth for an unwitting press. Writer Mark Hertsgaard, for example, has suggested that objective reporting, i.e., reliance on official sources, led to government officials' duping the press throughout the Reagan administration. "Although formally independent, in practice the American press functioned more often than not as an arm of the American state," says Hertsgaard.

There's probably some truth to the critique of the shoddy way that the press has wound up employing the doctrine of objectivity. But it now appears that doubts about the very concept of objectivity among journalists have led, increasingly, to a far looser, interpretive form of reporting and writing. Perhaps the epitome of this trend came in a story that has become well known in journalism circles. In June 1994, when Bill Clinton visited his Vietnam War–time alma-mater, Oxford, *New York Times* reporter Maureen Dowd wrote for a lead: "President Clinton returned today for a sentimental journey to the university where he didn't inhale, didn't get drafted, and didn't get a degree." Much of mainstream journalism nowadays frequently employs such chirpiness, a concoction of entertainment, news, and interpretation. And while newspapers still attempt to maintain the conventional distinctions between news, analysis, commentary, speculation, and opinion, the fact is that such distinctions have become quite arbitrary, and maintaining the distinctions has become pure fiction.

I found an obscure public acknowledgment of this trend in, of all places, a job announcement in the academic newspaper, the *Chronicle of Higher Education.* In the rather unusual ad of several hundred words, the Annenberg School for Communication at the

University of Pennsylvania was searching for a scholar to study THE FUTURE OF FACT. The ad plaintively wondered:

> *Classically, the genres of reporting—in journalism, law, history and the sciences—relied on their unquestioned ability to differentiate among facts, their representation, and their interpretation. But if facts cannot be told without narrators and narratives, and if these invariably affix imprints of their own, it follows that facts are accessible only through their interpretation and that there is no representation without interpretation. . . . Is the distinction between fact and fiction still tenable?*

3. Everything is a myth

Finally, according to *Books in Print,* there are nearly 1,800 books with the word "myth" in the title, and in the last five years alone, more than 650 myth books have been published. Commenting on the trend for *Newsday,* Fred Bruning says the bulk of these works reflect the rampant distrust sweeping America in recent years.

But besides cynicism in the mainstream political culture, the postmodern crisis of knowledge and power shows up in other, warmer and more cuddly ways. If modernity has got you down, if you can't trust science, politicians, professors, government, universities, or the media, or even the Lutheran or Catholic churches, if everything seems meaningless and nobody's telling you what's really going on, why not get yourself your own personal angel as your guiding power, warmly providing your inner child with peace and comfort, wisdom and joy?

I apologize if I seem to trivialize. In actuality, I find myself more in a state of wonderment and awe at the mushrooming of belief in anti-rationality, paranormal phenomena, and pseudo-science in our time. Although, to my knowledge, I haven't personally experienced angelic intervention, I see that tens of millions Americans have found their angels or otherwise embraced the light—or at least bought a book or a magazine or watched a TV show attesting to others' finding an angel or an alien from space. Commenting on the anti-rationalism sweeping America, author Wendy Kaminer says, "Rationality, in general, has been out of fashion in recent years. New-Agers condemn it as left-brain thinking, some feminists consider it male-identified, while some self-styled radical academics are apt to dismiss it as a pretense of objectivity; on the right religiosity is a much more potent political force than reason. I expect that we'll proudly become even less rational as the millennium approaches; more people will report being visited by aliens or abused by Satanic cults in childhood or graced by their guardian angels."

Thus, while the postmodern reaction for many people to the knowledge/authority conundrum has been cynicism and disgust with the institutions of modernity, other people (no doubt, many of the same ones) have encountered the postmodern question and seen the answer "out there" somewhere. To wit:

Exhibit 1: On the *New York Times* paperback best seller list, two books about near-death experiences are among the top ten most popular books, one *(Embraced by the Light)* having been a best seller for 29 weeks.

Exhibit 2: For $4.95, you can buy the Premier Copy of the magazine *Unexplained Universe,* whose colorful, glossy cover of space aliens and werewolves shouts: NEW EVIDENCE: ANGELS ARE REAL; PHOTOGRAPHIC PROOF THAT AN ANCIENT RACE EXISTED ON THE MOON! BEWARE, THE LIVING WEREWOLF! 1995 ENCOUNTERS.

Exhibit 3: The December 1994 issue of *Ladies Home Journal,* whose cover is adorned with two darling young girls, angels floating in white lace through the clouds. Read the cover story, titled, "Joy to the World: Perfect Angels and Other Stories of Real-Life Miracles."

Exhibit 4: A cornucopia of TV shows, all about the paranormal and the pseudo-scientific. Many hold themselves up to be fact-based documentaries, and they are called *Sightings, The Extraordinary, The Other Side, Encounters: The Hidden Truth, National Geographic Explorer's* "Mysteries of the Afterlife," and *Unsolved Mysteries.*

Exhibit 5: An entire issue of *TV Guide* devoted to "TV's New Supernatural Craze."

Exhibit 6: A *Time* magazine survey that shows almost seven in every ten American adults believe angels exist; that nearly one in two people think they have their own angel guarding over them; that Harvard and Boston College offer among them three courses about angels.

Exhibit 7: Sophy Burnham, author of the best selling *A Book of Angels,* says that my own angel is helping me write this, telling me only as much information as I really need to know.

Is our culture on some wild, collective acid trip? Anti-rationality has become so rampant, and so degraded have notions of reality become, that mere accusation, imagination, and wishful thinking are all many people need nowadays to establish what's true and what's real. Frequently, the "investigations" into the paranormal take on the trimmings—but ignore the substance—of scientific method, as if to appease the skeptics. But then again, perhaps truth and reality no longer matter in the postmodern epoch. What matters is that we feel good and safe from harm's way.

Remember Czechoslovakian President Vaclav Havel's 1995 speech to the World Economic Forum I referred to earlier, in which he condemned the objective, depersonalized thinking of the modern age? What possible connection might there be, then, between the message of this head of state and the rage of anti-rationalism that's engulfing the United States? I think it might be instructive to compare the language used by Havel with that of Eileen Elias Freeman, author of *Touched by Angels,* yet another best seller.

Freeman told the *New York Times:*

> As a species, we are unsure, fearful. Many thought with the cessation of the state of cold war with most of the Communist world, things would be totally harmonious. But there are just as many potential sources for disaster as there were before. And people ask, What does it all mean? The angels became more visible to reassure us. We've been worshipping an unholy trinity of money, power and prestige. These have a certain limited value, but they have absolutely no power to feed our soul. The soul is what continues.

Compare that to Havel's words:

> Sooner or later politics will be faced with the task of finding a new, postmodern face. A politician must become a person again, someone who trusts not only scientific representation and analysis of the world, but also the world itself. He must believe not only in sociological statistics but also in real people. He must trust not only an objective interpretation of reality, but also his own soul; not only an adopted ideology, but also his own thoughts; not only the summary reports he receives each morning, but also his own feelings.

Both Freeman, the believer in angels, and Havel, the head of a government, seem to be saying that modern societies haven't had much luck relying on rationality, objective science, or other trappings of modernity. And whether you call it a belief in angels or something else, they say it's time for a new way of looking at the world. Both writers suggest that answers to our problems reside in our individual subjective experience—our angels and our souls. Might both these writers also be issuing an open call for anti-rationalism in our times? Have we begun down this slippery and possibly dangerous slope? My contention is that we have, sometimes to alarming degrees, and that is part of our postmodern condition.

I realize what I'm about to suggest next opens me to vigorous attack. But I don't think it's too big a leap to consider the possibility that the increasingly widespread tendency to view institutions such as central government in conspiratorial terms is a logical next step along my suggested spectrum of responses to the postmodern crisis of knowledge and authority. I'm obviously referring to anti-government militia groups, the existence of which became widely known in the wake of the Oklahoma City truck bomb that was used to murder 169 people, including many children.

As I've discussed, in its milder forms the range of responses to the culture's legitimation crisis include a debilitating cynicism toward established authorities and power structures of modernity, as well as a flowering of anti-rational beliefs in such things as guardian angels, satanic cults, and the paranormal. In my view, at the far end of this spectrum lies outright paranoia of the institutions of modernity. Is it not possible that, while most people stop short of acting out such aggressions toward government, the same anti-modern revolt manifests itself in less well adjusted personalities as paranoia and absurd conspiracy theories? We hear of a United Nations plot with the U.S. government to establish a New World Order; how government authorities have secretly placed devices on traffic signals to help monitor U.N. troop movements; how secret codes have been affixed to our currency so government officials can drive by our houses to determine how much money we have; and that it was really the federal government itself, in order to justify a crackdown on the militias, that planted the deadly truck bomb in Oklahoma City.

Simply cases of radical white supremacist fringe groups? Not according to Chip Berlet, who has studied the militia movement. "What you have with this movement is a critique of the government that comes from the right based on the paranoid conspiracy theories of secret elites that plan an apocalyptic takeover of the United States," he says. "White supremacy is not a principle of unity of this movement. Because of that, it has the ability to draw from a much broader constituency."

Many observers of the militia movement have taken pains to point out, along the lines of historian Richard Hofstadter's 1964 study, that American politics and culture have historically been imbued with paranoid tendencies. But to suggest that the paranoid movements of today are no different than, for instance, the Antimasons or the Know-Nothings of the 1800s, is to ignore the vast changes in technology and communication that sustain mass movements and common ideology nowadays. It would seem that today's paranoid styles are fundamentally different than in the past because of their connections to much broader segments of the population. As Michael Kelly of the *New Yorker* has written, "In its extreme form, paranoia is still the province of minority movements, but the ethos of minority movements—antiestablishmentarian protest, the politics of rage—has become so deeply ingrained in the larger political culture that the paranoid style has become the cohering idea of a broad coalition plurality that draws adherents from every point on the political spectrum. . . . For one reason or another, and to one degree or another, the paranoid view of government and its allies has become received wisdom for many millions of Americans."

Of course, paranoid conspiracy theories of the far right and the cynicism of millions of mainstream voters differ profoundly in degree. Still, they share a common belief of betrayal by authorities in power against ordinary people—Republicans and Democrats betraying voters; government bureaucrats betraying citizens; fathers betraying weak and helpless children. In short, people's trust in the institutions of modernity, the progeny of the eighteenth century Enlightenment which have bound people together for more than two hundred years under the hope of freedom and progress, is in precious short supply, leaving people on their own to establish a plethora of new belief systems.

⌐   ⌐   ⌐

Am I suggesting that believers in such things as angels and the paranormal are wrong and simply unconcerned about truth? I don't believe so. True, like many I'm skeptical and perhaps a bit too cynical; but that these believers do seem to seek the truth might be among their most admirable virtues. My point is that, for many believers in the weird and paranormal, truth and reality appear to be highly subjective: They're pursuing their own version of truth and on their own terms—and damned what the usual suspects of modernity, such as teachers, scientists, and public officials, might have to say. Indeed, a defining characteristic of postmodernity is that the culture appears to be returning to pre-Enlightenment states of mind when such notions as witches, devils, satanic cults, angels, UFOs, and other unprovable explanations held so much power over people. By doing so, the culture appears to be letting go of modernity's central tenet: a reliance on a belief system whose claims to truth are based on what is provable.

Does this mean that science has lost all authority and credibility? Certainly not yet. But there appears to be a growing incapacity for, or unwillingness of, many people in postmodern society to think, if not in a strictly scientific way, at least in a critical way. And while science still holds power for many people, this power is curiously being employed to legitimize what amount to anti-scientific beliefs in the fantastic.

Consider, again, the TV show *The X-Files*. In the show's usual scenario, FBI agent Dana Scully, the scientifically trained M.D., plays the role of the rational skeptic against agent Fox Mulder's paranormal theories. But Scully is always a straw-woman: Whenever she serves up some scientific objection to her partner's hypotheses, the dashing, smooth-talking Mulder easily bats it down, with the backing of the unstated authority of anti-rationalism that lurks just beneath the show's surface. You can almost hear the audience in the background saying, "There she goes again, trifling us with those boring old laws of physics." Scully, the skeptic, can then do nothing but go along for the fantastic ride. Never mind that the logical gaps in Mulder's theories are big enough for Bigfoot or a flying saucer; those get glossed over in a quick cut to a new scene or to a car commercial.

One can find scores of similar examples in popular culture, where supposedly neutral observers and commentators will employ just enough scientific method to make a-priori beliefs in the fantastic appear to be legitimate and far more factual than the mere beliefs they really are. This is, of course, a complete bastardization of what science is supposed to be about.

Yet, it is the implications of the culture's growing reliance on subjectivism and the suspension of critical judgment that are most disturbing. As I have suggested, a belief in guardian angels or Bigfoot is probably harmless. But when mistrust in, and incapacity for, logic and reason in our culture results in radical conspiracy theories and paranoia of democratic institutions, then you can't help but wonder about the future stability of the society. As I've already suggested, the danger applies not just to the mistrust of politics among so many American taxpayers and voters. And the danger goes beyond grown men running around the backwoods in Army fatigues, training for the next United Nations takeover of the United States. The very capacity for people in this culture to reason might be in jeopardy when they are inclined to jump to the most outrageous conclusions to explain events in their lives.

A small example might illustrate my latter point. A physician I know told me about a young man who came to him complaining about a persistent stomach ache. The man explained that he got sick whenever he and his wife would go to his father-in-law's house for dinner. "My father-in-law is trying to poison me with Drano," the patient told the doctor in all sincerity. His wife stood with him in the examining room nodding her complete and enthusiastic agreement with this conspiracy theory. Both patient and wife told the doctor they also suspected that her father poisoned her mother with the same kind of suspicious-looking crystals in the berry pie. According to the doctor, it never occurred to the young man—who clearly wasn't mentally or emotionally ill—to consider that his upset stomach might have a less sinister explanation. "Sometimes, it seems like people have lost the ability to critically think about things," the doctor told me. (While the physician wouldn't let himself be engaged in a discussion about the man's father-in-law, he did advise the young man that Drano poisoning was unlikely because his throat would be severely burned eating it, symptoms the man confessed he didn't have.)

To be sure, this is an odd case. And I have no way of quantifying just how widespread the seeming devaluation of logic and reason in our culture might be. That's a huge question, really beyond the scope of this book. But you don't have to look far to find similar examples in which ordinary citizens readily jump to the most outrageous conspiracy theories and beliefs, or at least beliefs which aren't supported by known, concrete evidence. In this context, for instance, some observers might interpret the mostly black O.J. Simpson jury's almost non-existent evaluation of the evidence, much of it pointing to his guilt, as a quintessential event of the postmodern age, in that a racially charged conspiracy theory prevailed over science itself.

Also, as I discussed in the first part of this book, I didn't have to experience teaching for very long to observe a certain inability of many students to think clearly and critically—the problem was more than evident in their writing. I discovered that many educators have latched on to something called "critical thinking" in recent years, a movement that is becoming widespread at colleges and universities as well as K–12 schools throughout the country. Although some educators are trying to reform past practices that encouraged rote memorization, they also are attempting to counter the seeming inability or perhaps unwillingness of many students to think logically. While I confess confusion as to just what educators mean by "critical thinking," their motives seem well intended and justified given what I observed in the classroom.

In the end, the fearful young patient in the berry pie case might have been right to conclude that his father-in-law was trying to poison him. Believers in the weird and paranormal might some day prove the skeptics wrong and narrowminded.

What disturbs me is the seeming desperation with which postmoderns, in a giant leap backwards into the Middle Ages, seem so willing to grasp at mere straws as the basis of their claims to truth, and to do so in so many aspects of their lives.

Generation X, UFOs, and Teachers

If I seem to have dwelled on the adverse aspects of postmodernity, that's because those are undoubtedly what I encountered most frequently as a college teacher, which I related in some detail in the first part of this book. Yet, even while the culture appears to be so fundamentally re-inventing itself, there also seems to be a feeling among parents, legislators, taxpayers, and voters—the same ones who might have their own guardian angels—that institutions such as higher education can or ought to remain an untouched island stuck in the age of modernity. And so the society collectively complains about inadequate teachers and teaching, and wrings its hands over constantly declining academic preparation of students.

Has higher education been unscathed by the postmodern revolt that is delegitimizing the very foundations upon which colleges and universities were built—a belief in science and reason and the ability to sort out what's true from what's not? Hardly. Not only have institutions of higher learning been influenced by changes in the larger culture, colleges and universities have become a cauldron for the clash between the tenets of modernism and the fragmenting, "anything goes" influence of postmodernism. That would be true even if colleges were teaching fifty-year-olds, and even more so given that these institutions are largely trying to teach what is arguably the first postmodern generation of Americans, all born after the great postmodern break that probably occurred sometime in the 1970s.

I realize, of course, that there has been a loud backlash against the very notion of Generation X. It has become fashionable in both mainstream and alternative media to rail against myth-making and the stereotyping of Generation X. *Newsweek,* for instance, ran a cover story in June 1994 that it called, "The Myth of Generation X: Seven Great Lies about Twentysomethings." Critics denying the uniqueness of Generation X argue that the term is no more than a commercial invention of advertisers and the dominant media (like *Newsweek,* perhaps?), which have co-opted and exploited the Gen X label for the sake of profits.

To suggest that Generation X is just pure stereotype, that people born in the late twentieth century are unchanged from people of past generations, seems tantamount to saying that societies don't change, that American society in particular, despite its accelerated pace, hasn't much changed in the past twenty or thirty years. Such a denial seems equivalent to saying that people of the Old World were hardly different from their post-Enlightenment, modern counterparts. I think it's too soon to be calling Generation X just another myth or invention of the media. I'm open to the possibility that they really *are* different sorts of folks than my grandma.

At the same time, GenXers are creatures of popular culture, having learned to be who they are from the dominant society. Consider anti-rational beliefs, for instance. GenXers appear to be no less inclined to harbor beliefs in such phenomena as angels and near-death experiences as many of their New Age parents, aunts, and uncles. According to one representative survey of college students conducted by two University of Texas researchers:

- Nearly six in ten students agreed or were unsure that UFOs "are actual spacecraft from other planets."

- Half the students believed that some people have psychic power to accurately predict the future.

- Almost half agreed or were unsure that time travel into the past was possible.

- Some 56 percent believed that "seances can communicate with the dead."

What's more, researchers Raymond Eve and Francis Harrold discovered, these fantastic beliefs were quite unconnected to any predisposed religious attitudes the college students might have had.

From my conversations with many people in their late teens and twenties, they often proved to be thoughtful, articulate people. No, we can't stereotype them, and we shouldn't. Nor can we dismiss what they have to say themselves about their own generation regarding their trust in modern institutions and their notions of truth, knowledge and reality.

Lloyd, who is twenty-eight and a recent graduate from a well regarded liberal arts college on the West Coast, seemed to sound like a younger, more innocent version of many Americans when he said: "I don't think there's a whole lot of trust in anything. Cynicism is rampant. It might be a result from my generation seeing the failures of everything that has come before it. Maybe there is nothing left. Traditional values are bunk, rebellion is bunk, and if those are bunk, what's left?" Lloyd continued, "Generation X is not a thing; it's the lack of a thing, the lack of a positive theory, or an opinion about anything. They don't believe in anything, and everything is up for grabs."

Or listen to Frederick, a twenty-year-old former student of mine, who told me:

I'm an angry person. Living in America makes you angry. . . . We don't really trust anything anymore. That's why we're searching. If we trusted, we wouldn't be searching. Everything is so unstable and so unsure. There's always a big question after each answer. We can't trust anybody, not even ourselves. Look at this campus, for example. Integration means trusting another race, but blacks are with blacks, whites with whites and Asians with Asians. We don't feel like there's any security any more. . . . We're not satisfied any more with anything. That goes with being young, being an American. You go with the present. It's kind of scary what we're doing. Most of us kids don't know what our future is going to be. We're not sure of anything anymore. We don't know what the truth is. The only reason most of us are going to school is society says this is your meal ticket.

Then Frederick said something that seemed to verbalize the thought patterns and subtext of those situations in which students would question the very legitimacy of my position to evaluate their work—that my judgment was simply my opinion, no more worthwhile than their own.

"We're always suspecting something of you guys," Frederick said.

One hardly needs to scratch the surface to discover that teachers in our society don't get much respect. Teachers have been among the stalwarts of the modern epoch, but as parents and adults of the larger culture have become cynical toward modern institutions and methods, so have their children become cynical and suspicious. Parents, legislators, and others might admonish young people to respect their schools and their teachers, but the young have learned by example not to respect teachers and schools, and it now seems that this devaluation of teaching and education has spread to much of higher education as well.

And don't think that students haven't gotten the message from the larger culture about cynicism and distrust toward institutions of authority. Marsha, the twenty-year-old student I mentioned earlier, told me: "I think even as far as teachers' salaries go, that might be one reason students question their teachers. In general, in our society teaching isn't looked on as a really key part of the educational system. Even the school systems and the government don't put them in a position where students will respect them. If society doesn't look up to the teachers, why should the students? That's why students might question teachers' opinions and the grading system. 'You're just a teacher.'"

What's the Point?

And so, it's not just fancy academic philosophy that one's version of the truth is as valid as anyone else's. There are no more authorities. Everything is open to question and distrust. Millions of people appear to be searching—in unusual and sometimes weird directions—for answers and for comfort. Experts disagree, and people rightly wonder, Why should I trust the experts? Why not invent my own version of reality?

Does it really matter, for instance, that the enormously popular Rush Limbaugh has claimed, among his diatribes against evil-doers of the liberal elite, that the Iran-Contra affair produced no indictments? (It produced fourteen.) Or his claim that the Persian Gulf War was supported by "everybody in the world . . . except . . . the United States Congress"? (Both houses passed resolutions supporting the war.) In fact, that people really don't care about truth and falsity in public life, but rather its entertainment value, is the great ocean of cynicism and mistrust that Limbaugh has tapped into. He, more than anybody else, must know that he's become pure spectacle, and he knows that a spectacle in a spectacular society can't sustain itself without continually turning up the noise.

Throughout this chapter, I've been discussing the crisis of truth, knowledge, and authority that characterizes the society's movement into an uncertain and fragmented postmodern epoch. The crisis has shown itself as a broadside attack on modern institutions, and a turn away from the notion that the world is objectively knowable. There are many ways that people can chose to behave in the face of the postmodern Balkanization of knowledge and power. Reject, deny, and accuse. But there's another way, too. Might people—might my students—also just shut down and say, "What's the point? I think I'll just turn off my brain, sit back, and enjoy the spectacle." It's time to consider this possibility further.

CHAPTER 12

The Postmodern Spectacle and Generation X

When Mick was a third-grader, he gave an oral report to his class-mates about his travels to Europe as a youngster. For a few minutes, Mick says, he was the center of attention, the stories of his travels enrapturing his classmates. But afterward, nobody mentioned his trip again. Mick went on in later years to travel around the world, and when the subject of his traveling adventures would come up in casual conversation with his peers in junior high and high school, he says the common response was simply: "Oh." Then, like clockwork, the conversation would inevitably go on to the next subject. "This has been a huge influence on my life," Mick, a nineteen-year-old college student, told me. "The fact that I was a world traveler, that was just a bit of information about Mick." I asked him why his peers refused to dwell on anything for very long, such as his travels, obviously an important part of who he was. "Maybe it's because they never really had to think about something," he says. "It's like playing a video game; you just turn it off. You don't have to dwell on your defeat, you just start over again."

As Mick told me this, I suddenly felt a surge of empathy toward him. I never knew that I could feel such kinship for a guy who was born the year I graduated from high school. "Oh." The moment he uttered that sound of indifference, I felt the rush of horrible memories from my first days of teaching, when I hadn't yet developed that crusty layer that I imagine many teachers must have to grow in order to keep from having a nervous breakdown during class. Though I too have grown the crust, I've never really gotten over the feelings of inadequacy those brutal, passive stares can still give me.

That look of indifference that threw me into culture shock when I became a teacher might be the mirror image of the magnificent spectacle of images that have nurtured GenXers from childhood. Colorful, mesmerizing images and sounds flash and go; at a child's whim Big Bird metamorphoses into Mr. Brady, who in turn is transformed into an MTV sex object. The spectacle that Generation X was born watching is never boring—the hand-held remote guarantees that much.

In *Brave New World,* Aldous Huxley foresaw a society whose inhabitants had repudiated thinking and reflection for the constant desire to be amused. It seems that Huxley's world has arrived with a vengeance in the postmodern epoch of spectacular America. Generation X, like Huxley's babes who were nurtured with "hypnopaedia," have grown to expect amusement in virtually every aspect of their lives. Although the human desire to be entertained, to be provoked and engaged is good and natural, many of my students sometimes expected entertainment to the exclusion of almost everything else. Their desire to be entertained seemed at times a low but constant background buzz, providing the real cultural context that shaped virtually everything that went on in the classroom. It was as if I felt the constant force of Madonna's breasts or Michael Jackson's deft hand in his crotch, which I somehow had to live up to in order to hold my students' attention, in order to keep the brutal and indifferent "Oh" at bay.

To be sure, not all college professors would agree with the assertion that students just want to be entertained. Many might contend that they don't see direct evidence of students' desires for amusement in their classrooms. Besides the sea of indifferent stares I faced each day, I can point to my own modest survey in which four in ten students picked "entertaining" as the most important quality for their teachers (see chapter 6). I can cite a study of 135 students at one Midwestern university in which students equated learning and good teaching with "entertainment." I can point to the many complaints I heard from my colleagues, like this one: "The TV generation expects to entertained. With an attention span equal to the interval between commercials, that is not surprising." But I can also point to the words of students themselves, who in one way or another told me that the amusement culture has been a central force in defining their generation.

Lloyd, the twenty-eight-year-old recent graduate I mentioned earlier, who now works in computer sales, told me, "If there's a unifying force of our generation, it's TV." He gestured around the coffeehouse we were in, which was full of twentysomethings and students from the nearby college. "I could get a heated debate going right now if I blurted out, 'So who is more macho, Kirk or Picard?'" Lloyd said. "I find that kind of strange."

Marsha, a young woman who seemed mature beyond her twenty years, who was studying at a local community college, said, "We're a society that has grown up watching TV, going for the fast laugh, the quick entertainment. It's rare to find somebody who just sits and reads and goes bird watching. You're more likely to find somebody in front of TV nowadays. That has an effect on the classroom. Students expect to be entertained. If it's not entertaining, or something you feel passionate about, it's easy to tune out."

Angie, an eighteen-year-old freshman who wants to study marine biology, told me what she wanted from her teachers: "Last year, I took a speech class, which was completely boring. There are so many other ways it could be more interesting. Anything other than just lecture. Something more humorous, you know? Lectures are just one person talking, and it's kind of just not really any tone. Something that's loud and flashes or something like that, it grabs your attention. When somebody is just standing there just talking, it makes you want to fall asleep." Then, in the next breath, Angie said, "I think the media is out of control. Technology is moving so fast. We need to take a breath and stop for while and give people time to catch up."

When I asked Frederick, a former student of mine, what he wanted in his teachers, he was blunt: "We want you guys to dance, sing, and cry. Seriously, that is what we consider to be good learning. We expect so much more from everything now because of the media. You guys can't compete."

As I've already discussed, postmodernity has delegitimated the authorities of the modern era, not the least of which have been educators. There might well be numerous specific reasons educational institutions have been debased. But it seems plausible that some of the depreciation in the worth of teachers has been a consequence of our culture's abiding faith in entertainment. Like Denzel Washington's character well understood in *Crimson Tide,* reproduced images of reality had become more real, more meaningful, and far less scary than reality itself for Generation X. "Higher education doesn't work any more," Frederick told me. "It doesn't challenge. We (students) think the media is more substantial than you the teacher. We don't value what teachers say and do. We're afraid of what you will say and do; it's so personal. With media it's so impersonal. We don't want to be personal any more with anybody. We don't want to confront our emotions. Machines are easier. If we can get it from machines, we don't have to get it from a person. The media is passive, safer. It doesn't really affect us. But a teacher, it's real, it's close."

Marketing and media types have understood well Frederick's suggestion that mediated reality can be far more persuasive than reality itself for a generation that learned to read on *Sesame Street.* Protestations about the "myth" of Generation X notwithstanding, corporate America knows that Xers are perhaps the most media savvy, image-conscious cohort, ever. Never has a single age group been so well attended to and fussed over in the media, with entire television networks and much of the magazine industry devoted to the X group. There's the obvious, such as MTV, but also the upstart Fox network whose programming is dominated by shows predominately for Xers (that is, *Beverly Hills 90210, Melrose Place, The X-Files, Party of Five*— the list goes on and is getting bigger). There is cable's FX channel, sort of an MTV with half a brain and a toned-down sex drive, and a slough of magazines dedicated to Xers, drooling over the $95 billion they'll spend annually on everything from Teen Spirit to Mountain Dew.

But don't count out the establishment media as well. From *My So-Called Life* and NBC's *Friends* to the local daily serving up special "Teen" pages in their Saturday papers, presented in the Gen X code of what's cool, the old guard, too, is doing back flips to attract Xers. One of my favorite examples is *marie claire* magazine, which ran a series of full-pagers in the *New York Times* (aimed at advertisers, no doubt). In one ad, a cooly attired, very attractive X girl, shirt unbuttoned to her waist, is slumped in a chair, and she's complaining about all the useless white noise out there coming from other fashion and glamour magazines that she's now decided to shut out. But *marie claire,* on the other hand, "talks the talk." The X girl, she's very cool, and so by implication is *marie claire,* a joint venture backed by none other than the Hearst Corporation.

Indeed, so overpowering has become the force of amusement in our culture that institutions of modernity are, chameleon-like, clothing themselves in a postmodern guise, trying to "talk the talk." Take, for example, American religious institutions. Many are transforming themselves into corporate-like enterprises that are pushing sort of a "Bible-Lite" to attract Baby Boomers and Generation Xers. Some churches, not unlike a high-powered advertising agency might, are hiring marketing specialists savvy about the twentysomething mentality, to recruit new churchgoers bored with traditional church stuff. "How in the world could we ever create something so exciting in church, where people would wait four and a half hours to get in?" says the Rev. Walt Kallestad of Phoenix, referring to a line of people he once saw for a Batman movie. That experience inspired his new approach to religion as amusement. "Entertainment is really the medium of the day," he says.

For obvious reasons, elementary, junior high, and high schools have been far quicker to adapt the amusement culture to the educational setting than has higher education. Elementary education is, after all, the sort of environment where the phenomenon of teachers running around in chicken costumes is held up to be an example of "innovative" teaching. "Whether it is rented from a video store, purchased from a catalog, or taped off the air waves, visual media has become as common as textbooks and chalk in history/social science classrooms," says one California high school teacher. But primary education, having pandered to children's desires for amusement, has created a generation of twentysomethings who now expect the same treatment at colleges and universities.

Judging by educational journals, the demands by students to be entertained has produced a sharp split among educators in colleges and universities about how far teachers should go to pander to the new generation. The following is an example taken from a book for new college teachers, in which one professor offers advice on the "entertainment issue." As perhaps the dominant viewpoint in educational circles, the writer seems to suggest that it's the teacher's responsibility to deal with whatever students dish out in terms of low interest and motivation. Students' desires for entertainment has become a fact of life and teachers must cope with it—and better to be amusing than boring. The author writes:

*Most of the time what motivates faculty to discuss the entertain-
ment issue is not the role it does or does not play in student
learning but their own discomfort with this 'performance' dimen-
sion of teaching. Many of us find it hard to envision ourselves
doing a Johnny Carson or Joan Rivers routine, coming to class in
costumes, or dancing before students as some of our more dramatic colleagues have been known to do. But the question here is
really one of degree. There are lots of steps on the way to becoming a Carson or Rivers. Most of us have hardly taken more than a
step or two in that direction. We don't err on the side of too much
entertaining. We err more often on the side of boring.*

Reasoning such as this makes me afraid that college and university classrooms are in danger of becoming mere extensions of the
rest of spectacular, pop-America. And it appears that some people in
higher education are ready to go even further down the slippery
slope of amusement, beginning to adopt the same rhetoric as their
counterparts in elementary education, that good teaching *is* tantamount to entertainment. Indeed, to be entertaining is a sign of "professionalism," in the view of some. Take for example Richard
Wolkomir's assessment of "Old Jearl," as students called physics instructor Jearl Walker, who "has been known to lecture in costumes,
stick balloons on his forehead, and even plunge his bare hand into a
pot of molten lead," according to some observers. Says Wolkomir:
"Walker's antics may strike some pedagogues as a clear case of pandering to the modern student's desire for instant entertainment. But
at a time when the nation is once again reassessing its educational
means and ends, his commitment and creativity may suggest to others a new standard of professionalism and new possibilities for enliv-
ening curricula in the humanities as well as the sciences." In what
appears to be an increasingly common sentiment within higher education, the authors of one educational journal article concluded: "If
effective teachers are entertaining teachers, and today's media-satu-
rated students expect to be entertained and cannot tolerate boredom, then it is time to underscore the need for entertainment in the
classroom."

Of course, most of the students I talked to tell me they would welcome a proliferation of the spectacular in the classroom. They say,
for instance, that watching something on a video is easier and more
engaging than reading a book or listening to a lecture. From my

experience, many students have come to equate the mere fact that they're "engaged" with the illusion of real learning. But that students might be engaged—i.e., not bored—doesn't necessarily mean that they're doing any real thinking. The sad fact is that most students don't know how to think because, as Mick told me, they've never had to in almost any aspect of their lives. When you've grown up locked on to the spectacle, notions of truth, reality, and substance recede into meaninglessness. What is meaningful is what is momentarily before your eyes. Says the French writer Guy Debord, in his *Comments on the Society of the Spectacle:* "When social significance is attributed only to what is immediate, and to what will be immediate immediately afterwards, always replacing another, identical immediacy, it can be seen that the uses of the media guarantee a kind of eternity of noisy insignificance."

For the culture at large, but especially for Generation X, one more image or fact is all just "one more bit of information," as Mick would say. Whether it's about O.J. Simpson, the campaign for President, or the Bosnian War, each one engenders yet another collective "Oh." Says Mick: "I have an older friend who says when he was young, he'd watch a news clip at the movies, and he'd have a couple of weeks to think about it. Today we get that short bit of information over breakfast, three times a day, just driving down the street. There's so much information, we can't distinguish what to think about and what's just b.s. There's just too much of it, and we don't have time to think."

Cool Is as Cool Does

Of course, it's one thing not having time or inclination to think because there's too much to think about. It's quite another matter refusing to think, indeed, revelling in one's choosing *not* to think.

Once I had a student who did a movie review of the film, *Nobody's Fool,* about a cantankerous character living in a small town in upstate New York played by Paul Newman. The student panned the movie. Why? She said the plot wasn't entertaining. In fact, her *only* criterion for evaluating this film was that it wasn't entertaining enough, that there wasn't enough action. That there might be other ways to view a film, such as character development, mood, realism, etc., never occurred to her nor most others in the class. When I pointed out to students that there might be other ways to look at a film besides its entertainment value, blank looks of indifference swept though the room. It was as if they were reacting viscerally to the notion of complexity—that their set view of the world was being challenged. "Who cares?" seemed to be the collective response. But what was most disturbing for me was that they seemed *proud* of their ignorance.

Another time, I tried to underscore for students why it was important to read the newspaper every day. It was becoming obvious to me that, even though they had purchased the newspaper for my class, few were actually reading it, despite the fact that I quizzed on current affairs. On a five-question quiz, the clear majority would often get all five wrong. I wanted to shock them, to embarrass them actually, with their own ignorance of public life. So, I tried another little quiz, this one not based on any particular events. I asked students to tell me what G.O.P. meant and who it referred to. I also asked them how much welfare spending contributed to the federal budget. On the former I got such answers as "Great Old Politics," "Part of a Government," "Gross Product," and this winner: "Goofy Old People." And according to my students, the U.S. government is spending a whopping 30 to 50 percent of the federal budget on welfare. (It's actually just 1 percent.) But my students were hardly embarrassed. It seemed that the few students who got the answers nearly right were considered by their peers to be nerds and freaks. It was cool to be, if not dumb, to act as if ignorance of public affairs was a sign that you were too cool for all that serious grown-up garbage.

In the cafeteria-style approach to values that characterizes postmodernity, add a healthy serving of anti-intellectualism to the cynicism, paranoia, and anti-rationality that millions of Americans are adopting as their guiding principles nowadays. While the larger culture embraces anti-intellectualism as simply a sort of healthy, All American trait, Generation X is putting its own spin on the old idea that ignorance is bliss: It's also very cool.

To the extent that the postmodern generation traffics above all else in entertainment values, popular culture, and image, they are being inundated with the screwy idea that there's little to be gained from being smart. Why, you might end up being like Bill Clinton, the Yale Law School and Oxford grad whom media pundits flippantly refer to as "the smartest guy in the class." Educators, intellectuals, and opinion leaders commonly say that we live in an age of no heroes, which is perfect nonsense when you consider how extravagantly and unflinchingly our culture worships the likes of Michael Jordan, Bruce Willis, and Tom Hanks. I'm not saying actors and athletes aren't smart, but we surely don't idolize them for their beautiful brains. It's worth noting again that the smart guy who conceived and wrote the book and screenplay *Forrest Gump* earned for his work on the film about 1 percent of Hanks's $31 million as an actor in the movie. And let's not forget the Gump phenomenon itself. Among the most popular movies of all time, *Forrest Gump* idealizes naive stupidity as something to strive for in life. It pays handsomely.

Indeed, as opposed to the goodness of Gump, smart guys are often the bad guys in the movies. Really smart guys are either innocent buffoons, such as Walter Matthau's Einstein in *IQ,* mad bombers like Jeremy Iron's character in *Die Hard with a Vengeance,* or shrewd profiteers like Michael Douglas's character in *Wall Street.* You're not really up to hero quality in our culture unless you're someone of medium intelligence who is "able to get the better of the twisted genius," observes Phillip Lopate, a professor of literature at Hofstra University.

Of course, what I'm about to suggest might mean nothing of much significance. But then again, it might say something about the state of our culture when, as reported in the *New York Times,* celebrities, such as Neil Diamond, Michael Bolton, and Barbara Streisand, topped the charts as the most frequent speakers at college commencement ceremonies in the spring of 1995. Who says Generation X has no heroes?

The anti-intellectual juggernaut that Generation X watches at the movies and on TV is one thing, but also consider what they get increasingly from my own field of journalism, which—to the surprise of many of my students—traditionally has stood alongside higher education as one of the pillars of modernity. At its best, the American press has stood for emancipatory values, justice, and truth-seeking. But much of mainstream journalism is becoming just another aspect of the spectacle, pandering to audiences that demand amusement. In what former *Washington Post* writer Carl Bernstein has called the "triumph of the Idiot Culture," the ideals of truth, justice, and emancipation have become almost meaningless, mere verbiage that professional journalism organizations quaintly place in their codes of ethics. "For the first time in our history, the weird and the stupid and the course are becoming our cultural norm, even our ideal," says Bernstein, the guy who helped uncover the Watergate scandal. Of course, one reason newspapers have turned to gross simplicity and the sensational is to attract younger people who don't read, and so print journalism has tried to be more like TV, becoming more simple to attract readers who *still* won't read the paper. Most newspapers' brilliant response to this trend is to try to become even more entertaining, and so on in a vicious circle.

Indeed, the postmodern generation could be the most disengaged cohort in the history of the republic. According to a recent study by the Higher Education Research Institute at UCLA, today's college freshmen are the least interested in public affairs of any group of freshmen in the institute's twenty-nine-year history of measuring this trait. Just one in three college freshmen indicated that keeping up with public affairs was important to them, compared to six in ten freshmen who thought so in 1966.

Robert Pollack, a professor of biology and former dean at Columbia University, says young people are rationalizing their ignorance because the world is too complex to cope with. Pollack might be a bit more charitable than I when he says he's noticed many students maintain a "willful naivete . . . in the face of a complicated world," a "wish to remain innocent: If I don't understand the complexity, it doesn't bother me," says Pollack. Students nowadays, he says, would rather see the world as "a place to outwit, not a place to help run."

Meantime, Xers are inventing their own postmodern journalistic forms in an effort to talk their own talk, quite apart from the co-opting influence of corporate media. GenXers have typecast newspapers and traditional print media as boring, and mainstream papers won't attract the postmodern generation unless they transform themselves into something entirely new. Recognizing this obviousness, Xers themselves are giving us new magazines and newspapers like Dallas's *The Met.* Who is *The Met* trying to reach? "My reader doesn't care that city hall is stealing from us," twenty-four-year-old publisher Randy Stagen told the *Columbia Journalism Review.* "He cares that there's a great band playing tonight and that there's cold beer at Phil's Bar."

Or consider *Project X* magazine, subtitled "your global guide to tomorrow's scene." That subtitle says volumes about Generation X culture. We're not talking about *today's* scene here; just getting "now" right used to be what one wishing for cool could ever hope for. But in today's accelerated culture, we're seeing the spectacle unfold of an absurd competition for coolness in a world in which everybody has already seen and heard everything, and coolness has come to be defined as newer than new and beyond the now. Cool is *post*-postmodern, post-cyberspace, post-Internet. Cool is anti-present.

And the past? Well, it never existed, except perhaps in vintage clothing stores. Commenting on the latest, coolest, X-oriented magazines it had anointed, *Project X* wrote, "The hottest magazines of this season are here; they're post Generation X, post teen, post anything that marketing analysts can even begin to identify."

But try as the new Gen X media might to "cool" their way out of dominant culture's shadow, there's no escaping it. *Project X*, for example, using the fashionably convoluted, sometimes unreadable formats for its printed pages, despises the printed culture of modernism for a postmodern, anti-print design. But it's still print. It despises the commercialism of the dominant culture, but it still runs ads for Dewar's. But (slap me, I generalize), I would guess that the intended audience for this magazine and others like it are quite oblivious to such contradictions and, I dare say, manipulation. Growing up in a spectacular society that constantly reinforces the "ideals" of anti-intellectualism and vacuity, one learns not to see anything beyond its pretty face value. That's what the spectacle is all about—pure pleasure and pure entertainment. Which is why *Project X's* gambit that it can out-manipulate the masters of manipulation on Madison Avenue, won't work: In a spectacular culture, consumers don't care much that *marie claire* is really published by a bunch of boomers at the Hearst Corporation. Born into the postmodern spectacle, GenXers know no other language than the language of the spectacle; they know no other talk nor walk other than that of the spectacle; and by definition, the spectacle knows completely the language of the youth culture, who despite their efforts, will remain naive prisoners of conformity to the amusement society. Guy Debord says:

> *The individual who has been more deeply marked by this impoverished spectacular thought than by any other aspect of his experience puts himself at the service of the established order right from the start, even though subjectively he may have had quite the opposite intention. He will essentially follow the language of the spectacle, for it is the only one he is familiar with; the one in which he learned to speak. No doubt he would like to be regarded as an enemy of its rhetoric; but he will use its syntax. This is one of the most important aspects of spectacular domination's success.*

We've come a long way, then, since the days of Voltaire and Rousseau, when *enlightenment,* of all things, was cool. But then, ignorance and naivete might be a natural response to the wild spectacle of information and images careening out of control in postmodern America. Although I personally recoil at the "willful naivete," in Robert Pollack's words, that I observed in so many students, aren't these children of postmodernity simply a predictable creation of a larger culture that itself is recoiling from thinking and reflection? I'm unfortunately reminded of Aldous Huxley's words in *Brave New World* when he's describing the long-lasting results of the new society's conditioning of its offspring: "They'll grow up with what the psychologists used to call an 'instinctive' hatred of books and flowers. Reflexes unalterably conditioned. They'll be safe from books and botany all their lives."

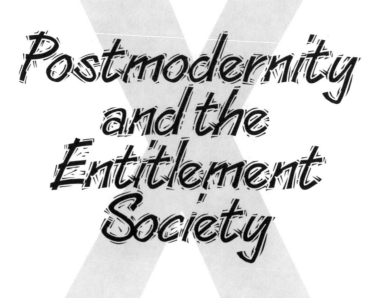

CHAPTER 13

Postmodernity and the Entitlement Society

During my journey into teaching, as recounted in some detail in the first part of this book, students provided me with much feedback on my teaching, in the form of student evaluations at the end of each quarter. Here is a paragraph from one of those evaluations, which seems to capture the sense of consumerism and entitlement that characterized the mind-set of many students:

"I hated this class and found it hard to get up in the morning to get here. I would have dropped it except that I am graduating in June," the student wrote. "You must understand that we are beginning college writers and not graduate students. Your attendance grading is 'BS' because we pay for our school and should choose whether to attend or not. . . . If I don't get a decent grade because of your critical attitude, I will be speaking to your superiors."

Consider, also, the following descriptions of certain kinds of people that one encounters with increasing frequency nowadays. The first refers to the *"I have it coming because you owe me"* person:

> *Panics with risk. Emotion high if there is the perception of any risk, including that of accountability. With risk, this person needs a life-saver. Tendency to deny the loss of entitlement or the*

*requirement for performance. Follows and memorizes the
rules. Avoids risk. Apathetic, passive and dependent though that
can be hard to discern under the overt 'You owe me' attitude.*

And here is the *"I did the best I could so I don't understand why
you're crabbing at me"* sort:

*Resistant to increased risk or accountability. Projects causes from
the self and rationalizes failure: 'Circumstances were out of my
control.' May say: 'This is good enough." Blames others . . . for
nonperformance. Very judgmental and frequently verbal. Pre-
sumptuousness. Greedy. Avoids assessment. Tries to look good.
Is prone to justify performance, saying 'Look at the time and effort
I put in!' Very difficult and time-consuming to deal with because
the anxiety is high but so is the denial of any responsibility. Hard
to budge from Entitlement.*

When management consultant Judith Bardwick wrote those descriptions of entitlement-bound employees common to contemporary corporations, she wasn't referring to college students. But she
might as well have, for those descriptions exactly fit the sort of attitudes I encountered on a daily basis as a college teacher.

In the dark days of the modern era when industrial capitalism was
its meanest and nastiest, ordinary people were lucky to get what was
coming to them from institutions of authority. The old saying "buyer
beware" was probably an apt characterization of the mood of the
times. But so profound has been the delegitimation of the institutions
of modernity, so thoroughly has economic and political power shifted
from these institutions to the hegemony of cultural populism, that we
can change that old saying: Nowadays, call it "The System, beware,"
or some subset of it, like "Seller, beware" or "Politician, beware." In
my case, it might be "Teacher, Give me an A or I'll call your boss." As
a result of the degree to which power has continued to shift in the
postmodern epoch, many people now seem to believe that "the system" in all its various guises owes them, and owes them far more
than what many are willing to give back to the system.

Indeed, the spreading social and economic power seems to have
manifested itself in the postmodern epoch as various sorts of entitlement, regardless of one's social and economic position. At one level
of analysis, we've witnessed a widening sense of popular entitlement

to at least a middle-class existence, sort of a quasi-constitutional birthright that one might suppose comes with being an American. Thus, for most Americans, higher education, as the main route to economic success, is considered an entitlement, not unlike Social Security or Medicare benefits.

On another level, we see an intensifying consumerism, a "hyper-consumerism," as perhaps *the* defining characteristic of postmodern human beings. The prominent French thinker Jean Baudrillard captured the flavor of this idea in his 1970 essay, "Consumer Society." But by today's accelerated standards, the notion of consumerism, shopping malls, drug stores, and a zillion objects to buy seems a bit quaint. Postmodernity has taken consumerism to where no man has gone before: hyperconsumerism is transforming realms of social life once considered off limits to the consumption mentality. And so, for consumers who "buy" an education, the notion of "success" is increasingly treated as a quasi-negotiable exchange; you pay your money and you get what you pay for, regardless of what you put into the deal. Indeed, some consumers of education seem to invest no more personal responsibility in the transaction than a McDonald's customer buying a Quarter Pounder with cheese.

Also inherent in the power shift, it seems, are various related phenomena we've all observed with some frequency in recent years. Increasingly, the postmodern person is relinquishing his responsibility to others and the larger society; she has an expectation of immediate gratification without necessarily having to work for it; and he's a "victim" of the system if his gratification is thwarted or isn't immediate.

But the existing institutions of modernity play a key role, too, in the power shift. To sometimes an alarming extent, we see them pandering for mass appeal in vain and absurd attempts to win back or to maintain their failing legitimacy. And thus we see such abominations as teachers pandering to students by giving lots of A's, and we see U.S. politicians pandering to voters with promises of ever lower taxes—already among the lowest in the industrial world.

Entitlement's Humble Beginnings

To be sure, the roots of popular entitlement in the United States go back to the vast inequities that no-holds-barred capitalism had created during the birthing pains of industrial society. But when the United States faced its worst economic crisis in its history during the

Great Depression and nearly one in three workers was without a job, economists and politicians woke up to the harsh reality that industrial capitalism had to be tempered in order to survive. Franklin D. Roosevelt's vast reforms of unemployment insurance for the jobless, health care for the poor and aged, welfare for the poor, securities and banking regulation for small investors, and Keynesian economic policies for the stability of the economy—these became the pillars of the modern government's protection of its citizens from the economic disasters that free markets were capable of.

It is well known that, after these necessary foundations for economic and social stability were erected, the United States saw an explosion of economic capacity after World War II. With citizens back into the fold of the American promise, and the threat of socialism beat back by capitalism's reformation, a middle-class consumer culture took root and flourished. An explosion of mass communications, particularly television and advertising for consumer goods, provided rocket fuel for America's post-War consumer culture. The United States economy became the biggest jobs machine the world had ever seen. You could hardly say "American" without also saying "success" in the same breath.

But while the children of the Great Depression saw capitalism's reforms as establishing an entitlement not to starve or freeze to death, that view would change with succeeding generations. By the time the nation's Baby Boomers had grown up and gone off to college or to a job at auto and steel mills, you were no longer entitled to mere survival as an American: you were entitled at least to a middle-class life. By the time Generation X was born in the late 1960s and early 1970s, America's entitlement society had become deeply entrenched. Unlike any generation before it, America's X babes grew up with mighty powerful images of comfort and style to live up to.

By the 1980s, the constant images of a glossy, perfect life, false though they might have been, proved to be at least as persuasive for a generation reared on amusement and glitz as the reality of increasing homelessness, poverty, and weakness becoming evident in the U.S. jobs machine. Indeed, the powerful contradictions between unreal images of the amusement culture and the reality of diminishing economic prospects would become the basis of great fear and uncertainty for much of Generation X.

Probably no better illustration can be found of the degree to which popular entitlement has become entrenched in American culture than higher education. Assisted by such post-War efforts as the President's Commission on Higher Education in 1947, the Servicemen's Readjustment Act (GI Bill), the National Defense Education Act, the Vocational Education Act, and the Higher Education Act, the democratization of higher education became official U.S. policy. The clear purpose of those official acts was to open up access to higher education to all Americans, regardless of economic class and privilege.

They worked exceedingly well. In 1955, there was roughly a one-to-one ratio of public-to-private enrollment in U.S. colleges. By 1995 enrollment in public colleges and universities was four times that of private institutions. Attendance at colleges and universities by 1995 had surged nearly 500 percent from that of forty years ago. In the twenty-year period from 1971 to 1991, the number of bachelor's degrees awarded rose 30 percent. And while just half of high school graduates went to college in 1980, some 63 percent of school graduates had enrolled in colleges and universities in the fall of 1992—a record high.

Another key barometer of the degree to which American higher education has been democratized is enrollment in community colleges, institutions that have minimal or no admissions requirements. In 1994, attendance at public two-year colleges stood at 5.5 million, roughly equal to that at public four-year schools. But open admissions haven't been limited to community colleges. Some 205 four-year institutions, or 12 percent of such schools, will accept virtually any high school graduate.

But we now face some disturbing consequences from the noble goal of unlimited access to higher education. Greater access has coincided with the intensifying hyperconsumerism in the larger culture, which has devalued the entire higher education enterprise. Just as many Americans have come to view a middle-class existence as an inalienable right, success in higher education as the principle means to achieve that level of material existence has risen to near entitlement status. Responding to the demands of the consumer culture, educators have gone far beyond the principle of more egalitarian access to higher education; they have sold the fiction to the American public that success is achievable upon an economic transaction, regardless of one's skills, motivation, or talents. I'll explore in more detail the student-consumers' demands for "success" and the institutional back flips the educational establishment has undergone to supply this success. But first I need to explain the evolution of "hyperconsumerism" in our time.

My admittedly simple and abbreviated version of the evolution of a postmodern, hyperconsumer culture goes like this: During the modern era in Europe and the United States, when nation-states provided the legal infrastructure for a surging industrial capitalism, producers dominated society in the form of such stalwarts as General Motors, Standard Oil, and AT&T. The role of citizens in this scheme were primarily as workers for such industrial enterprises. As workers first and consumers second, people learned, as it were, the ABC's of consuming, from buying new cars to washing machines. But being a consumer was a new way of being on the human landscape; mainly, people earned and consumed enough to fulfill their roles as good, stable workers. This era might be symbolized in the novelty of the early Sears-Roebuck catalog, sort of a training manual for the American Consumer in adolescence.

But the balance of power between producers and consumers slowly began to shift as incomes rose beyond what people needed to survive as workers, and the demand for consumer goods surged. Americans graduated from the Sears-Roebuck Consumer Training Academy to graduate-level consumerism. With consumption growing to account for two-thirds of economic activity, the fate of the nation's economy became hog-tied to the fickle attitudes of consumers. Entire research organizations were founded just to check the temperment of the American consumer on a quarterly basis, so dependent were the nation's economic fortunes on something as amorphous as "consumer sentiment."

I don't think it's much of an exaggeration to say that, eventually, being a consumer and being human had become in many ways indistinguishable. Consuming the things, services, and popular images of the culture had taken up virtually all one's waking moments. "We have reached the point where 'consumption' has grasped the whole of life," Baudrillard wrote in "Consumer Society." By the time Generation X had come of age some twenty years after Baudrillard wrote those words, Americans had become something far more intense than mere consumers. We were superconsumers from the tips of our Chicago Bulls hats to the toes of our Nikes, and hyperconsumerism characterized the postmodern condition. Consumption, says the postmodernist writer Z. Bauman, seeming to take Baudrillard a step further, had become "the cognitive and moral force of life, the integrative bond of society."

Indeed, hyperconsumerism has played a key role in revolutionizing the society's power arrangements from the institutions of modernity to forms of popular power. Therefore, we see that traditional dividing lines between elites and popular masses being disintegrated, not via political action of citizens, but through the hegemony of consumers. As one example, in recent years the venerable auction houses Christie's and Sotheby's have vastly broadened their clientele from wealthy elites to middle-class consumers, known as "street people" in the auction trade. Nowadays, about half of the 200,000 to 300,000 items Christie's sells each year go for less than $5,000 and one-quarter for no more than $1,000, a "terrifying" fact, Christie's chairman, Christopher J. Burge, told the *New York Times*.

The individual logic of the superconsumer is straightforward. One earns or otherwise obtains money, and commands absolute sovereignty over its disposition. Payment *entitles* one to that power and discretion. No moral or ethical responsibilities to others bear upon the decision of what to consume or when to consume it. Consumption is an absolutely egalitarian act. One pays money for a consumable item; one receives the item. Consumption is an act of individual empowerment. Invoking the magisterial nature of the exchange from the consumers' point of view, market-oriented economists have a value-laden term for the consumption act: They call it "consumer sovereignty."

Of course, that set-up works rather well for buying something like a parka at L.L. Bean or a flatbed truck from Ford. Things would become overly complicated and muddled if matters of individual ethics and responsibility to others got mixed up in the purchase. But nowadays, hyperconsumerism has wound up in segments of society that once seemed off-limits to its logic, raising important questions whether these spheres of activity are compatible with the superconsumer mentality. For example, we watch the rise of the "customer-driven" church, trying to make its "product" more appealing and entertaining in response to changes in American culture. Is such an approach conducive to spirituality? One theologian has doubts: "The deeper meaning of the tradition is blanded out as the church is democratized," says Charles McCoy, of the Center for Ethics and Social Policy at the Graduate Theological Union in Berkeley.

The quaint notions of responsibility for one's actions and a sense of obligation to the public good are completely laundered out of the consumption equation. As hyperconsumerism has come to dominate our postmodern existence, we've seen a collapse in the ethic of individual responsibility. And, the flip side of that has been a notable rise in the ethic of victimhood. If I live thoroughly within the mind-set of a consumer who is to be serviced by the system, and I feel entitled to immediate gratification of my desires, then I feel cheated and victimized if I don't get what I want. Unfortunately, this feeling of being cheated, that an organization or the system or people of authority are to blame if I don't get what I want—this world view has become pervasive in a society based on the near absolute right to consume one's way into happiness, or into the middle class, or wherever consumption might lead one.

Conservatives, of course, have railed against the collapse of individual responsibility that seems to characterize our times. But even people in such bastions of conservatism as Orange County, California, are not immune to the flight from responsibility. Thus, after the county suffered huge losses on speculative investments—investments that substituted for the property tax hikes that would otherwise have been necessary to fund county services—voters in the largely conservative, wealthy Southern California county rejected a plea in 1995 to raise the state sales tax by half a cent in order to pay off municipal bondholders. While voters enjoyed public services, they weren't willing to pay for them, and their collective refusal to make good on the county's obligations threatened to wreak havoc in the entire municipal bond market. The move not only damaged Orange County's ability to ever raise money again for public purposes, but also the ability of all local governments to do so.

Success as a Consumer Service

The very same hyperconsumerism that has taken hold of the larger American culture has also gripped higher education by the throat, threatening to render meaningless such traditional notions as hard work, responsibility, and standards of excellence. Students nowadays were born into the culture of hyperconsumerism, and many, I'm afraid, don't fiddle with fine distinctions between going to college as an act of consumer sovereignty and many other types of consumer purchases. The responsibility for one's success, then, lies with the institutions and the teachers who staff them. Failure, i.e., consumer dissatisfaction, is ruled out upon payment of one's tuition.

David Reisman, the Harvard sociologist and long-time observer of trends in higher education, took note of the transition from faculty controlled universities to student-dominated consumerism several years ago. "This shift from academic merit to student consumerism is one of the two greatest reversals of direction in all the history of American higher education; the other being the replacement of the classical college by the modern university a century ago," Reisman says.

What do student-consumers want? According to my own modest survey (which I discuss in detail in part one) at the college in which I taught, by and large, students view themselves primarily as consumers who intended to study just a handful of hours a week for all their classes, and who expected, at a minimum, solid B's for their efforts. Students raised in a postmodern society of hyperconsumerism appear to want facile knowledge, served up in easily digestible, bite-sized chunks. They have little tolerance for messy thinking or expansion of their frames of reference beyond the routine and predictable. In short, they view themselves as consumers who pay their teachers to provide "knowledge," regardless of how superficial that knowledge might be. After all, how hard should a consumer have to work at buying something?

"Adapt-a-Chapter"

As an example of the sort of superficial knowledge I'm talking about, consider what are known as "study guides" in educational circles, which are page-by-page summaries of textbooks—which themselves are often simplified versions of more substantive works and ideas. Thus, these study guides represent a dumbing down of the already dumbed down. When I first started teaching and found out about the existence of these guides, I was surprised that they were needed for college-level studies. That surprise turned to near disgust when I actually saw one from an undergraduate psychology course that a student provided me. The example shown is somewhat modified from a small segment of that guide.

The student who shared this guide with me said that tests for the course in question were taken almost directly from the study guide itself. If this strikes you as cookbook education, you're right. In the same spirit of dumbing down the already dumbed down, an

> ### A College Textbook Study Guide
> *page from text*
>
> xx   *Since 1900, the average U.S. life expectancy has increased*
>   *from ____ to __. In 1900 __% of reported deaths involved*
>   *persons under age 15.*
> xx   *Know the three main causes of death and their percents.*
> xx   *Today about ___ % of deaths occur in an institutional*
>   *setting.*
> xx   *Give at least five examples of the way we use language to*
>   *avoid the reality of death.*

instructor I know who compiled a textbook study guide called it "Adapt-a-Chapter." But such methods were far from unusual. Several students told me about these study guides, a few believing that they constituted an unwarranted degree of hand-holding. But from what I gathered in talking to teachers and students, most students expected this sort of spoon-feeding and were upset with their teachers if they didn't get it.

Of course, college students nowadays have their junior high and high schools to thank for never having been weaned from the hand-holding and spoon-feeding that they first learned in kindergarten. Consider the tale of a Tacoma, Washington, newspaper columnist, C.R. Roberts, who tells us about a request he received from a Puyallup, Washington, high school student—by fax, of course. The day before his assignment is due, the student informed "To Whom It May Concern" at the newspaper that he has to write a report on Sri Lanka. "Please help me!" the student's fax implored. With his tongue firmly in his cheek, Roberts writes in his column: "How proud I am to help, albeit a bit late. How pleased I am with an educational system that would encourage students to have others do their work for them. . . . I am delighted to be of assistance!" Then Roberts, hopefully, teaches the kid a lesson to remember, offering the high schooler reams of made-up, beautifully crafted garbage about Sri Lanka.

For their part, college teachers and the institutions who employ them might also take a cue from C.R. Roberts. As opposed to taking Roberts's approach to douse the entitlement mind-set with cold water, institutions are doing back flips with double twists in what strike me as often Herculean efforts to ensure that student consumers' expectations for success be satisfied. As consumers of educational service, students—along with the skills and motivation they present—literally end up shaping their own curriculum and standards. Amid the postmodern shift in power from authorities to consumers, the institutions themselves appear unwilling to draw firm lines in the sand. Instead, they have re-defined themselves in the age of hyperconsumerism as providers of consumer services, while paying lip services to their traditional roles as gatekeepers and vanguards of academic standards. "Again, it is consumerism—the rise in societal demand and the interplay between that demand and the university's traditional ideals—that is defining what we do," acknowledges Robert Zemsky, founder and director of the Institute for Research on Higher Education at the University of Pennsylvania.

An example of the rising tone of consumerism in higher education can be found in the notion of "TQM" or Total Quality Management, an approach to business developed in the early 1970s, later adopted by the American auto industry, to improve quality. Here's a partial description of TQM taken from the Educational Resources Information Center:

> TQM is based on the principle that the customer is the most important person. The major tenet of TQM can be summed up in nine words: Satisfy the customer, satisfy the customer, satisfy the customer.

While TQM might work fine for making cars or toaster ovens, it strikes me as naive practice in the face of a postmodern popular culture that is largely based on amusement and hyperconsumerism. What the student-customer born and bred in such a culture wants is success; he wants it now, and he doesn't want to have to struggle to achieve it. But this phenomenon often seems lost on the devotees of TQM and customer-driven education (who I would guess more often than not tend to be enrollment-maximizing educational administrators rather than teachers).

Besides the TQM mentality, the dominant world view in much of higher education is that students ought to succeed in college—at any cost. One illustration is found in a newsletter called *Innovation Abstracts,* published by the University of Texas College of Education in Austin. From what I can ascertain, these newsletters often amount to tips by teachers for teachers on how to bend over backward just a little bit farther to appease unmotivated, acutely passive students. Here are a few such examples from the newsletter, in which college instructors related, in all earnestness, how they have devised schemes to help students "succeed." Their suggestions for innovative teaching include:

- Creating assignments that encourage students to participate in group-written essays.

- Allowing students to have questions for essay tests days before an examination.

- Permitting students to re-take exams until they get the grade they want.

- Devising scored "drills" at the beginning of each class that collectively amount to one major assignment, which students can work on cooperatively. This is to encourage attendance. "While it does not solve all problems (some students have not yet learned to take responsibility for their learning), it does seem to get more students to class and on time," the instructor advises.

What's more, the size of the non-academic infrastructure institutions have built to assist in the virtual underwriting of student success is indeed imposing, and, arguably drains resources from the academic side of institutions. The plethora of student services at most colleges and universities includes entire departments devoted to such things as psychological counseling, disabled student services, educational planning, financial aid, health services, men's and women's resources, multicultural student services, tutoring, etc. The trend for institutions of higher education to become social service providers is not unlike the rise of "nannyism" in the American corporation. Companies are providing employees with "a broad array of goodies, ranging from the sensible shoes variety (job training and tuition reimbursements at $35 billion annually) to more exotic offerings" such as employer provided legal services and wellness programs, says Laura L. Nash of Boston University.

Not to miss an opportunity, textbook publishers have exploited the nannyism in higher education, creating something akin to a mini-industry for success texts. Houghton Mifflin, as one example, has launched an entire "Student Success Programs" series. The program offers several texts, variously titled, *College Study Skills, Essential Study Skills, Study Skills in Practice, Becoming a Master Student,* and *The Confident Student.* These and texts such as Wadsworth's *Your College Experience: Strategies for Success* are intended for what has become a vast market—a generation of students that lacks the attention spans, social skills, and study habits needed for college work. According to a 1991 survey by the National Resource Center for the Freshman Year Experience, roughly 692 of 1,064 institutions offered college credit to freshman for orientation courses. These covered such basic topics as study skills, "learning styles," time management, diversity, writing papers using word processors, and other less than rigorous subjects.

Beyond the great efforts institutions are making to assist students in college-level classes are those offered to students who need remedial work. The significant scope of remedial education in the United States, often at taxpayer expense for college students who still have difficulty composing coherent sentences or solving simple math problems, underscores the practically non-existent academic barriers to entering and succeeding in college. Fully 30 percent of the nation's students in colleges and universities are enrolled in remedial courses of some type, and one-third of institutions offer remedial course work. Between 1975 and 1980, enrollment in remedial math courses at public, four-year colleges surged 72 percent. These now make up one-quarter of all math courses taught at these colleges. At one urban campus of the California State University system, fully eight of ten freshman in 1993 were unprepared for college-level English classes.

But even those figures don't account for the unknown amount of remedial work that takes place daily in supposedly college-level courses—the "Adapt-a-Chapter" kinds of things. The teachers I've talked to do so willingly on an informal basis, but it's a vast commitment of their time and energy. And now pressures are building at the institutional level for teachers to formally incorporate remedial work into their college-level classes. As one small example, the U.S. Department of Education spent some $255,000 on a three-year grant for California State University purporting to show that integrating remedial language skills in courses significantly improved performance of a test sample of students compared to those who didn't get the extra help. But a close look at the study's data, provided in an appendix, makes that claim doubtful. In the second year of the study, for instance, 37 percent of the special test group of 46 students received A's compared to 42 percent of a regular group of 177 students. Some 13 percent of the special group got B's—half the rate of those who didn't get remedial help.

A's for All Comers

But whether the students are getting remedial assistance at the lowliest of public community colleges or doing advanced studies at an elite university, they are being paid handsomely for their efforts in terms of lots and lots of A's and B's, grades that once upon a time had some relationship with excellence. Indeed, easy grading has become part of the entitlement bargain in higher education, and as I discussed at length in the first part of this book, few if any players in the system have much incentive to break the cycle of grade inflation. In fact, student consumers demand it, administrators seem to encourage it, and teachers who try to maintain rigorous grading standards expose themselves to ruinous student evaluations, dwindling class sizes, and possible loss of a job.

Thus, we see how administrators at a college in Austin, Texas, overruling an English instructor, permitted a student to retake a test and then changed his final course grade from an F to a C. The instructor maintained that students have a right to succeed, but that they should have to work for it. An unreasonable demand? Apparently so. "Campus officials said privately that (the instructor's) expectations of his students were too high," according to the *Chronicle of Higher Education*. Or, consider the case of one Boston University professor. Once, over her "strong objections," the chairperson of her department changed a student's F to a pass. Asked to justify the change, the chairperson told the professor, "Both of his parents are lawyers." Or, hear the frustration of Daniel Kazez, an associate professor of music at Wittenberg University in Ohio. "No prudent, career-minded professor dares risk infuriating students by giving out anything but A's or B's. Students who receive a C, D or F on a test or paper tend to hold the teacher personally responsible. Rare is the professor who can afford to adhere to high standards, give students the grades they deserve and accept the personal, professional and financial consequences." And, we can read the laments of a Yale graduate teaching assistant, who says: "I can honestly say that for one of these (Yale) kids to get below a C would require a major federal offense. As long as they hand in 'something,' no matter how cliche, plagiarized, poorly punctuated or sloppy, they will pass, usually at 'B' level. It's infuriating but that's how the system works."

In a system like this, then, it's hardly surprising that college freshmen in 1994 reported the highest ever proportion of 'A' averages in high school, at 28.1 percent. That means nearly one in every three students got A's—compared to just 16 percent who earned 'A' averages in 1970. Nor should it be surprising that, at the college where I teach, nearly nine of ten students, or 85 percent, get grades of B or higher. That might sound extraordinarily high, but it's not unusual, regardless of the selectivity of the institution. At Stanford University, for instance, 90 percent of the grades are A's and B's; at Harvard, more than 40 percent of students get A's alone.

Could these trends possibly mean that young people have just gotten smarter and harder-working over the years? That possibility seems quite remote, given the inexorable, continuous decline since the 1960s in scholastic achievement scores at all points of the socioeconomic spectrum. Verbal scores on the SAT in 1993 were 42 points below their levels nearly thirty years ago, and average math performance was down 14 points. Simply artifacts of greater numbers of disadvantaged students taking the test? Perhaps. But consider: American high school seniors taking advanced placement biology, who presumably consist of mostly middle-class students competent in English, in one international competition placed *last* out of thirteen other nations, including Japan, Taiwan, Mexico, Canada, and Thailand.

Rather than grade inflation being the result of students' finer work ethic and greater brilliance, it seems more likely that it's an artifact of a desperate educational establishment choosing to play make-believe games. Educators are trying to engage a generation of young people that, in large measure, has lost heart and will. Many GenXers are, deservedly so, quite frightened about the future and their ability to make their own way in an economy that seems to be offering ever fewer opportunities for them. But instead of demanding the sort of excellence students will need to really succeed in the world, educators have responded to the crisis in motivation by making achievement easier and easier, hoping that lots of A's and B's might help young people feel good about themselves and thus, propel them toward excellence, or at least mediocrity. Perhaps it's time to consider the possibility that this approach isn't working: the flip side of grade inflation is a ruinous deflation of academic standards, and that can't be good for the country, let alone all the individuals who can't find a job because they have never really learned how to think.

But the irony is, most students realize that they've been living their lives in a never-never land where nobody is below average and where "success" in school is virtually guaranteed, no matter how little they had to work for it. And if you ask them, most will give you some startling admissions. News analysts looking for new angles can jump on the "Generation X as myth" bandwagon till the cows come home, but *something* is going on here that cute new story angles won't dispel.

Listen to Frederick, a twenty-year-old student I talked to at length. Here was an obviously bright guy who almost always showed up late to class, if he came at all, and might be described as the quintessential Gen X "slacker." As always, he was characteristically blunt. "From my perspective, we are there (in college) to warm the seats, basically," he said. "That is what we're doing. . . . Our generation is very lazy. Very, very lazy. We don't work a tenth of what our parents did. Maybe we're so sick and tired of everything, the result is laziness."

Listen to Kelly, eighteen-year-old freshman: "Yeah, kids want it handed to them," Kelly told me. "Kids see people like (Microsoft Chairman) Bill Gates who gets rich out of nowhere, they just kind of expect it, expect it to come out of the sky somewhere. It seems a lot of people get it that way, by not having to work. They just come into it real quick, like the lottery . . . . I have friends who expect to get good grades and they don't study. They get mad at the teachers and blame them if they don't. For example, once I had an English class and the instructor was very strict. Students would call him names and make him seem like he was the enemy. The system has often made it too easy to succeed."

And listen to twenty-year-old Marsha: "A lot of times students think, 'I'm paying this teacher, it (learning) should just happen. I think our entire society is like that right now. . . . Teachers pander to that mentality. I remember the first couple of months in my program, there was a test coming up. The teacher would go over every question on the test. . . . There were no surprises. As long as you could memorize you were fine. That's part of the consumer mentality—I paid for it so I shouldn't have to work for it."

So Long, Horatio, Hello, Forrest

As Marsha suggests, GenXers seem to understand implicitly what I've tried to illustrate throughout my discussion of education in postmodern America: their sense of entitlement as consumers of education or anything else wasn't something they just up and invented one day. They understand that their behavior is fundamentally no different than the ways most people exposed for very long to postmodernity have come to behave. Xers are simply younger and more thoroughly postmodern than somebody like, say, me, who as baby boomer, was filled with Huxley-like "hypnopaedia" of a different sort during my formative years. But as I suggested before, we're all postmodernists now in some fashion. We are skeptics, if not cynics, toward traditional sources of knowledge and authority; searchers for larger, more soulful meanings about the world than what scientific rationalism seems to provide; superconsumers of amusement or anything else the spectacle puts before our eyes. We are people who have seen it all, who want it all, but are up against a world that won't give it to us.

And so we are collectively mesmerized by the make-believe. An innocent, virtuous, IQ-challenged waif named Forrest Gump comes along, and he strikes an amazingly receptive cord among Americans. Many critics have suggested he represents the triumph of ignorance in our culture. There's surely enough willful vacuity in our midst to make that a valid interpretation. But I think Forrest Gump represents something much more basic. He's the guardian angel who floats into our lives through a movie screen. His presence strikes at the wishful hearts of a weary culture whose people have all but given up on the hopes and dreams of modernity. The rhetoric of modernity—trust in the struggle for progress, belief in science and reason, and a reliance on hard work—still fills up our heads. But people sense a hollowness in those ideals, that modernity hasn't lived up to their hopes. Living up to the ideals of modernity is such a struggle, and for what?

America willed Forrest Gump into being. As Forrest Gump's innocent image is mixed and morphed on screen amid the horrors we blame on modernity, such as Vietnam and racial strife, we're witnessing the birth of our new angel, of a new, postmodern hope. He is a reflection of the new Everyman we wish were possible in an overly complex, technological age. He is the antithesis of Horatio Alger, modernism's symbolic offering to the collective psyche. Wouldn't it be nice? Wouldn't it be nice if you could just simply *be*, however dumb to this world, and still have the fruits of its bounty? Wouldn't it be nice if Gump could just happen?

CHAPTER 14

Adapting to a Postmodern World

Of course, I'm not alone in many of my observations about declining standards, consumerism, entertainment, and anti-rational beliefs of the larger culture threatening higher education as one of the few remaining pillars of sober analysis, deep reflection, and belief in reason. In recent years there has been a notable backlash among some writers, intellectuals, academics, and others who in their many disparate ways have, in effect, mounted something of a counter-revolt against the influences of postmodernism in academia and elsewhere in our culture.

We see books attacking postmodern ways of thinking, such as philosopher James Harris's *Against Relativism,* an indictment of postmodernity's relativistic notions of truth and objective reality. At one point, Harris confides: "I have chosen to throw my lot with the remnants of Modernism, and this book represents something of a 'rear-guard action' for modernists who will hopefully gather their forces and mount some kind of counterattack in defense of reason and rationality against the onrushing tide of pernicious relativists." Similarly, we see books attacking anti-science stands within academic circles, such as Paul R. Gross's and Norman Levitt's *Higher Superstition: The Academic Left and Its Quarrels with Science.*

Or, there is the former *Time* culture critic William A. Henry's *In Defense of Elitism,* a manifesto for restoring such "elitist" notions as hard work and meritocracy in the larger culture. Regarding education, Henry writes: "There was a time, not so very long ago and still fondly remembered by most who lived through it, when schools taught discipline, self-denial, deference to one's betters, and other elitist values. Teachers had little time for encouraging students' self expression and consumerist self-assertion because it was understood that schools were preparation for life and that very few jobs indeed offered much scope for self expression or self-assertion. School was boot camp, not therapy."

We see organized movements of scientists and academics, essentially defending modernism's virtues against various manifestations of postmodernity, such as pseudo-science in the larger culture and multiculturalism in academia. Among these is the Committee for the Scientific Investigation of Claims of the Paranormal and its journal, *Skeptical Inquirer.* The group's very existence is to defend science from the science bashers and also to do a bit of Bigfoot and space-alien bashing itself. Similarly, there is the National Association of Scholars launched in 1987 and its journal *Academic Questions,* which target what essentially are postmodern influences in academia, such as political correctness and multiculturalism. In a May 1995 letter to prospective members, Steve Balch, NAS's president, says, "Though our colleges and universities still embody much that is exemplary, the last twenty years have witnessed the steady erosion, and sometimes the abandonment, of academic standards. Worse yet, the very concept of standards has come under attack."

We also see conservative writers like Gertrude Himmelfarb, a former history professor at City University of New York, who flicks her own spit wads at the academic left. In an October 1994 article in *Commentary,* Himmelfarb proposes, in essence, that educators need to restore the values of modernism to higher education. "Bored with trivia, with specious relevance, with a smorgasbord of courses, with the politicization of all subjects and the fragmentation of all disciplines," Himmelfarb writes, "professors and students might welcome a return to a serious, structured curriculum and to a university that is intellectual and educational, not a political or therapeutic, community."

I could go on listing the significant number of groups and individuals forming a "rear-guard action," as Harris would say, against the behaviors and values associated with postmodernity, both in education and in mainstream culture. Given my own experiences as a teacher, I wish these various writers and groups success with their efforts. I, too, am probably a modernist at heart, as I would suppose many people are who harbor certain nostalgic notions about days past. But something bothers me about modernism's advocates engaging in a rear-guard action against postmodernism, because doing so strikes me as utterly futile in the face of an overpowering cultural transformation that shows few signs of petering out. The institutions of modernity are rapidly withering in their influence, while the forces of popular culture and power appear to be staging an irrevocable revolution of Western post-industrial societies.

I'd say those longing for the good old days of modernity might have a chance of success but for one minor detail: technology. Rapid advances in the technology of communication now allow anybody with access to a $995 computer and a $100 modem (at current prices) to literally become an author/publisher by creating one's own World Wide Web page. This means that the former gatekeepers of knowledge and authority have become just more insignificant voices trying to be heard in the din of information and entertainment. Nowadays, the White House can hardly get a press conference covered on prime-time TV. The U.S. government's Home Page on the Web is just one of thousands competing for the world's attention. For a government official to get much attention nowadays, he's got to talk the talk—say, go on MTV and play the sax.

In dealing with the postmodern world, it would seem that educators have three obvious choices: First, they could continue to cave in to popular culture and consumerism, spoon-feeding a post-modern nation's insatiable demand for mediocrity. That's a clearly unwholesome choice that will do nobody any good in the long run. Or, educators could hunker down and attempt to "re-modernize" higher education, whatever the cost. That's also a strategy that seems doomed to failure. The postmodern age has arrived in pervasive and powerful ways, and modernists probably won't accomplish much engaging in knee-jerk, neo-conservative backlash, trying to preserve the past at any cost.

It seems to me that, when you're swimming against the postmodern tide, good old American pragmatism is the only real choice. Perhaps modernists need to confront the reality of postmodernity and explicitly account for it in their educational reforms. Higher education could abandon certain features of modernity that no longer work, while drawing firm lines in the sand on academic standards. And, colleges and universities should be encouraged to adopt certain, judiciously chosen guises of postmodernism. Here, educators might take a lesson of sorts from Madison Avenue. It would be like Coca-Cola talking Generation X's talk by packaging pop in the form of a product it calls OK (actually a real product Coke test-marketed with the reassuring slogan, "Things are going to be OK"), and then instead of filling the bottle with heaps of high fructose corn syrup and other gunk, you actually put something good for people in the bottle.

Before elaborating on these points, I'll say again what I've maintained throughout this book: I'm in no sense an educational policy expert nor a postmodern scholar. I'm a journalist who adventured into the world of teaching, and I'm reporting my experiences and my observations of that subculture, while trying to place them into the context of the larger society. Based on my experience, might I modestly suggest that it's time for higher education to clearly and explicitly acknowledge that many of the problems of higher education in the 1990s are rooted in the culture's break from modernism, to recognize that education as we've known it might no longer be relevant for a postmodern age.

Adopting Postmodern Guises

It's time, perhaps, to finally acknowledge that the standard teaching and classroom structures of most colleges and universities reflect modernistic power arrangements between institutional authorities and people—structures of power that have not survived in the larger culture. The professor as the classroom monarch, playing both the boss and provider of knowledge and wisdom to roomfuls of passive, bored consumers seems at times a frustrating, unworkable, and quaint remnant of a bygone era. Trying to retain modernistic classroom arrangements and forms of authority in the face of the postmodern mind-set produces the ugly spectacle of teachers adopting a performance and entertainment mode of teaching. This set-up might "work"—in the sense that students are entertained—for a few gifted, performance-oriented teachers. But such an arrangement doesn't work for most professors who want to teach college because of a love for their fields, not because they enjoy contorting themselves into Jim Carrey look-alikes.

Americans love technological fixes, but technology alone won't improve educational standards in the postmodern age. Educators need to consider completely rethinking the idea of the "classroom," and even whether the classroom as we know it should continue to exist. In the jargon of postmodernity, a classroom is little more than a cultural "text" whose content and meaning is created both by teachers and students. Postmodern students enter higher education from a cultural climate in which authorities are no longer permitted to impose meaning from on-high about the world. Citizens, consumers, voters, and the students of postmodernity shape their own meanings; they become "authors" of meaning in their own right. David Harvey, a geographer at Oxford University, says that in a postmodern environment, "the cultural producer merely creates raw materials (fragments and elements), leaving it open to consumers to recombine those elements in any way they wish. The effect is to break (deconstruct) the power of the author to impose meanings or offer a continuous narrative."

What this sort of analysis means exactly for the shape of the "classroom" and the power relations between teachers and students is not clear. But one can imagine some possible forms that might be encouraged. For example, a postmodern classroom might be simply a space for teams of students to work with raw materials of learning, provided by anything from a teacher to a CD-ROM, in order to create something new and apply their knowledge. It's sort of a "lab," but traditional usage of that term implies a place for interaction quite apart from the more "important" place where teaching and lecturing occur. This new kind of space for interaction, creation, and applied knowledge might be encouraged to displace the lecture room as the dominant way that the classroom is organized. People reared in a postmodern environment—and I've found this applies especially to Generation X—often could not care less about abstract, theoretical knowledge or knowing for the sake of knowing. Being able to *do* something with knowledge in a way that connects to their past experience or might relate to some future job—that tends to ring the intellectual bells of many Xers. As Jean-François Lyotard, the French postmodernist thinker, phrased the point, "The question (overt or implied) now asked by the professional student, the State, or institutions of higher education is no longer 'Is it true?' but 'What use is it?'"

As I've suggested, a polyglot of new electronic sources of information, served to one's desk at Net speed, are reinforcing the postmodern revolt against prior forms of knowledge and institutional authority. Colleges, universities, and the know-it-all professor now have competition in the knowledge business: electronic data bases and multimedia "do" knowledge faster, to far more people, and in many cases, perhaps better than most professors.

This casts a new light on how colleges and universities might use new technologies. They can install lots of new gadgets. But if educators were to examine their proposed improvements for higher education through the lens of postmodernity, they would easily see that some kinds of technological fixes don't make a lot of sense. Among these would include computerized audio-visual equipment that helps professors make more glitzy presentations. I'll get to the professor's role in postmodern education in a bit, but I would suggest here, for the reasons I've already mentioned, that doing more lecturing and presenting is the antithesis of what professors ought to be doing in the postmodern age.

As an example of how modernists seem bent on maintaining their paradigms in a changed world, consider what was called the "Technology Proposal," a summary of plans to upgrade the technology in the classrooms at the college where I taught. The wish list included multimedia *presentation* systems, CD-ROM's for *presentations,* and audio-visual display systems for—you guessed it—more presentations. At one small faculty meeting to review the proposals, it became clear what basic belief systems were imbedded in the plan. Technologists and administrators at the college were blindly adhering to the habits of modernism even when trying to think futuristically. Adhering to modernity's customary arrangements of authority and power, the institution was placing technology into the hands of the faculty for transmitting knowledge to passive audiences of students. A postmodern approach, on the other hand, would explicitly acknowledge that the culture's basic concepts of knowledge and authority have been irrevocably changed. Instead of teachers being like shop floor managers at the head of the class, and commanding the attention of a roomful of passive listeners, the postmodern classroom might be splintered into technology-based modules for students to create their own multimedia presentations, individually or in teams.

One teacher at that meeting, commenting on the belief systems inherent in the technology proposal, remarked to the small gathering of instructors, "We're all afraid of becoming irrelevant."

His concern was a valid one. The culture's turn toward postmodernism has made teaching and learning as we know it in many respects irrelevant and ineffective. And those steeped in the ways of modernity are fighting to retain control. Which reminds us that modernity is not yet dead, by any means. Although postmodern influences have irrevocably altered large segments of higher education, the habits of modernity that were reflected in that technology proposal remain the dominant ideology and practice at most colleges and universities. I'm not saying that's necessarily bad, but such habits do possibly blind them to seeing better routes.

Postmodernity aside, economics alone would suggest that professors are too expensive (and too talented in other ways) to waste their time imparting information that is more cheaply and more effectively transmitted with machines, particularly multimedia presentations. This is a point that corporations, such as Hewlett-Packard, Xerox, Apple, Chrysler, and Ford have already discovered in their own training programs, and they now envision paring actual classroom instruction down to almost nothing. Corporate studies indicate that multimedia technologies slash learning time and costs by half; and that it boosts by 80 percent the ability of employees to retain information. Companies like Hewlett-Packard and Apple have eliminated anywhere from 75 percent to 90 percent of their classroom training. "We aim to get (classroom instruction) down to zero as soon as the technology is ready," says Lucy Carter, a training instructor at Apple.

Beyond the obvious economic advantages of such technologies, educators probably should accelerate the pace at which students are given direct access to these new tools. The postmodern use of electronic information is not simply for imparting information, but so students can apply, interact, and create—in short, to take direct control of their own learning, without the intermediary of the institution or the professor.

To be sure, some individual institutions and professors and their students are already putting these insights into practice, but evidence suggests that most of the rest of the students and teachers get left out, a result of the inertia of tradition and the woefully inadequate training of educators in using new methods. Still, at Trinity University in San Antonio, Texas, for instance, biology professor Robert V. Blystone has students create multimedia "term papers," an assignment which seem to excite students about learning. "All of a sudden, a term paper is not some sort of report," he says. "It represents something they've created." And at Hamline University, English teacher Richard Smyth requires students to publish stories on the Internet's World Wide Web.

Both the examples above illustrate what I mean by suggesting that educators should consider adopting certain "guises of postmodernism." While publishing a piece on the Web says nothing about the quality of the work, doing so is a brave, postmodernist act, suggesting that the student's work has some connection to the outside world and a meaning beyond the abstractions of the classroom. And, unfortunately, most students—unless they plan to be writers—don't see the ability to write a term paper as something they'll ever use in the real world. But in the age of amusement and the spectacular, they do see the ability to create a multimedia project as somehow useful. To educators, I say, go with it, and in time there will be clear standards by which to judge good multimedia from bad multimedia.

Of course, in the extreme case, a postmodern analysis of knowledge and institutional authority would suggest that, for an increasing number of students, classrooms as physical spaces are no longer necessary nor even desirable in higher learning. Indeed, any discussion in any forum nowadays about technology and education will eventually end up on the topic of so-called "distance education" or the "virtual campus," which means that people can, in essence, attend school from their home computers. It's hard to say where this impulse will lead, but already an estimated 25,000 students are pursuing degrees in this manner, according to the National Distance Learning Center.

Linda Harasim of Simon Fraser University in British Columbia, who has been working on a $1 million project to create a virtual campus, says: "Online education is evaporating all the old boundaries, the things that kept people apart." Somewhat gushing about the possibilities of such technology, she adds: "The old models came from 19th Century technology and they're based on transmission models. One-to-many broadcast: the TV, the radio, the newspaper, the lecture! New computer networking technology requires and enables a whole new way of teaching and learning. For the first time in human history we can have many-to-many communication across time and across space."

And so, tele-commuting to college would seem to be one postmodern guise that educators ought to consider placing on the front burner of their new technology efforts. For the many students who nowadays have jobs that demand twenty hours to thirty hours a week or more of their time, and for students who view attending class as a monumental waste of effort, attending college with a Mac and a modem would seem a promising alternative. And, educators could get rid of the debilitating influence of bored and unmotivated students by removing the opportunity for boredom. Such students could be passive and unmotivated on their own time, in their own homes, without wasting the time and effort of their professors and their more motivated peers.

What, then, is the role of the professor in postmodern education and in the application of these new technologies that reinforce postmodern arrangements? As I've already suggested, there would seem to be little place for the traditional role of professor as the disseminator of information when a student can get it more quickly and perhaps better with the punch of a button on a CD-ROM drive. Information technology has turned knowledge into a mass-produced commodity, accessible to all, and conceivably allows anybody to become an expert in virtually any subject. Lyotard himself predicted the demise of teaching as we've known it when he wrote that postmodernity's delegitimation of authorities and its equating knowledge with what one can do rather than what one knows "are sounding the death knell of the age of the Professor: a professor is no more competent than memory bank networks in transmitting established knowledge," says Lyotard.

To be sure, traditional technologies such as books and encyclopedias might have allowed people to educate themselves without the benefit of teachers. But doing so was probably relatively inefficient compared to what is now possible. The new information technologies seem to represent a quantum change from the past because of the immediacy and ease with which they allow so many people at once to learn. In the past, it was probably cheaper and easier for students to gather general, summarized knowledge from a professor than from a library full of books; teachers acted as gatekeepers to the storehouse of knowledge in their fields of expertise and filtered the relevant from the irrelevant for their fledglings. But one wonders whether the professor as the principle gatekeeper to knowledge is any longer of significant value. It is now probably cheaper and easier for one to go directly to the knowledge well itself. Compared to the professor as gatekeeper, new technologies such as multimedia, on-line databases, CD-ROMs, and the World Wide Web make knowledge simultaneously and immediately accessible to far more people. Indeed, instead of what now seem to be quaint sounding words such as "readers" and "writers." we now call those who gather computerized information mere "users," and those who supply it "content providers." This change in the language seems indicative of the degree to which new technologies have "commodified" knowledge.

But when knowledge becomes a commodity the only interesting game in town then becomes what new things one can dream up to do with that knowledge. It follows that using one's imagination *while* working on one's skills then become the twin philosophical pillars of the postmodern educational enterprise. And there you have it: at last, the marriage of praxis and theory, which I imagine many educators would view as educational nirvana. In a postmodern sense, any given course would be one in learning how to do something, and at the same time you'd be thinking about what you're doing, wondering why you're doing it, and imagining new ways of doing it.

Instead of a transmitter of knowledge, the postmodern teacher in higher education is more akin to an expert consultant, who has two primary roles: (1) guiding students in the use of information-gathering tools, i.e., helping them learn how to learn; and (2) helping students imagine new ways of looking at knowledge, while prodding them to appreciate subtle complexities about a discipline not obtainable from machines and databases. These will be the only real benefits—and they are often intangible—that teachers can add to an educational enterprise in which all information is equally accessible. Thus, quite unlike the commonly heard adage nowadays that "knowledge is power," it would seem that, in the postmodern epoch, it would be more accurate to say, "imagination is power."

Says Lyotard: "It is possible to perceive the world of postmodern knowledge as governed by a game of perfect information, in the sense that the data is in principle accessible to any expert: there is no scientific secret. Given equal competence (no longer in the acquisition of knowledge, but in its production), what extra performativity depends on in the final analysis is 'imagination,' which allows one to either make a new move or to change the rules of the game."

In the end, the reality of our postmodern condition means that the educational establishment needs to understand and fully articulate to itself and to the public that it is trying to teach people of a new, postmodern sort. Modernists might not fully like it or want to, but recognizing postmodern realities might provide them with powerful tools for creating pragmatic, effective policies and reforms. Otherwise, we persist in reproducing an education system that doesn't work for an increasingly dominant segment of the population.

Drawing Lines in the Sand

But while pragmatism would suggest that higher education needs to adopt certain features of postmodernity in order to simply survive the onslaught of hyperconsumerism and amusement in the dominant culture, the pivotal question, as posed by the prominent German thinker Jürgen Habermas, is whether Western societies and its institutions should simply "abandon the project of modernity" and be done with it.

But if education, and higher education in particular, is to have any meaning in our culture, we should vigorously say no to Habermas's rhetorical question. The suggestions I outlined above are necessary but hardly sufficient steps for stemming the rising mediocrity in higher education. From my vantage point, many of the problems of upholding standards in higher education stem from an unwillingness of student-consumers themselves to do what it takes to succeed at real, college-level work, because they've grown up viewing the world as a place to consume and to be entertained. Sure, educators should first make the sorts of postmodern adaptations I suggested above. But I would also suggest that educators need to simply refuse to cave in to postmodernity when it comes to academic standards and meaningful criteria for success. If our society wants to defend higher education as a worthwhile enterprise, then it would seem that policymakers need to attack the notions of entitlement and consumerism which are threatening to destroy the very notion of "higher" education.

Grade inflation is an obvious, first place to attack the cancer of consumerism and entitlement. And the fact is, educators know how to fight grade inflation, but often they lack the will power, so intimidated have they become in the face of popular culture and consumer power. Some obvious steps that colleges could take immediately to once again make grades actually mean what they purport to mean include:

- Publishing a student's course grades along with the class averages and class sizes in grade transcripts. This simple step alone would allow anybody looking at a transcript, including

employers or graduate and professional schools, to determine if a student's work was truly outstanding or simply ordinary. Dartmouth College announced just such a new disclo-
sure policy in 1995, and soon discovered that professors
were already being more stingy with A's and B's.

- Placing reasonable restrictions on the last date at which students can withdraw from a class without the withdrawal being
  indicated on a transcript. At many colleges, students are allowed to bail out of a class at the last minute if they're not getting a good grade. At public colleges and universities, this
  amounts to a monumental waste of taxpayers' money, because
  these student "grade shoppers" consume significant amounts
  of instruction and grading time before they check out.

- Stipulating a meaningful grade distribution for all courses on
  campus. For example, this might mean a policy mandating
  that class averages should be a C or B– and that no more than
  10 percent of a class can receive an A. Such a policy is not
  uncommon at law schools. A friend who attended one law
  school in the West told me that the institution stipulated
  grading curves for all core classes and for sections of upper-
  division courses taught by several instructors. My friend was
  delighted by the arrangement because his good grades will
  actually mean something to future employers.

In addition to these reforms that restore some rigor to grading
systems, educators might review procedures they use for granting
tenure to professors. I'm referring especially to how institutions use
student evaluations when deciding whether a faculty member is
granted tenure. To be sure, feedback from students is important to
consider, but I fear that in this epoch of hyperconsumerism, placing
significant weight on student evaluations produces the unwholesome incentive in all-too-human teachers to give out lots of good
grades in order make students happy customers. Somehow, institutions need to break apart the unholy trinity among faculty, students,
and administrators, in which all seemingly benefit by handing out
good grades: Professor Smith gets tenure; Marcy gets into grad
school; and the dean avoids the low-enrollment blues.

Indeed, any reforms that break the hyperconsumer mentality of
students should be encouraged. For instance, grade shopping, in
which students literally shop around a campus or even a metropoli-

tan area, looking for easy-grading instructors, is not uncommon. Institutions could discourage grade shopping by not publishing in course schedules which teachers are scheduled for multiple sections of classes.

Yet another tactic to deal with grade inflation is to officially de-emphasize the significance of grades. After all, almost everyone knows that grades no longer mean much, realistically, and yet grades still have an enormous amount of official legitimacy. Short of doing away with grading altogether, educators could, de facto, place relatively less importance on grades by elevating the stature of *ability*. This means establishing rigorous performance criteria for completing any course and for graduation. Recognizing that institutions are graduating people who aren't competent in a wide range of abilities, some leading educators and path-breaking institutions are turning to performance assessment as a way to restore credibility to their enterprises. One highly regarded proponent of this approach is Alverno College, a small private institution in Milwaukee, Wisconsin, which launched its performance assessment efforts in the early 1970s. Alverno faculty believed that students should actually be able to do something with their abstract knowledge. Thus, the entire college curriculum is set up to measure student competence on such abilities as communication, analysis, problem solving, decision making, social interaction, and citizenship. Is such a program one that works for just an elite population of students? Evidence suggests that's not the case. Alverno says that more than half of its students are the first in their families to attend college; that a staggering 81 percent of its incoming minority students returned to school after their first year (as against an 86 percent return rate for all Alverno's students); and that fully 90 percent of its graduates have obtained jobs they were trained for.

But besides attacking grade inflation and the hyperconsumer mentality that feeds it, policymakers might also consider that it's probably time to address Americans' sense of entitlement to higher education. As I discussed previously, the democratization of American higher education has worked well in terms of tearing down barriers to college for the poor and disadvantaged. But maybe we've made it too easy when anybody who is passed out of an American high school with a D average can get into virtually any community college in the country. With access to college guaranteed with even poor achievement in high school, there is little incentive for many high school students to excel or to even care about academics. Too many young people get passed through the public schools without any sense of individual responsibility for their success, figuring that the system will take care of them regardless of their motivation and effort. And, as I've discussed at length, colleges and universities often end up adapting to the poor habits of students, rather than students adapting to the demands of the institutions. It seems that weary taxpayers have grown accustomed to such a waste of resources in public high schools. But I doubt that many taxpayers, if they were to see it first-hand, would tolerate subsidizing the flight from responsibility that occurs daily in many so-called college classrooms.

Maybe it's finally time to place at least some minimal restrictions on access to higher education. Public community colleges should perhaps require applicants to have at least a C average in high school—which in the current environment is almost impossible *not* to achieve. Or, if public schools eventually do adopt more ability-based evaluation systems instead of grades, then community colleges might consider admitting only students who have demonstrated minimal competency in high school. Perhaps more institutions, inundated with people who need remedial education, should follow the lead of the City University of New York, which has limited to just the freshman year the length of time a student can remain enrolled in pre-college, basic education courses. Again, if we're serious about maintaining high quality colleges and universities, even at "A-Mart" College, then high school teachers, administrators, parents, and students—especially students—need to get the message that going to college might not be possible if you do next to nothing to contribute to your own success.

In the same spirit, policymakers might need to bite the bullet and concede that the current system of high school graduation standards being defined by individual states and localities doesn't work. The nation's largest teachers union, the American Federation of Teachers, in July of 1995 finally acknowledged as much: The union came out in favor of a national competency exam for high school graduation, following the model of many European countries. But predictably in the current political climate of devolution of power from federal authorities to the states, Labor Secretary Robert B. Reich was less than enthralled with the proposal.

But it would be unconscionable for American society to place tougher restrictions on access to higher education without also joining the rest of the industrialized world and create a comprehensive, national system of vocational and technical education. It's probable that enormous numbers of American students wind up trying to pursue bachelor's degrees for no other reason than there are too few other options. By and large, Americans are inflicted with ideological blinders toward the validity of technical and vocational credentials, for the sake of the American ideal of "a college education." As a result, the pressing needs of scores of young students are ignored in many educational reform efforts.

Dale Parnell of Oregon State University, who has written widely and convincingly about this dilemma, says most educational reformers are professional educators who want the rest of the world to look like the world they came from and ignore the "neglected majority." Reformers "ignore the fact that three out of four students in the U.S. educational system are unlikely to ever earn a four year college baccalaureate degree," Parnell says. He adds that policymakers need to redefine notions of excellence in education to revolve not just around university education, but first-rate technical and vocational studies as well.

Meanwhile, our European counterparts are far more aggressive and systematic than the United States with vocational training for those not pursuing university degrees. In a Brookings Institution study comparing the American system of vocational education with those of Germany, Sweden, Great Britain, and France, William Nothdurft concluded that the United States performed admirably—at experimental programs and demonstration projects. As for the universally recognized, comprehensive features that make the vocational systems of European countries work so well, the United States comes up far short. Unlike Europe, Nothdurft says, American policymakers talk a good game about work force competence and yet fail to enact "coherent, universally available action programs capable of ensuring that high school graduates are ready, willing, and able to enter and succeed in the working world."

In addition to attacking consumerism and entitlement in higher education through systemic reforms, there are the trenches to also consider, the classrooms in which students and teachers interact each day. Already, increasingly frustrated with changing student attitudes about hard work, study habits, and individual responsibility, scores of colleges and universities are asking—and in some cases demanding—that new students take college orientation courses, variously dubbed, College 101, the Freshman Experience, and so on. Such courses have had some success in nudging up retention and graduation rates. But I think they could be improved by also turning them into a forum for some frank dialogue between students and teachers about Generation X, about modernism versus post-modernism, consumerism and entitlement, and about what students and teachers want from higher education compared to what they get.

For example, Oregon State University hints at this sort of frank communication with students in a pamphlet given to all newcomers. The university's pamphlet advises, among other things, that: *"There is nothing wrong with a 'C' grade if that is all you can achieve in a given course. Why some students consider 'C's' despicable is beyond reason."* The pamphlet also says: *"The best way to impress your instructors and peers is to complete your academic work without fanfare or loud-mouth bragging. You will not be taken seriously if all you can do is talk a good story and show little productive effort. . . . If you want to beat the system: study."*

In short, colleges and universities need to add a pinch of postmodern salt to their freshman orientation programs—inspired no doubt by the modernistic desire to uphold academic standards. Besides teaching useful skills for adapting to college life, educators need also to turn their College 101 into a course in *abstract thinking,* into a course that also lets the imagination run.

◢   ◢   ◢

Now that I'm near the close of this chapter and to the end of my report about education in postmodern America, I can't finish without also making a final plea to the people who run higher education. I'm thinking now about one student I encountered in my journey into teaching named Andie.

One day, in a writing class I was teaching, we had broken up into small groups, and with about five minutes before the end of class, I asked one young Xer a question about an article we were discussing. He answered that he'd already put his things away; he didn't budge an inch to get them back. In other words, he wasn't going to think another second about this class. It had been a bad week for me. At that point, I just picked up my things and left the room, disgusted.

A few minutes later, Andie stepped into my office. She was a good student, constantly picking my brain for information and feedback on her work, and we had developed some rapport with each other. It was apparent that she'd come to express her sympathy toward me about what had just happened in class. "That really got me," she said, referring to the guy who had put his stuff away and turned off his brain.

Apparently, my anger and frustration with teaching were evident, because she asked me some personal, penetrating questions, like why I had left newspapers, why I had gone into teaching, and was I going to keep teaching. She talked about her own frustrations with many of her fellow students, who she said shopped around for "nice and easy" teachers, and she expressed her disdain for the system that encouraged teachers to be that way, afraid to demand excellence from their students in the prevailing climate of entitlement, litigation, and victimization.

"How are you going to live your life being angry and losing your interest in teaching?" she asked me. I told her, "You develop a crust, so nobody can penetrate you with those vacant looks, so students can't hurt you any more with indifference." Then she said something quite startling, and which I had not entertained as being possible. "One of these days, a truly interested student will come up to you and you will no longer be able to recognize it, because you'll be just as dead as your students," she told me. "That vacant look will come over you, too. It's contagious."

A few days later, Andie wrote me a letter. She told me how she didn't learn much from the actual class ("due to the fact that the class consists of a bunch of morons") but that she did learn a lot from our discussions in my office, which "have given me incentive to analyze, to look at both sides of the coin and, much to my surprise, to show a slight interest in research. . . . I want you to know that I appreciate the extra time you've spent with me and that I did learn a lot from you," she said.

Then, Andie wrote, "Please don't give up. Give the few of us who want to learn a chance."

That was Andie's plea to me, which I now pass along to the people who care about the future of higher education. Let's create a system that encourages people like Andie at least as much as the ones who don't give a damn. Let's create an environment that doesn't make teachers indifferent because they're overwhelmed by a sea of indifference. And for the wonderful, special, lovely people who *want* to learn, let's bend over backward and show them how.

Epilogue

It has now been nearly four years since I quit my newspaper job and began my journey into teaching. I am still teaching at The College, about the same subjects, and in many respects, to the same students—although the individuals whom I've described in these pages have long since left The College.

To be sure, some things did change. One aspect of teaching in particular changed—and for the better. After I became tenured, the pressure on me to perform—and I do mean perform in the most pejorative sense—diminished dramatically. I believe that is because I was no longer required to take student evaluations each term, and because no official decisions were based on evaluations I did take. Doing evaluations was completely up to me. Once, a few semesters ago, just out of curiosity, I did do student evaluations. I regretted it. From what I could tell through casual observation, my students seemed satisfied with my teaching, and they did seem to be learning. Still, some students wrote the same stinging remarks that hurt me to the bone. It was the same old story: No matter how well my classes seemed to be going, always lurking beneath the surface were some students' complaints that neither I nor what I taught was entertaining enough for them.

With the official pressure diminished, I did tone down the aim-to-please act of my Sandbox Experiment. I wasn't quite so accommodating to students' every whim, knowing they no longer had as much leverage over me with their stinging comments on evaluation forms. But I also knew that this pleasant state of affairs was only temporary. Post-tenure evaluation would be coming eventually, and if I wanted to remain at The College, I would have to keep my student customers satisfied.

Indeed, it was curious to me that I had, more or less, permanently changed from the early days of my journey when I was determined to uphold standards at almost any cost. I noticed that my grading policies had permanently adapted to my surroundings, and that I was still giving mostly A's and B's, just like all the other instructors. Doing otherwise was a battle I was not prepared to fight—the odds were simply stacked against me or any other instructor who might try.

Events subsequent to those I've described in my story underscored my sense that already low standards at The College were at risk of being de-valued further. The "Save Our Standards" Committee, the cadre of instructors who tried to fight to uphold collegiate standards, finally disbanded for good, its members demoralized. In its place were instituted what seemed to many of us expedient efforts, sanctioned by the administration, to attract more student consumers to The College. Bandied about were suggestions to toss out course prerequisites, placement testing, and anything else deemed to be barriers to more enrollment.

Looking back, there was a time at the beginning of my journey, fresh from the non-academic world, when I would have been far less sympathetic to students in this unfortunate milieu. I would have reasoned that they got what they deserved, by essentially demanding mediocrity. But these days I'm more sympathetic to them. I now believe the students are the real victims of this systematic failure of the entitlement mindset.

From time to time, I see students at my college wearing a Harvard or Yale sweatshirt, and the bitter irony of such an unconscious act saddens me. While Harvard or Yale students might also see academic standards slipping and A's and B's relatively easy to get, they'll do just fine; mushy standards surely won't significantly affect their prospects in life or in the workplace. But for ordinary students at the "A-Mart" colleges of the country, solid standards and real learning are all they've got. The Harvard name on the sweatshirt won't help them.

And yet, my students are quite unconscious of this irony, gladly will-ing to display the emblem of an exclusive club they'll most likely never be admitted to.

I suppose it would be possible for a truly good teacher to get that message across to students. But I don't see much evidence that such a message would be well received by students, parents, or adminis-trators at such institutions. Perhaps this state of affairs is endemic to what is supposed to be a class-neutral, meritocratic society, where anybody can be anything regardless of your parents' income bracket or where you went to school.

In any case, I'm afraid that I am not that inspiring teacher. I am certainly not the kind of teacher you'll see portrayed in movies like *Dangerous Minds* or some other uplifting Hollywood production. My journey into teaching is nearing its end. It's perhaps time for me to move on, and leave teaching to the more gifted among us.

But I am not unchanged by or regretful of my experience as a teacher. My journey has exposed me to the critical challenges educa-tion faces as our society approaches the millennium. I want to con-tinue to write about education and the role it will, I hope, play in a society that strives to remain free and democratic.

Peter Sacks
San Miguel de Allende, Mexico, 1996

Notes

PART ONE

Chapter 9

Page

88   **But while I felt shameless, I had to remind myself that
. . . :** From "In a Change of Policy, and Heart, Colleges Join
Against Inflated Grades," *New York Times,* July 4, 1995, p. 10.

PART TWO

Chapter 10

109   **A movie about a good natured idiot . . . :** From *New York
Times,* "Forrest Gump's Creator Isn't Supid," May 28, 1995, p. E2.

109   **In a *Time* magazine poll . . . :** From "Angels Among Us," *Time,*
Dec. 27, 1993.

111   **I could be wrong . . . :** From "In the Region: Westchester;
Yorktowns's Stalled Projects Now Selling," *New York Times,* Dec.
6., 1992.

112   **"And the terrain is contested precisely because . . . ":** Quoted in Barry Smart, *Postmodernity* (New York and London: Routledge, 1993), p. 19. Originally from "Mapping the Postmodern," *New German Critique,* p. 33.

112   **In 1992, the Czechoslovakian President . . . :** From Vaclav Havel, "The End of the Modern Era," *New York Times,* March 1, 1992, Section 4, p. 15.

114   **Historians Will and Ariel Durant describe the kind of backward world . . . :** From Will & Ariel Durant, *The Age of Voltaire (New York:* MJF Books, 1965), p. 493.

114   **" . . . the edifice (of superstition) is sapped to its foundations . . . ":** Quoted in Will & Ariel Durant, *The Age of Voltaire,* p. 785.

114   **Voltaire also declared the triumph of reason . . . :** Quoted in Will & Ariel Durant, *The Age of Voltaire,* p. 785.

114   **From the Age of Enlightenment onward, modernity became synonymous . . . :** Quoted in Barry Smart, *Modern Conditions, Postmodern Controversies* (London and New York: Routledge, 1992), p. 148. Originally from Z. Bauman, *Legislators and Interpreters: On Modernity, Post-modernity and Intellectuals* (Cambridge: Polity Press, 1987).

115   **Indeed, modernism has become the "focus of increasing critical reflection . . . ":** From Barry Smart, *Postmodernity,* Routledge, p. 91.

115   **David Harvey, an Oxford geographer . . . :** From David Harvey, "The Condition of Postmodernity," *The Post-Modern Reader,* ed. Charles Jencks (London: Academy Editions, 1992), p. 299. Originally appeared in *The Condition of Postmodernity* (Cambridge, Mass., and Oxford: Basil Blackwell Inc., 1989).

115   **Paolo Portoghesi, a professor of architecture in Rome . . . :** From Paolo Portoghesi, "What is the Postmodern?" *The Post-Modern Reader,* ed. Charles Jencks, p. 208. Originally from *Postmodern, The Architecture of the Postindustrial Society* (New York: Rizzoli, 1983).

115 **While stopping short . . . :** From Andreas Huyssen, "Mapping the Postmodern," *The Post-Modern Reader,* ed. Charles Jencks, p. 42. Originally from *After the Great Divide* (London: Macmillan, 1984).

116 **"Of all the terms bandied about . . . :** From Linda Hutcheon, "Theorizing the Postmodern: Towards a Poetics," *The Post-Modern Reader,* ed. Charles Jencks, p. 76. Originally from *A Poetics of Postmodernism, History, Theory, Fiction* (New York: Routledge, 1988).

116 **Robin Usher and Richard Edwards suggest that . . . :** From Robin Usher and Richard Edwards, *Postmodernism and Education* (London and New York: Routledge, 1994), p. 7.

116 **"What we can say positively . . . :** Usher and Edwards, *Postmodernism and Education*, p. 7.

118 **"Here we are now/Entertain us," :** From "Smells Like Teen Spirit," on *Nevermind,* by Kurt Cobain and Nirvana, recorded 1991 by DGC Records, Los Angeles.

120 **Charles Jencks, an architectural scholar . . . :** From "The Post-Modern Agenda," *The Post-Modern Reader,* ed. Charles Jencks, p. 12. Originally from "The Values of Post-Modernism," *Post-Modernism: The New Classicism in Art and Architecture* (London: Academy Editions, 1987).

120 **Postmodern scholar Z. Bauman adds that postmodernity is . . . :** Quoted in Barry Smart, *Postmodernity* (New York and London: Routledge, 1993), p. 101. Originally from Z. Bauman, *Modernity and Ambivalence* (Cambridge: Polity Press, 1991), p. 272.

120 **"Electicism is the degree zero . . . :** From Jean-François Lyotard, "Answering the Question: What is Postmodernism," *The Post-Modern Reader,* ed. Charles Jencks, p. 145. Originally from "Answering the Question: What is Postmodernism?" trans. Regis Durand, from *Innovation/Renovation: New Perspectives on the Humanities,* ed. Ihab Hassan (Madison: University of Wisconsin Press, 1983).

Chapter 11

124   **But as Erich Fromm suggested in the afterword to the book, Orwell . . . :** From *1984,* George Orwell, Afterword by Erich Fromm (New York: Penguin Books USA, 1984).

125   **"We have for millennia accepted the distinction between fact and fiction . . . :** From Hilary Lawson, *Reflexivity: The postmodern predicament* (La Salle, Ill.: Open Court Publishing Co., 1985), p. 10.

125   **Susan Haack, a professor of philosophy at the University of Miami . . . :** From Susan Haack, "Puzzling Out Science," *Academic Questions,* Spring 1995, pp. 20–31.

125   **In the face of this onslaught, one defender of scientific method . . . :** From James F. Harris, *Against Relativism: A Philosophical Defense of Method* (La Salle, Ill.: Open Court Publishing Co., 1992.), p. 17.

126   **According to Goodman, no theory or view of the world is uniquely true . . . :** Quoted in Harris, *Against Relativism: A Philosophical Defense of Method,* p. 66. Originally from Nelson Goodman, "The Way the World Is," in *Problems and Projects,* (Indianapolis: Bobbs-Merrill, 1972), p. 30.

128   **The reporter talked to a couple of construction workers . . . :** From *New York Times,* "Other Party to the Contract Isn't Impressed," April 12, 1995, A1.

128   **"It's this ominous mix of the paranormal and the paranoid . . . ":** From "Paranormal and Paranoia Intermingle on Fox TV's 'X-Files', *Skeptical Inquirer,* March/April 1995, p. 18.

128   **Consider a full-page advertisement in the *New York Times* . . . :** From "WHAT THE AIRLINES WON'T TELL YOU," April 2, 1995 advertisement in *New York Times,* E16.

129   **"Although formally independent . . . ":** From Mark Hertsgaard, *On Bended Knee: The Press and the Reagan Presidency* (New York: Farrar Straus Giroux, 1988), p. 76.

130   **"Is the distinction between fact and fiction . . . ":** From *Chronicle of Higher Education,* Nov. 30, 1994, B30.

130 **"Rationality, in general, has been out of fashion . . . ":** From Wendy Kaminer, *It's All the Rage: Crime and Culture* (Reading, Mass.: Addison-Wesley Publishing, 1995), p. 9.

131 **A *Time* magazine survey that shows almost seven in every ten American . . . :** From "Angels Among Us," *Time,* Dec. 27, 1993.

132 **Freeman told the *New York Times* . . . :** Quoted in "Standing up For a Growing Belief in Angels, *New York Times,* Sept. 25, 1994.

132 **Compare that to Havel's words: . . . :** From Vaclav Havel, "The End of the Modern Era," *New York Times,* March 1, 1992.

133 **Not according to Chip Berlet . . . :** Quoted in "Fearing Conspiracy, Some Are Prompted to Answer a Call to Arms," *New York Times,* Nov. 14, 1994, A1.

134 **As Michael Kelly of the *New Yorker* has written . . . :** From Michael Kelly, "The Road to Paranoia, *New Yorker,* June 19, 1995, p. 63.

138 **According to one representative study of college students . . . :** From Raymond Eve and Francis Harrold, "Differential Etiology of Pseudoscientific Beliefs: Why Creationists Don't Go to Psychic Fairs," Paper presented to the American Association for the Advancement of Science Annual Meeting, Atlanta, 1995.

140 **Does it really matter, for instance, that the enormously popular Rush Limbaugh . . . :** From "Rush Limbaugh's Reign of Error," *Extra!,* by Fairness and Accuracy in Reporting, New York, July/August 1994, p. 10–18.

Chapter 12

143 **I can cite a study of 135 students . . . :** From Russell F. Proctor, Richard Weaver II and Howard Cotrell, "Entertainment in the Classroom," *Educational Horizons,* Spring 1992, p. 148.

145 **. . . drooling over the $95 billion . . . :** From "To Find Out What's on Generation X's Mind, Hire an Xer as Marketing Director," *New York Times,* Oct. 24, 1994, p. C11.

146 **"How in the world could we ever create . . . "**: Quoted in "Religion Goes to Market to Expand Congregation," *New York Times,* April 18, 1995, A1.

146 **. . . teachers running around in chicken costumes . . . :** From a posting on America Online, April 1995.

146 **"Whether it is rented from a video store . . . ":** From Bill Payne, "A Word is Worth a Thousand Pictures: Teaching Students to Think Critically in a Culture of Images," *Social Studies Review,* Spring 1993, p. 38.

147 **"Most of the time what motivates . . . ":** From Maryellen Weimer, *Improving Your Classroom Teaching* (Thousand Oaks, Calif.: Sage Publications, 1993), p. 72.

147 **Take for example Richard Wolkomir's assessment of "Old Jearl" . . . :** Quoted from from Russell F. Proctor, Richard Weaver II and Howard Cotrell,"Entertainment in the Classroom," *Educational Horizons,* Spring 1992, p. 150.

147 **"Walker's antics may strike . . . ":** Quoted in Russell F. Proctor, Richard Weaver II and Howard Cotrell, "Entertainment in the Classroom," *Educational Horizons,* Spring 1992, p. 150. From Richard Wolkomir, "Old Jearl Will Do Anything to Stir an Interest in Physics," *Smithsonian,* Oct. 17, 1986, pp. 112–20.

147 **"If effective teachers are entertaining . . . ":** From Proctor *et al.* "Entertainment in the Classroom," p. 147.

148 **Says the French writer Guy Debord . . . :** From Guy Debord, *Comments on the Society of the Spectacle,* trans. Malcolm Imrie, (New York and London: Verso, 1990), p. 15.

149 **And according to my students, the U.S. government is spending a whopping 30 to 50 percent . . . on welfare. It's actually just 1 percent . . . :** From "A Citizen's Guide to the Federal Budget of the U.S. Government," FY 1996, Office of Management and Budget, on the Internet at www.doc.gov/inquery/budgetFY96.

150 **You're not really up to hero quality . . . :** From Phillip Lopate, "It's Not Heroes Who Have Bad Grammar: It's Films, *New York Times,* June 18, 1995, H13.

150 **"For the first time in our history. . . ":** From "Trash Journalism," *Editor and Publisher,* Oct. 29, 1994, p. 10.

151 **According to a recent study by the Higher Education
Research Institute at UCLA . . . :** From "Disengaged Freshman: Interest in politics among first-year students is at a 29-year
low, survey finds," *Chronicle of Higher Education,* Jan. 13, 1995,
A29.

151 **Robert Pollack, a professor of biology . . . :** Quoted in "Half a
Wit Meets Technology," *New York Times,* May 14, 1995, Section 4,
p. 1.

151 **Who is *The Met* trying to reach? . . . :** Quoted in "Showdown
at Generation Gap, *Columbia Journalism Review,* July/August
1995, p. 38.

152 **Commenting on the latest, coolest X-oriented magazines . . . :** From "Hot Off the Press," *Project X,* Issue 29, p. 11.

152 **"The individual who has been more deeply. . . ":** From
Debord, *Comments on the Society of the Spectacle,* p. 31.

Chapter 13

154 **Consider, also, the following descriptions of certain kinds
of people . . . :** From Judith M. Bardwick, *Danger in the Comfort
Zone,* American Management Association, New York, 1991, p.
67.

158 **In 1955, there was roughly a one-to-one ratio . . . :** From
the 1994 *Statistical Abstract of the United States,* U.S. Government
Printing Office.

158 **Another key barometer . . . :** From *Chronicle of Higher Education,* Almanac Issue, Sept. 1, 1994. p. 5.

158 **Some 205 four-year institutions, or 12 percent of such
schools . . . :** From Judith S. Eaton, *Strengthening Collegiate Education in Community Colleges* (San Francisco: Jossey-Bass Publishers, 1994), p. 168.

159 **"We have reached the point where 'consumption' has
grasped the whole of life . . . :** From Jean Baudrillard, *Selected*

Writings, edited and introduced by Mark Poster (Stanford: Stanford University Press, 1988), p. 33.

159 **Consumption, says postmodernist writer Z. Bauman . . . :** Quoted in Smart, *Postmodernity,* p. 64. Originally from "Sociological Responses to Postmodernity," *Thesis Eleven,* 1989, No. 23.

160 **As one example, in recent years venerable auction houses . . . :** From "New Auction Gems: Common Folks," *New York Times,* April 23 1995, p. 19.

160 **One theologian has doubts . . . :** Quoted in "Power Shift in Protestantism Toward a New Church Model," *New York Times,* April 29, 1995, p. 1.

162 **"This shift from academic merit to student consumerism . . . ":** From David Reisman, *On Higher Education: The Academic Enterprise in an Era of Rising Student Consumerism* (San Francisco: Jossey-Bass, 1981), p. xi.

163 **Consider the tale of a Tacoma, Washington, newspaper columnist . . . :** From C.R. Roberts, "With help like this, a student will go far—toward self-reliance," *Morning News Tribune,* Jan. 17, 1995, B1.

164 **"Again, it is consumerism—the rise in societal demand . . . :** From Robert Zemsky, "Consumer Markets & Higher Education," *Liberal Education,* Summer 1993, p. 17.

164 **Here's a partial description of TQM . . . :** From AskERIC InfoGuide, March 9, 1993, retrieved via the Internet, May 1995.

165 **Devising scored "drills" at the beginning . . . :** From Barbara Adams, "The 5-4-0 Drill," *Innovation Abstracts,* University of Texas at Austin, Sept. 3, 1993.

165 **The trend for institutions of higher education to become social service providers is not unlike the rise of "nannyism" . . . :** From Laura L. Nash, "The Virtual Job," *Wilson Quarterly,* Autumn 1994, p. 72.

166 **Fully 30 percent of the nation's students in colleges and universities . . . :** From Educational Resources Information Center Digest No. ED317101, 1989, retrieved via Internet May 1995.

166 **Between 1975 and 1980, enrollment in remedial math courses at public, four-year colleges . . . :** From "Hearing on the Status of Education in America and Directions for the Future," U.S. House Committee on Education and Labor, Nov. 13, 14, 1989. Government Printing Office, 1990.

166 **As one small example, the U.S. Department of Education spent some $250,000 . . . :** From *Learning English for Academic Purposes at California State University, Los Angeles,* Final Report to Fund for the Improvement of Postsecondary Education, U.S. Department of Education, Nov. 1994.

167 **Thus, we see how administrators at a college in Austin, Texas . . . :** "Faculty Notes," *Chronicle of Higher Education,* March 2, 1994, A19.

167 **"Both of his parents are lawyers . . . ":** From "Grade Inflation Demeans Good Students," letter to editor, *New York Times,* July 7, 1995, p. A16.

167 **Or, hear the frustration of Daniel Kazez, an associate professor of music . . . :** From "'A' Is for Anybody," Letter to the Editor, *Newsweek,* Aug. 8, 1994. p. 10.

167 **And, we can read the laments of a Yale graduate teaching assistant . . . :** From the Internet, soc.college newsgroup submitted by nobody@yale.edu, May 20, 1995.

168 **In a system like this, then, it's hardly surprising that college freshmen . . . :** From "Disengaged Freshmen," *Chronicle of Higher Education,* Jan. 13, 1995, p. A29. Also from *1994 Statistical Abstract of the United States*, U.S. Government Printing Office.

168 **At Stanford University, for instance . . . :** From "In a Change of Policy, and Heart, Colleges Join Against Inflated Grades," *New York Times,* July 4, 1995, p. 10.

168 **American high school seniors taking advanced placement biology . . . :** From "Excellence in Science Teaching," a hearing of the U.S. House Committee on Science, Space and Technology, May 15, 1992. Government Printing Office, 1992.

Chapter 14

171   **"I have chosen to throw my lot . . . ":** From Harris, *Against Relativism*, p. 1.

172   **Or, there is the former *Time* culture critic . . . :** From William A. Henry III, *In Defense of Elitism* (New York, Doubleday, 1994, p. 35.

172   **"Bored with trivia, with specious relevance . . . ":** From Gertrude Himmelfarb, "What to Do About Education, 1: The Universities," *Commentary*, Oct. 1994, p. 29.

175   **David Harvey, a geographer at Oxford University . . . :** From David Harvey, "The Condition of Postmodernity," *The Post-Modern Reader*, ed. Charles Jencks, p. 299. Originally from *The Condition of Postmodernity* (Cambridge, Mass. and Oxford: Basil Blackwell Inc., 1989).

175   **As Jean-François Lyotard, the French postmodernist thinker . . . :** From Jean-François Lyotard, *The Postmodern Condition: A Report on Knowledge* (Minneapolis: University of Minnesota Press, 1984), p. 51.

177   **This is a point that corporations, such as Hewlett-Packard, Xerox . . . :** From William E. Halal and Jay Liebowitz, "Telelearning: The Multimedia Revolution in Education," *Futurist*, Nov.-Dec. 1994, p. 22.

177   **Still, at Trinity University in San Antonio, Texas, for instance . . . :** Both examples are from "Term Papers Go High Tech, *Chronicle of Higher Education*, Dec. 7, 1994, p. A23.

178   **It's hard to say where this impulse will lead . . . :** From Halal and Liebowitz, "Telelearning: The Multimedia Revolution in Education," p. 26.

178   **Linda Harasim of Simon Fraser University . . . ":** From "Shaping Cyberspace Into Human Space," ed. Barry Shell. Internet document from The Centre for Systems Science, Simon Fraser University.

179   **Lyotard himself predicted the demise of teaching . . . :** From Lyotard, *The Postmodern Condition*, p. 53.

180 **"It is possible to perceive the world of postmodern knowledge . . . ":** Lyotard, *The Postmodern Condition,* p. 52.

181 **. . . the pivotal question, as posed by the great German thinker Jürgen Habermas . . . :** From Jürgen Habermas, "Modernity: An Unfinished Project," *The Post-Modern Reader,* ed. Charles Jencks, p. 163. Originally from *Critical Theory, The Essential Readings,* ed. David Ingram and Julia Simon Ingram (New York: Paragon House, 1991), first published in Kleine politishe Schriften I-IV c Suhrkamp Verlag, Frankfurt am Main, 1981, all rights reserved.

182 **Dartmouth College announced just such a new grade policy in 1995 . . . :** From "In a Change of Policy, and Heart, Colleges Join Fight Against Inflated Grades," *New York Times,* July 4, 1995, p. 10.

183 **Thus, the entire college curriculum is set up to measure student competence . . . :** From Alverno College, *Ability-Based Learning Program,* backgrounder, 1994, p. 1.

184 **The nation's largest teachers union, the American Federation of Teachers . . . :** From "Union Seeks a National High School Exam," *New York Times,* July 6, 1995, p. A8.

185 **Dale Parnell of Oregon State University . . . :** From Dale Parnell, "The Tech Prep Associate Degree Program Revisited," Paper presented at the Annual Conference on Workforce Training of the League for Innovation in the Community College (2nd, New Orleans, Jan. 30-Feb. 2, 1994, ERIC Document No. ED369441.

185 **In a Brookings Institution study . . . :** From William E. Nothdurft, *SchoolWorks: Reinventing Public Schools to Create the Workforce of the Future,* German Marshal Fund of the U.S., Brookings Institution, 1989, p. 6.

Index

A

academic standards, 110
age of amusement, 178
Age of Enlightenment, 113
Age of Modernism, 112
aliens, 118
Alverno College, 183
American Federation of
    Teachers, 184
amusement, 146, 181
  culture, 146
angel(s), 107, 109, 126, 131–35
anti-government militia, 133
anti-intellectualism, 149
anti-modernist, 113
anti-rational beliefs, 133
anti-rationalism, 125
anti-rationality, 125, 130, 132,
    149
anti-scientific beliefs, 135
Apple, 177
architecture, 111, 115
art, 115
artistic criticism, 111
AT&T, 159
authorities, 118, 126
authority, 118, 123, 127

B

Baby Boomers, 157
Balch, Steve, 172
Balkanization, 141
Bardwick, Judith, 155

Baudrillard, Jean, 156, 159
Bauman, Z., 114, 120, 159
Berlet, Chip, 133
Bernstein, Carl, 150
Bigfoot, 126, 135
Blystone, Robert V., 177
Brave New World, 153
Brookings Institution, 185
Bruning, Fred, 130

C

California State University, 166
capitalism, 156
Captain Kirk, 117, 119
Carrey, Jim, 174
CD-ROM, 175, 179
Center for Ethics and Social
    Policy at the Graduate
    Theological Union 160
Chicago Bulls, 159
Christie's, 160
Chrysler, 177
City University of New York,
    172, 181
Clinton, Bill, 119, 129, 149
Cobain, Kurt, 118
Coca-Cola, 174
Cold War, 115
college freshmen, 168
Columbia Journalism Review, 127
Committee for the Scientific
    Investigation of Claims of
    the Paranormal, 172

Communism, 113, 124
community colleges, 158, 167, 184
Conservatives, 161
conspiracy, 108
conspiracy theories, 133, 136
consumer culture, 157
consumer power, 181
consumer sovereignty, 70–71
consumerism, 121, 166, 181, 185
consumers, 156
consumption, 160
consumption mentality, 156
corporations, 118, 127
Crimson Tide, 117, 119, 145
crisis of truth, 141
critical thinking, 137
customer-driven education, 164
cyberspace, 151
cynicism, 126–27, 129, 131, 133, 139, 149

D
dawn of modernism, 114
Debord, Guy, 148, 152
Descartes, 118
delegitimation, 116, 121, 155
    of knowledge, 121
democratic institutions, 136
democratization, 158
Diderot, 113
distance education, 178
distrust, 129
Dowd, Maureen, 129
Durant, Will and Ariel, 114

E
economics, 115

Educational Resources Information Center, 164
Edwards, Richard, 116
elementary education, 147
Emery, Gene, 128
Enlightenment, 113, 129, 152
entertainment, 118, 121, 143, 146–47
entitlement, 121, 154–55, 157, 170, 181, 186–187
epistemology, 126
Europe, 113–14
Eve, Raymond, 139

F
federal budget, 149
Ford, 177
Forrest Gump, 109, 150, 170
Fox, 145
Frederick the Great, 114
Freeman, Eileen Elias, 132
Freshman Experience, 186
Friends, 145
Fromm, Erich, 124

G
G.O.P., 149
Galileo, 125
Gates, Bill, 169
General Motors, 159
Generation X, 108, 110, 112, 118, 124, 138–39, 143, 145, 148–50, 157, 159, 174
Goodman, Nelson, 126
government, 118, 130
    conspiracies, 118
grade(s), 183
    inflation, 167–68, 181,183
"grand narratives", 112
Great Depression, 157

Gross, Paul R., 171
guardian angels, 133

H
Haack, Susan, 125
Habermas, Jürgen, 123, 181
Hackman, Gene, 119
Hamline University, 177
Harasim, Linda, 178
Harris, James F., 125, 171
Harrold, Francis, 139
Harvard, 168
Harvey, David, 115, 175
Havel, Vaclav, 112–14, 120,
      132
Hearst Corporation, 146, 152
Henry, William A., 172
Hertsgaard, Mark, 129
Hewlett-Packard, 177
high schools, 163
higher education, 110, 112, 116,
      137, 145–46, 150, 158, 161,
      180, 183
Higher Education Act, 158
Higher Education Research
      Institute at UCLA, 151
Himmelfarb, Gertrude, 172
Hofstadter, Richard, 134
humanities, 111
Hutcheon, Linda, 116
Huxley, Aldous, 143, 153
Huyssen, Andreas, 112, 115
hyperconsumer, 183
hyperconsumerism, 156, 159–
      61, 164, 181

I
industrial capitalism, 155
Information Superhighway, 116
Innovation Abstracts, 164

Institute for Research on Higher
      Education, 164
institutional authority, 175
institutions, 118
Internet, 151

J
Jackson, Michael, 143
Jencks, Charles, 120
Jordan, Michael, 149
journalism, 110, 129, 150

K
Kaminer, Wendy, 130
Kelly, Michael, 134
Keynesian, 157
kindergarten, 163
knowledge, 116, 121, 123, 126,
      141, 173, 178–80
Knowledge Crisis, 126

L
L.L. Bean, 160
Levitt, Norman, 171
Limbaugh, Rush, 140
literary criticism, 115
literature, 111
Lopate, Phillip, 150
Lovell, Jim, 119
Lyotard, Jean-François, 120,
      175, 179–80

M
Madison Avenue, 174
Madness of King George, The
      114, 117
Madonna, 143
marie claire, 145, 152
McCoy, Charles, 160
media, 144–45

Medicare, 156
Met, The, 151
"meta-discourses," 112
Middle Ages, 137
middle-class, 158, 160
millennium, 120, 131
modern, 109–10, 116
Modern Era, 109, 118, 120
modern institutions, 123
modern/postmodern split, 116
Modernism, 109, 112, 113, 115–
    16, 152, 186
modernist(s), 176
modernistic, 174
modernity, 110, 119, 131, 155, 160
Montesquieu, 113
Mountain Dew, 145
MTV, 143
multicultural, 165
multiculturalism, 110
multimedia, 176–77, 179
Murphy Brown, 119
myth, 130

N
nannyism, 165
National Association of
    Scholars, 172
National Defense Education Act,
    158
National Distance Learning
    Center, 178
National Resource Center for the
    Freshman Year Experience,
    166
near-death experiences, 131
New-Agers, 131
New World Order, 133
New York Times, 110, 117,
    119, 127, 150

Newman, Paul, 148
Nirvana, 118
Nobody's Fool, 148
Nothdurft, William, 185

O
objective knowledge, 113
objective reporting, 129
objectively knowable, 141
objectivity, 113, 118, 129–30
Oklahoma City, 108, 133
online databases, 179
open admissions, 158
Orange County, 161
Oregon State University, 186
Orwell, George, 124
Orwellian, 120

P
paranoia, 126
paranormal, 134–35
paranormal phenomena, 107
Parnell, Dale, 185
performance assessment, 183
Persian Gulf War, 140
philosophy, 111, 113, 115
politicians, 130
politics, 110
Pollack, Robert, 151
popular culture, 107, 119, 135,
    149, 181
Portoghesi, Paolo, 115
post-Enlightenment, 138
post-industrial, 173
postmodern, 110, 111–13,
    116–17, 120–21, 123, 131,
    151, 156, 159, 170
postmodern
  age, 112, 137, 176
  break, 115

classroom, 176
condition, 133, 180
crisis, 133
education, 179
epoch, 141, 155
generation, 110, 149, 151
revolt, 123, 137
spectacle, 152
split, 115
world, 173
postmodernism, 112–13, 115,
    118, 171, 186
postmodernist(s), 110, 118, 126
postmodernity, 110, 120, 144
power, 121
pragmatism, 181
pre-Enlightenment, 135
pre-modern, 114
President's Commission on
    Higher Education, 158
press, 118
professor, 179
progress, 113, 115, 120
Project X magazine, 151

R
rationality, 133, 171
reality, 118, 124, 135, 139
reason, 113–15, 120, 131, 171
Reisman, David, 162
relativism, 125
religion, 110
religious institutions, 118, 146
right-wing extremists, 123
Roberts, C.R., 163
Roosevelt, Franklin D., 157
Rousseau, 113, 152

S
satanic cults, 126, 131, 133

science, 113, 115, 120, 126, 135
scientific method, 113, 125, 129,
    132
Sears-Roebuck, 159
Servicemen's Readjustment Act,
    158
Sesame Street, 145
Simon Fraser University, 178
Simpson, O.J., 136, 148
slogans for modernity and
    postmodernity, 118
Smart, Barry, 115
Smyth, Richard, 178
Social Security, 156
sociology, 111
Sotheby's, 160
spectacle, 143
spectacular culture, 152
spectacular society, 141
Stanford University, 168
Star Trek, 108, 119
student-consumers, 162, 167, 181
study guides, 162
subjectivism, 135
success, 156, 158, 161
superconsumer, 160
superstition, 114

T
teachers, 140, 146, 163, 174
teaching, 116, 120, 138
Teen Spirit, 145
Times Mirror Center for the
    People and the Press, 126
Tom Hanks, 109, 119, 149
Total Quality Management, 164
Trinity University, 177
truth, 118, 123, 125–26, 134
"The Truth is Out There," 128
TV generation, 143

U
UFO's, 107
Unexplained Universe, 131
United Nations, 136
United States, 114
universities, 118, 130
Usher, Robin, 116

V
victimization, 187
virtual campus, 178
vocational and technical
    education, 185
Vocational Education Act, 158
Voltaire, 113–14, 152

W
Washington, Denzel, 117, 119,
    145

welfare spending, 149
White House, 173
Willis, Bruce, 149
Wolkomir, Richard, 147
World Economic Forum, 112,
    132
World War II, 157
World Wide Web, 173, 178,
    179

X
Xerox 177
X-Files, The, 118, 128, 135

Y
Yale 167

Z
Zemsky, Robert 164

92953